TOGETHER IN BIAFRA

by

Leslie Jean Mitchell
(Previously Ofoegbu)

To Joan, my daughter
Adaora's friend,
with Very Best Wishes

Leslie J. mitchell
25/1/2020

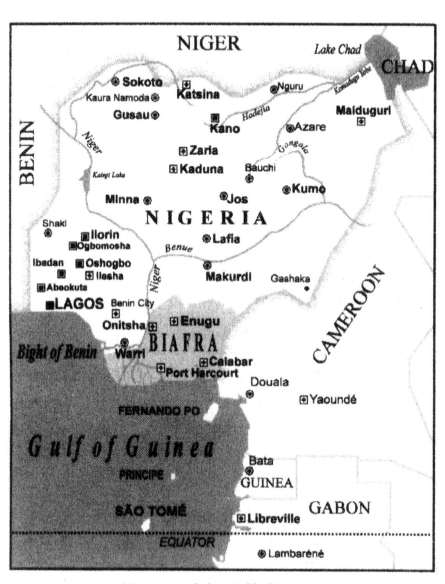

Nigeria and the Gulf of Guinea

Biafra 1969

Together in Biafra

Leslie Mitchell

ISBN: 978-1-9161590-1-3

Published by Dunort Publications in conjunction with Writersworld. This book is produced entirely in the UK, is available to order from most book shops in the United Kingdom, and is globally available via UK-based Internet book retailers and www.amazon.com.

Copy edited by Ian Large

Cover design by Jag Lall

www.writersworld.co.uk

WRITERSWORLD
2 Bear Close Flats
Bear Close
Woodstock
Oxfordshire
OX20 1JX
United Kingdom

☎ 01993 812500
☎ +44 1993 812500

The text pages of this book are produced via an independent certification process that ensures the trees from which the paper is produced come from well managed sources that exclude the risk of using illegally logged timber while leaving options to use post-consumer recycled paper as well.

'Old Paper with Burned Edges' image © Janaka Dharmasena | Dreamstime.com

Front cover: Family photo of Ada, Uche and Nnenna in Ogbor; Biafra in early 1969; Flags of Nigeria, Scotland and Biafra; Biafran stamp and five shilling note; Nigerwives first logo of linked rings.

Back page: Top left, Biafra stamp; Right from top, Emeka, Ada, Nnenna, Uche in Apapa, Lagos early 1980s; Leslie and Len wedding photo, Dunfermline, Scotland. 1963; Leslie and Elizabeth ready to leave for village clinic in Biafra early 1969; Leslie's Residence Permit; Elizabeth Ihebom, Ada Iwenofu and Leslie in Apapa 1971.

Contents

Acknowledgements

Firstly I have to thank those who made the first edition of *Blow the Fire* possible. Had I not married Leonard Ofoegbu in 1963 my life would have been very different and I would probably never have lived and worked in Nigeria for almost twenty-one years. Without the humanitarian actions of Fr. Donal O'Sullivan in 1968 it is extremely unlikely that I would have survived life in Biafra. His steadfast support and encouragement until his death in 2013 continue to motivate me. My good friend Elizabeth Dee took on the voluntary role of editing and encouraged me through several re-writes. She has spent countless hours fine-tuning and tweaking this manuscript and its sequel. Rose Umelo, an old friend from Biafra days and a respected author gave the manuscript a professional edit along with lots of encouragement. My thanks also extend to Penny, Meriel, Amanda and my children who have all made valuable comments and suggestions. Nigerwives, an organisation offering support to foreign wives and partners of Nigerians, played a major role in my life in Nigeria from its inception in the late 1970s. Graham Cook, Jag Lall and Ian Large from Writersworld have done sterling work in guiding me through the publication process. I would also like to thank Fr. Tony Byrne, the author of *Airlift to Biafra* for his kind permission to use the maps on pages 2 and 3.

Any errors and omissions are mine. I have tried to be as accurate as possible.

Dedication

This expanded version of my earlier book of my family's life in Nigeria was written as part of their heritage. It is dedicated to my children, grandchildren, family, friends and all those who walked part of my life's journey with me between 1944 and 1985 whether mentioned in these pages or not.

I believe we all keep learning from one another all of our lives.

I dedicate it also to the people who lived and died during the events which led to the Nigerian Civil War and the creation and demise of the Republic of Biafra.

Introduction

Ogbor-Ugiri, Biafra. Monday 5th January 1970.

Early in the morning, my husband Len and I had a visit from a friend, Pat, who told us that his wife Kate was very ill. He had managed to borrow a car and a gallon of very precious petrol and Len and I went with them from the small village where we had been living as refugees for over a year to the little makeshift hospital at Amaimo a few miles away. On arrival we were told that there was no doctor there that day and an Irish nun advised that we go to Amaigbo Joint Hospital a bit further away. We hadn't enough fuel to get there and were afraid that it was even too late to go now because outpatient cards were generally given out before 9am. Sr. Gabriel Mary gave us two gallons of petrol and a letter to one of the nuns working there. Travelling mainly on untarred roads we were lucky to get to Amaigbo in time to be seen as we had stopped on the way to pick up our three-week-old son Emeka, and to give instructions about lunch for the older children. We did not know how long we would be gone, several hours at least.

Using a little bit of 'long leg' (the euphemism for using undue influence to overcome obstacles), we were able to get a doctor to see Kate at Amaigbo and treatment was prescribed. Seeing how tired she was I took the prescription card from her. There was a clamour of people around the palm-thatched hospital dispensary building across the open space from the outpatients department and wards.

"Take the baby and wait in the shade over there," I said. "I will go for the medicine."

As one of the very few white wives of Biafrans still inside the country I thought my chances of being attended to quickly would be better. Len led them out of the blazing sun to the shady veranda of a ward as I crossed the red dusty few yards towards the dispensary door.

Courtesy prevailed and I was soon able to reach the front. I had just managed to hand the prescription to a dispenser when I heard my baby's cry. Turning instinctively towards him, to my horror I saw a plane flying very low towards us. It was approaching from behind the hospital out of sight of the crowd. My mind whirred round. I must not run across the open ground to where Len and the baby waited with Pat and Kate. If I did so I would start a panic and the whole mass of people in these makeshift buildings would scatter, drawing the attention of the pilot to the number of people and presenting a fine target. In a second the plane drew nearer and lower and now we could all hear its engines. A burst of firing set our hearts pounding. The anti-aircraft gun in the corner burst into life as the plane flew over the hospital and as soon as it passed I ran the few yards to the main outpatients department in the nearest substantial building. In the same moment we heard bombs exploding and the building shook. I dived into a small consulting room and stood in the corner behind the open door.

A nurse in a blue uniform was weeping. She was sure the nearby market had been bombed and she had sent her child there a few minutes earlier to buy something. I tried to calm her. I really wanted to get back to Len and the others but the corridor was now full of noise and people, shocked and panicky. We half expected the plane to come back for a second run.

The noise of its engines faded and I managed to force my way along the veranda to where I had left Len, Emeka, Kate and Pat. They had moved from the building to a steep embankment overhung by trees a few yards away. While I was still making my way through the crowd a bicyclist rode up with a casualty sitting on the carrier supported by someone running alongside. A Peugeot car also arrived with badly wounded men. The bombs had indeed fallen in the market.

Most of the outpatients immediately left the hospital whether treated or not. Meanwhile I returned to the dispensary but couldn't see the man to whom I had given the prescription card. We had had quite a journey to get here and I wasn't giving up now. Eventually he returned from where he had been taking cover and I collected the medicines. More casualties were arriving, some in a Red Cross car which had been in the thick of the raid, some on bicycles and a few on foot. We left as soon as we could, still feeling pretty shaky, and made our way back to Ogbor. Thankfully Kate made a full recovery.

I could not voice how angry I felt that nations of the so-called civilised world in the middle of the 20th century were allowing this crisis to continue. Biafrans had been driven out of the rest of Nigeria, the country they had helped to gain independence from Britain in 1960. Hundreds of thousands were killed, maimed or became refugees returning to the land of their ancestors from other parts of Nigeria yet still they were attacked and bombed, starved and isolated. The British High Commissioner had seriously underestimated the situation in 1967, predicting the fighting would all be over in less than three weeks. If it had not been that the former Eastern Region of Nigeria, which became Biafra, was rich in oil, surely they would have not fought so hard to re-unite the country.

It is to the eternal credit of Biafrans that, conspicuous as I was, being white and British, there was never any animosity shown towards me, apart from a drunken accusation of one man. Indeed they were grateful that I was one of a very few who had remained with them in this difficult time. I on the other hand did my best to assist them in any way I could.

In the back of my mind I never forgot that I had been born during World War 2 in Dunfermline and had grown up hearing about the losses of loved ones and homes, shortages and rationing, of making do and never losing hope!

Now, thousands of miles away in West Africa and aged 25 I was right in the middle of the Nigerian Civil War, married to a Biafran and a refugee, 'running' more than a dozen times since 1967 with my husband and children.

The events I witnessed and the experiences I had in the 21 years spent in Nigeria still return in dreams and flashbacks 50 years later. Awake I ask myself "Could I have done more?" but deep down I know I couldn't. Without enough food, medical care or decent living conditions so many died or were separated from loved ones never to be re-united. No one knew when an air raid would target a market or a stream of refugees walking along a road. The Biafran soldiers were ill-equipped and unprepared for war conditions. Like them I did what I could with what skills I had, working voluntarily in return for food for my family, bartering for what we needed.

When the hostilities finally ended in January 1970, it was said that the efforts of the relief agencies who, from 1968, had flown in food and supplies under constant threat of bombing, had prolonged the war. "Starvation is a legitimate weapon of war," we were told. That's not what it felt like to me or the millions affected.

Why did I then, a Scot through and through and former student nurse, defy the discrimination in the early 1960s to marry a Nigerian and accompany him back to his country? I was naive and swept off my feet by this handsome young man who was a very good dancer and who was always very smartly dressed in one of several made to measure three-piece suits. He was very persuasive too, brushing aside any doubts or concerns I might have. He was the same height as me, 5' 6". He told me that he had completed a Charles Atlas exercise course to build up his muscles and had attained a gold star award in ballroom dancing. He was a very determined man. We first met at a dance in June 1962 just as I completed a three-year pre-nursing course. I became a student nurse and six months later we were engaged. Despite several requests the matron of the hospital refused to allow me to marry with my family and friends present, and to continue and complete the course after marriage.

We knew this would not be easy because Len would complete this part of his training seconded from the Nigerian Navy to the Royal Navy, at HMS Caledonia Artificer Training Establishment in December 1963. He would then, along with the other newly 'passed out Artificers', be sent to sea for three months. The Nigerian Navy had agreed that their men should be scheduled after that for short courses on internal combustion engines, air-conditioning and refrigeration at another shore base, HMS Sultan in Gosport before he was to return to Nigeria in August 1964.

Late in 1963 I realised I was pregnant and the die was cast. My resignation was accepted and we were married. The nursing knowledge I had already gained has stood me in good stead since on many occasions and in retrospect fate took a hand in setting me on a different career direction many years lately. So in August 1964 I left behind my parents, younger sister Sheila, a close extended family and my friends to take a leap of faith into a world about which I really knew very little.

Chapter 1

This Is Nigeria

The Nigerian Navy had given Len the choice of returning to Nigeria by air or by the mail boat. He chose to go by sea as he had accumulated quite a lot of possessions, including a 10kW ex-US army generator and a three-piece suite (two armchairs and a settee which converted to a bed), which he had purchased in a sale in Portsmouth, as well as his Lambretta scooter, which had been his main means of transport while in Britain. His fare back to Nigeria was paid for by the navy but they would not pay for me and the baby so I used my savings to buy our tickets. We had arranged for all of our the luggage to be delivered to Liverpool and put on MV Aureol, the Elder Dempster flagship for its West African service. I said an emotional goodbye to my parents. My mother's parting words to Len were to make sure to look after me. I left in a taxi to the station where Len and his scooter joined us. We travelled to Liverpool Docks to board the ship.

The passengers were mainly Nigerian, Ghanaian and Sierra Leonean young men as well as a few from Gambia returning home after completing degrees and courses in Britain. There were also a large number of expatriates who worked for the government or private companies. They travelled first class. The actual difference in price per ticket was only about £10 per passenger but it made a big difference in access to amenities on board.

We travelled in 2nd class and after we had made our first stop in Las Palmas, started calling in round the coast of West Africa where steerage passengers joined and left the ship. At the start of the voyage there were only two white people in our dining room. The other was a lady missionary who moved to first class when a cabin became available at Las Palmas. At the same table with Len and I were other Nigerians who had been studying under government scholarships in Britain, including one who had just completed studies in Military Music and had his piano on board too. Len was very happy to be able to speak his native language, Igbo, on a daily basis and Hausa, which he had learnt while living in the north of Nigeria.

I had never been with a group of Nigerians, having previously only met a total of fewer than a dozen. Africans were still a rarity in my part of Scotland. On the ship to me they all spoke very loudly and at times it seemed to me aggressively. I felt a bit left out as my time was largely taken up with looking after my infant daughter.

Pushing Uche in her pram round the deck one day I met a Welsh woman with a mixed-race baby. We started to chat. Her name was Irene Jones and she was travelling with her husband Tunde and baby son Fidel on to Lagos. As they were travelling first class we could only converse over a gate across the deck keeping the classes apart. We kept in touch until her death a few years ago.

Before we sailed from Liverpool we had been informed that there was a general strike on in Lagos which had virtually brought the country to a standstill with imports and exports greatly affected. Fortunately it ended while we were on the voyage as we had been told we might all have to offload our own luggage from the hold when we arrived!

On the morning of 27th August 1964, our 13-day sea journey to Lagos ended.

Across the lagoon, on Lagos Island, I could see the fine modern buildings of Marina. Plodding back and forward across the water were two green and white ferryboats full of people and bicycles. MV Aureol was firmly berthed at Apapa Docks opposite Lagos Island and a noisy melee on the quayside prepared for us all to disembark. Gangways and cranes were all busy. Men swarmed on the dockside, some in khaki uniform, others in crisp white tropical uniforms, most wearing shorts. The air was filled with unfamiliar aromas and the sun was already strong and bright. Further along the quay were berthed cargo ships of varying sizes.

Great bales were being loaded on some ships. Some I was told were full of cotton, others with cocoa beans or groundnuts. Uche lay in her pram sound asleep as we gathered up our cabin luggage, remaining belongings and joined the mass throng noisily making our slow way forward to step on Nigerian ground. Soon we were ashore rounding up our various cases and crates of belongings and arranging to clear customs. The generator remained crated up at the docks in the meantime; Len would have to arrange for it to clear customs and be transported to his village.

Len had been unconcerned that when MV Aureol docked in Apapa, the main port of Lagos, we did not know where we would be staying or if we would be met. He had closed his bank account in Britain and transferred the money to Lagos. Having spent the previous five yours organised by the Royal Navy he assumed the Nigerian Navy would be as efficient. He expected that he would be paid by the navy on arrival and that he would have a period of leave before starting work at the naval base.

To my great relief a lorry painted dark blue and with 'Nigerian Navy' on the side was waiting at the docks with a driver and a familiar face for Len; it was one of the Nigerian naval trainees with who he had been in Scotland and who had returned before him. Our cases and trunks were loaded into the canvas-covered stowage at the back and I was hoisted up with the pram and baby. Len and the other two Nigerians got into the cab and we were driven to the naval base, passing lorries with wooden sides, which lined the road and the central reservation. They were loaded with sacks which I was later told were likely to be groundnuts from the Northern Region, waiting to get into the port to be transferred to ships for export. Men, presumably the drivers, either lay on mats under the lorries out of the heat of the sun or sat chatting with plastic kettles beside them. I was told these were for drinking water and for their preparations for prayers. It was very hot and noisy. Because of the recent strike some had been waiting for weeks. There were also little tables along the roadside selling foodstuffs. Mechanics were working on the engines of some of the lorries. Itinerant traders with trays on their head walked by trying to sell their wares either calling out or trying to attract attention with a hand bell. There was a cacophony as vehicle horns blared while people shouted and gesticulated. This was to become part of the daily scene for me in Lagos and its environs. Lean cows with very big horns were walked along the road accompanied by a man in a grubby, once white, nightshirt-like garment. He walked, wielding a long stick, prodding them to keep them moving while another man brought up the rear. They plodded along seemingly unfazed by the traffic and the general noise.

It wasn't what I was expecting but then I actually had very little idea of what to expect. Len had not been very forthcoming when I had asked him about living conditions in Nigeria.

"What is Lagos like?" I had asked him several time during the past two years. "I don't know," he answered. "I was only there for the interview and then went back to the North. When we were preparing to depart for the UK it was all rushed. I had thought I would just be in Lagos to sign papers and have medical tests and then I could go to the East to say goodbye to my parents but I didn't have the chance." I got similar vague answers when I asked about his home in the village.

"My father sent me to live hundreds of miles away with my brother in Jos when I was still in primary school. I went to secondary school in the North too. It has probably all changed now."

At the base our arrival seemed to be a surprise for the Officer of the Day. There were no married quarters accommodation allocated and Len had no family or friends living in Lagos who could accommodate us temporarily. I was taken with baby into a back office while arrangements were made for most of our luggage to be taken to a store for safekeeping.

Eventually a small sum of money was given to Len for immediate expenses.

We ended up spending our first night together as a family in Nigeria in a local hotel which had a noisy band playing late into the night. The next day after Len had returned to the base, arrangements were set in motion for him to get some money as the account he had transferred from the UK was not yet available to him and we moved to a small quieter guesthouse off Ikorodu Road. The first night there I awoke to find Len standing by the bed clapping his hands above his head.

"What on earth are you doing?" I asked.

"Killing mosquitoes," was the answer. "There are holes in the mosquito net and they are getting in. We don't want to get malaria."

I had had several injections before leaving Scotland to protect myself against tropical diseases and had been taking prophylactic tablets for two weeks, which were to help protect against malaria which was, and is, endemic in Nigeria. We soon learned that Moon Tiger and other brands of mosquito coils were a deterrent. These were packaged in twos in a little carton, the lid of which became a tray once the metal stand that was supplied had been set up, the coils separated and the outer edge lit with a match. These coils would burn for about six hours, releasing an incense-like smell. Once it had burned out the mosquitoes returned so another coil was lit which would be half burnt by the time we rose in the morning.

Within a few days Len had been granted several weeks leave and been paid for that period. He also arranged for the generator, which had now cleared customs, to be transported by Armel's Transport to Onitsha, the largest town near to his village from where it would be taken to his home in Azigbo. He had also taken the opportunity to meet up with some of the other Nigerians who had trained in the Royal Navy and returned before him. We had sorted through our luggage for what we would need for the trip to the East leaving the rest, including most of our wedding presents like the china and linen, at the naval base in a store. One, Nick, kindly put us up in his flat for a few days till the formalities were completed.

Early one morning in September, we arrived at the Iddo Motor Park from where wooden-sided lorries with bench seats known as 'mammy wagons' (which conveyed both goods and people), along with buses, minibuses and taxis both local and long distance all loaded and unloaded. It was already hot and dusty and the smell of food cooked by the roadside mixed with petrol and diesel fumes, scented pomade, cheap perfume and sweat mingled in an ever-changing intoxicating mix of aromas. As taxis arrived with passengers preparing to travel, touts pushed forward loudly trying to entice passengers to their particular vehicle.

"Where to madam?"

"Ibadan, Ibadan, Ibadan."

"Ikorodu, Shagamu, Benin!"

"Madam, make I help you?"

"This way! Where to?"

"Ijebu-Ode!"

"Onitsha, two more?" This could be a ruse as one or two of the men sitting in the car would get out when the 'two more' were found!

"I get fine new car take you. This way."

"Daily Times, New Nigerian." (These were the daily papers.)

Conductors shouted out the destination of their own vehicles while other men pounced on luggage, offering to help. Cars, lorries and buses revved their engines, tooting and sounding their horns to indicate they were almost ready to move out.

Hawkers, each with a tray on his or her head, entreated passengers to buy small loaves of bread, hardboiled eggs, oranges, bananas, bottles of soft drinks and bottles full of shelled-roasted groundnuts. Adding to the melee were goats bleating plaintively and chickens either with legs tied together being carried upside down or several in round wicker baskets waiting to be transported. Women with babies carried on their back secured with a piece of cloth, children of all ages and scores of people with luggage: suitcases, bundles wrapped in fabric, cartons often tied up with wire, or bulging sacks all travelling or arriving.

Nearby were sellers of convenience foods like akara balls (fried bean cake) and puff puff (a fried doughnut type snack), as well as sausage rolls, chin chin (small pieces of a sweet fried pastry), bottles of soft drinks and small pyramid-shaped cartons of cooled Fan brand milk.

The discord was further shattered by a woman's voice shouting, "Ole! Ole!" (Thief!) A young man in ragged clothes ran through the melee and was pursued by several others. I had been warned that petty thieves and pickpockets were also milling around in the assembled throng. I had a large bag with tins of Lactogen powdered milk, flasks of boiled water and feeding bottles for Uche as well as a readily accessible bundle of nappies and a change of clothes for her. In front of me was Uche's pram which was really a carry-cot on wheels which could be lifted off and the wheels folded down and put in the boot. I clutched all firmly and refused every effort of those anxious to assist and be rewarded with a few pennies.

It was a scene of what appeared to be chaos with no queuing and with everyone trying to get the best price for their journey. The long-distance taxis were mainly Peugeot 404 estate cars which took up to seven passengers. It was in one of these that we were to travel to Onitsha. Eventually a deal was struck and we were settled in the taxi with the other travellers. Len was keen for us to get to Asaba on the banks of the River Niger, from where we would take a ferry across the river to Onitsha, before nightfall. A road bridge across the river was under construction at the time and would be completed in 1965, until then the government-run vehicle ferry only ran during daylight hours. Canoes would also do the crossing for those with little luggage both day and night.

The road journey would take us most of the daylight hours. The distance, as the crow flies, is under 300 miles but the routing of the roads meant that we covered a much longer distance and the road surface varied from good to barely passable. Our journey took us through varied landscapes of forest or farmland with small villages peppering the way between larger towns. I noticed that as we went through Western Nigeria the women were most often wearing blue and white patterned cloth which I later learned was called Adire meaning 'tie and dye' and which used indigo as the dye. Men wore traditional long flowing robes or shorts or trousers with a shirt. As we went further east people wore more brightly coloured clothes; predominately red and yellow patterns known as Dutch wax prints became more popular. I had already noticed in Lagos the intricate hairstyles many women sported. Often a pattern was etched on the scalp as the hair was divided into small sections then plaited or wrapped round with strong cotton thread. It could take several hours to do. Many women wore head-ties. Some were very simple in construction but others, made for more formal occasions from stiff brocade, were works of art.

When we reached Asaba, after a long and bumpy journey, we joined a queue of vehicles for the ferry and were surrounded by more hawkers. At last it was our turn to drive aboard and cross the river and soon we were in Onitsha. Len directed the driver to the home of one of his kinsmen only to learn that he was in the private Toronto Hospital with a broken leg. We visited him there and Len thanked him for arranging for his late father's house to be painted inside and out in preparation for our arrival. We spent the night in Onitsha and the following day we were driven on to Azigbo in a more local taxi. Although there were no phones in rural areas at that time, and we had been unable to write and say when we would arrive, word had already reached Azigbo that we would arrive that day.

His mother had decided to go to the market that morning and had not returned before we arrived. Cars were still quite a rarity on the last few miles of our journey which was now on an un-tarred road and the sound of a car or motorcycle engine could be heard some distance away. Before we had even stopped as near as we could get to the family compound people started appearing from all directions to greet us. Len and I were embraced by a crowd of people all speaking Igbo and Uche was much admired. Len's sisters Helen and Rhoda appeared but there was so much going on it was hard for me to remember who was who. Then the group parted and his mother appeared. She had been on her way back from the market when the news reached her so she had left her purchases at a house on the way to hurry home. My first impression was of a small, slim woman traditionally dressed and delighted to welcome home her son, the first in their village to have travelled overseas for further studies and now returned. The fact that he had done so and with a white wife was also most unusual in those days and there were many who would have been disappointed that he had not waited and married a local woman on his return.

Nevertheless, she welcomed us and spoke the few words of English she knew while I tried the few words of Igbo I had learned. Igbo is a tonal language meaning that a written word with the inflection on different parts of the word had sometimes several different meanings. After about half an hour we were able to walk the final hundred yards along a footpath to a carved wooden door set in the high wall made from the local clay, which surrounded his family home as was the local custom. On top of the wall were layers of spiky palm fronds which made an effective burglar deterrent. Just outside the entrance to the walled compound, to the right, was the grave of Len's father who had died while Len was in the UK.

For the rest of that day and over the next few days there was a constant stream of visitors from early morning until late at night. For the first few days we were not supposed to go out as Len and I had not been formally welcomed back after his five years abroad. A big official welcome was being organised near the centre of the village about a mile away. I think it was in the sports field of a primary school. Benches were brought from the two schools and both churches, one Roman Catholic, the other CMS (Anglican Church Missionary Society). Some tables and chairs were arranged for honoured guests and a small generator supplied power to a microphone.

We walked in a noisy procession to the venue, Len's relation Chilo walking in front of us proudly pushing Uche in her pram. This was a great novelty as the tradition was to carry a baby on the back of the mother or an older sibling, held in place with a length of cloth folded and tied in front so that only the baby's feet and head were visible. As the village paths, and in this case roads, were sandy, pushing a pram was not easy anyway.

The reception involved the whole village and featured welcome prayers and the breaking and sharing of cola nuts, which is a feature of all special Nigerian occasions. There were long speeches, some translated into English for my benefit by the catechist; groups entered the arena singing and swaying, others came and performed traditional dances, and there were drummers and Juju masqueraders. There was also the presentation of gifts by various groups, which included live goats and chickens, yams, beautiful hand-woven Akwete cloth for me which I later made into a traditional outfit, a gold-coloured coffee set and a large carved ebony elephant. Soft drinks, beer, stout, biscuits and bread as well as more traditional foods were enjoyed by all. Len's other sister Irene, who had married a man from the neighbouring village of Amichi, with her family were present along with all his mother's and father's extended family. His oldest sister Caroline, who was living with her husband and children in the Northern Region, even made the long journey home with her twins Janet and Jerome; they were still babies and her older daughter Grace was with her to help. She brought me two very pretty dresses for baby Uche. Caroline was the most educated of Len's sisters so her English was good. His youngest sister, Helen, who lived in Azigbo, had completed her primary education so we could converse without too much difficulty which was a godsend to me, indeed Helen and I had exchanged letters while I was still in Scotland.

The big 10kW generator which Len had shipped from England was deposited as near to the compound as the lorry could get and an appeal made for the men of the village to come and help push it into the walled compound, using large pipes as rollers, to where it was to be installed and a palm-roofed shelter was erected to keep the rain off. Len had soon rigged up cables and we had electric light in the house. The generator was big, weighty and very noisy. He organised a cinema evening using the cine films he had bought in the UK such as Charlie Chaplin short films as well as some footage he had taken of the family in Scotland. This was a great success but then, whenever the generator started up, people would turn up expecting another film show! At that time there was neither electricity nor piped water in Azigbo. People came all the time wanting to speak to Len and sometimes, when he went to see them off at the end of their visit, it would be hours before he returned. As we slept in the main living room, where a curtain gave us some privacy, I would often be unable to stay awake until the last guests had gone in the evening. Also Uche was waking every two hours so I had very little sleep.

Water for cooking and drinking was fetched from a stream some distance away and rainwater was also collected from the corrugated iron roof and stored in large clay pots although later we bought some large water tanks. After a few weeks Uche and I both became unwell and were taken to a mission hospital north of Onitsha where we were prescribed liquid medicines although we had to buy some bottles for the medicine to be put into before it could be dispensed!

Shortly after we returned to Lagos with Len's niece Paulina who was to help with cooking and housework, and Len started looking for a place for us to live. The navy married quarters were very basic blocks of rooms which opened on to common corridors. Several families shared kitchens, toilets and bathrooms at each end of the block on each storey and there was very little privacy. This was not the only disappointment, as the salary Len was now receiving was less than that which he had had when training with the Royal Navy in Britain while also being accommodated and fed by them. Consequently, we couldn't afford the deposit and rent for a flat in the better area of Surulere where we first looked.

However, he eventually found a place in Fasanya Street, in Lawanson which was just over the border separating Lagos from the Western Region. The only sign that this was no longer part of Lagos city, to begin with, was that the tarred road ended at the Lawanson bus stop. The flat was on the first floor of a recently completed building. We had three rooms plus a kitchen, bathroom and toilet to ourselves in this, our first home of our own. Two of the rooms had a connecting door. They became respectively our living room (known locally as The Parlour) and our bedroom. Next in line was the third room, which in time had a dining table and chairs but initially was simply where most of our bulky luggage was stored. This was also the sleeping quarters for Paulina, one of Len's nieces then in her late teens, who had come with us from the East to help look after Uche as well as to shop in the market and cook the traditional food we would all eat. This and the rest of the flat were reached from the corridor. The communal corridor and stairs were open to all comers and we had to lock the rooms as we stepped out of them. The kitchen had a sink with a cold water supply and we bought a wooden cupboard in which to store provisions. A small Calor gas stove for cooking sat on a little wooden table. An essential piece of kitchen equipment was the grinding stone, a piece of roughly flat granite with a smaller rounded stone which was used to grind some of the ingredients for the regularly eaten stews. We also bought a large wooden mortar and pestle which was also put to good use to pound yams etc. to eat with the stews. A small corridor led to the bathroom which was just a narrow space with a tap and shower head fixed to the ceiling. Most Nigerians washed using a bucket of water. Sometimes the water pressure was insufficient to reach the first floor so then we filled the buckets from a tap in the back yard. Next to the bathroom was the toilet. The end wall of this corridor had decorative open brickwork.

On the other side of the first floor lived a married Hausa couple and a single Hausa man. Both men worked for Radio Nigeria. The wife was a young girl who only left the building wearing a burka and with a female chaperone. Downstairs lived a large friendly Igbo family. The matriarch was known as Mama Bose; she was a nurse working in the Lagos University Teaching Hospital. They had a television set which was still quite a rarity in 1964, so neighbours used to make a point of visiting them on a Saturday evening when 'Ukonu's Club' and 'The Village Headmaster' were shown on TV. There was also a little provision shop downstairs in what could have been a garage. The rent was £15 a month, almost a third of Len's salary. It was several miles from the navy base but on his scooter he managed the commute.

Directly opposite our building was the Estate Hotel with a live band which practised during the day and played at night at an open air dance hall. The hotel rooms, we later discovered, were actually used as a brothel! Next to the hotel was a large refuse heap which was periodically cleared but was a haven for rats which also came into our building in the rainy season when, like all the surrounding roads, it flooded. The storm gutters could not cope and the whole street was under water. Sometimes people walked on planks laid on bricks or across stepping stones in an effort to keep their shoes dry. Others carried their shoes or changed them at the bus stop before continuing on their journey. On the plus side, however, we were only a few hundred yards from the Lawanson market and the nearest tarred road which was the terminus for the Lagos Municipal Transport System buses. Those travelling further into Lawanson could take a minibus. A former classmate of Len's lived very close to the bus stop and showed us great kindness in those early days.

Gradually we began to furnish our home. We started off with the bed settee and two armchairs which had been brought from the UK. We had plenty of bedding, towels, cutlery and crockery given to us as wedding presents. Len found a very good Yoruba carpenter who had been trained in Ghana; when he went to his workshop Len was impressed that he finished off the unseen parts of the furniture, which many carpenters didn't. Shown a photograph of what we wanted he could make fine replicas. He made us a bed, wardrobes with sliding doors, a dining table and chairs, a proper cot for Uche, some side tables (very important in Nigeria as guests were usually offered a drink) and the cupboard and table for the kitchen. It took us a while as money was still tight. We also bought a very powerful standing fan. For the first few months I kept the windows on one side of the flat closed, as there was another house only a few feet away and if I opened the windows the occupants would openly stare into our rooms. For Christmas 1964 Len gave me the material for one pair of curtains and I gave him the material for the other pair so the two windows in the lounge were curtained once I had sewed them by hand and the windows could finally be opened, allowing some air circulation. While I frequently wrote airmail letters to my family in Scotland I didn't tell them how bad the situation really was.

For my 21st birthday in April of the following year, Len bought me a treadle sewing machine which I put to good use. I made dresses for Uche, clothes for myself and even a sports shirt for Len. There were many shops in Nnamdi Azikiwe and Balogun Streets on Lagos Island selling material for clothes, curtains etc.

One in particular, trading under the name Sibrosco, was owned by people Len knew from his home area so we usually went there first.

In May 1965, less than a year after we had arrived in Lagos, Len was told he would be posted to Holland where the new flagship of the Nigerian Navy, NNS Nigeria, was being built. The navy wanted the crew to see how the ship was assembled and they would then sail it back to Nigeria when it was completed. He would be away for several months, perhaps a year so we discussed the situation and agreed I should remain in Lagos with Uche and Paulina and Len arranged for some of his salary to be paid into our bank account each month so that I could pay the rent, the household bills and feed us. It was quite a struggle as half would go straight to the landlord as rent. A further £5 would cover electricity and Calor gas for cooking and I would have £10 a month for food and other household expenses. I also had to get to the bank by bus to collect the money each month.

Before he left there were some formalities to be attended to at the naval base. When he joined the navy in 1959 he had sworn allegiance to the Queen as it was then Her Majesty's Nigerian Navy and he also agreed to serve in the navy for a period at least equal to the time he had been in training. In 1960, Nigeria became an independent nation and all of the armed forces then had to swear allegiance to the president but somehow those studying overseas had been overlooked. Now they were all asked to sign up again by completing a new set of forms but Len said he did not want to re-engage. He was very disillusioned with conditions, feeling that his years of training abroad were not being utilised and that the remaining expatriate officers, mainly British or Indian, who were meant to be training Nigerians to succeed them were more interested in remaining in their present positions where they were earning much more than they would in their own navies. The official response was that they still had the original forms he had signed in 1959 and would hold him to the terms therein.

The process included a medical examination and chest X-ray. Len was duly sent to the military hospital in Yaba for the procedure but when he presented himself he was told they were short of X-ray films and were only using them for dealing with emergencies. He reported back and in all the practicalities of the departure the matter was overlooked and he was told to carry on and set off for Holland which he did. As they were being paid at a higher rate while out of the country Len, like many of the fledgling crew, took the opportunity to purchase a refrigerator. Others had also bought televisions and other electrical equipment. All of these would come to Nigeria when the ship was sailed home.

In August a message reached him that his re-engagement paperwork could not be found and he was told to complete a new set of forms. Len was sure that he had completed and signed the new forms and they would soon turn up but in any case he was so unhappy with the conditions in the navy that he refused to sign any more documents. This effectively meant that he was a civilian on a naval ship so he was returned to Nigeria and discharged. He had managed to get out through a loophole or technicality which was then swiftly closed and the regulations amended to prevent others from following him.

At the time there were a lot of British expatriate engineers in Lagos who knew that the training which the Royal Navy gave its artificers was among the best in the world. Pressure was being put on foreign companies employing expatriates to actively participate in training Nigerians to take over from them. The cost of employing expats was much higher than that for local employees. Not only were they paid much more but they had to be accommodated in furnished houses, with their spouse if they had one, and have paid home leave every year. Understandably, many of these people, who were also able to remit to their home country a large part of their income, were not keen to give up their employment as they had a comfortable lifestyle in Nigeria. The Nigerian government was, however, keen to promote indigenisation and was tightening up on expatriate quotas. I had already lost one job as the company where I worked could no longer employ me as they would have needed an additional expatriate quota which they did not have. The fact that I was married to a Nigerian and was being paid a local wage did not count. Around the same time a message was brought to us to say that Paulina should return to the East as her aunt wanted her to help there. Arrangements were made and we then had to employ one of a series of house helps to look after Uche, as well as to cook and clean while I looked for another job.

Len was offered two positions, one by Barclays Bank who needed an engineer to maintain the air conditioning in their Lagos Headquarters, branch banks and staff houses. The other was from Esso Petroleum and this was the one he accepted. He was based in Apapa at the oil terminal, not far from the naval base and was given a company car, a brand new Fiat. For the first time in Nigeria we had a car! Up to now Len had been using the Lambretta scooter brought from UK, which had meant that I could go out with him riding on the pillion seat but we had to leave Uche with the house girl. The car made a big difference to us and meant we could now take Uche out and about. We took her to the Federal Palace Hotel Gardens in Victoria Island where I took her hand and led her on to the grass and she screamed! At first I did not realise what was the matter then I realised that, although she was over a year old, she had never stood on grass before. There were no parks local to where we lived and most houses that did have a little bit of space had a concrete hard standing which could be swept clean and used to park the car, if they were fortunate enough to have one, off the road. We reassured her that there was nothing to be afraid of and that other children were running around on the grass quite happily. After we had all sat on a blanket laid on the scary grass for a while she tentatively touched the strange green stuff around us and in time walked about happily on it.

I found a new job working in the air travel section of a travel agency on Lagos Island. It was part of the Elder Dempster Shipping Line on whose ship we had travelled the previous year. Their main business was the mail boat and passenger service they operated between Liverpool and West Africa, which terminated in Apapa, the main port for Lagos. It had become worthwhile to open an air booking service as well. Reservations were made by us consulting in large reference books and timetables from the different airlines operating in Nigeria, and it was possible for many expatriates to take a detour on their flight to their own country, paid for by their employer, for very little extra money. Tickets were written out by hand after we had made the booking by phoning the Lagos office of the relevant airlines, all of whom were keen to boost their business. I joined the commuters using the crowded LMTS buses five days a week.

At the time BOAC were about to introduce a new type of passenger plane to the London/Lagos route and they were keen for local travel agents to promote this new service. A trip was laid on to London for Nigerian-based travel agents to introduce the new VC10 plane and I was asked if I would like to go, to represent my company ED Lines. The general manager knew my circumstances and that it would normally not be easy for me to visit the UK. He suggested that I skip the organised tour to the factory where the planes were built and, for a few extra pounds, I could fly from London Heathrow to Edinburgh and spend a couple of days with my family before re-joining the group for the return flight to Lagos. Len agreed and for my first ever flight I flew to London first class!

It was lovely to see my parents and sister and they were happy that I had managed to get back to see them less than eighteen months after moving to Nigeria.

"You are not very brown," was my sister's comment when she saw me.

"Sheila," I replied, "it is so hot that I spend most of my time trying to walk in the shade. It's not like here when you will cross the road to walk on the sunny side."

"Why are you walking so slowly?"

"Because in Lagos I realised you have to walk slower or you sweat buckets." It was difficult to try to describe what life in Lagos was like to people who had never been out of the UK.

I had been feeling a little unwell and while at home in Dunfermline I made an appointment to see the family GP who informed me that I was pregnant again.

All too soon it was time to fly back to Nigeria, this time economy class, so I had experienced the comforts of the VC 10 in both classes! Back in Lagos I met, by chance, two other British women who were married to Nigerians and through them I heard of and started to attend a monthly meeting of women from other countries who were married to Nigerians. We met in each other's homes on a Sunday afternoon once a month, taking it in turns to host; it was all very informal but was useful to us all. Later this type of contact was to become a major part of my life.

A few months later the 'too many white faces in the front office' argument was raised again and, as the last one in, naturally I was the first one out. My next employment was with a small family-run Italian building contractor. There were very large German and Italian construction firms operating in Nigeria at this time and in turn smaller firms emerged. This company ran the business from their home with the wife managing the office. After lunch the office closed for a siesta and I was provided with a settee where I could lie down and rest. My pregnancy was advancing without complications and I was near to starting my maternity leave when Len, who now usually collected me from work at the end of the day as I was working on the mainland rather than Lagos Island and it was relatively easy for him to drop me off and collect me, phoned to say that he had been called to the head office of Esso and told that he was being dismissed. His car keys were taken there and then and he soon arrived at my office in a taxi with his briefcase and the car mats he had bought for the car. Len got on well with the Nigerian staff he had supervised at the oil terminal but I knew that he had not always been agreeing with the English engineer under whom he was working. I had not realised, nor had Len, that the situation was so serious. I put down the phone and sat stunned at my desk, trying to take in the news.

"What is the matter?" asked my boss. "You have gone very pale."

"That was my husband," I replied. "He has lost his job and is coming to collect me in a taxi."

"Oh dear," she said, "especially as I have to tell you that we won't be able to have you back here to work after the baby is born as a relative from Italy is coming out to help us and he will be working here in the office."

It was a traumatic time for us. In a few weeks, once I began my maternity leave, we would both be out of work. We even considered going back to live in Britain. Eventually though, Len started writing applications and we bought a second-hand Volkswagen 'Beetle' car. Len was called for interview by the mighty UAC (the United Africa Company), whose origins reached back to before the time when Nigeria became a nation. Over the years it had merged with other companies and expanded and by the 1960s it had many divisions, including the Kingsway stores and chemists, Niger Motors, Lever Brothers (Omo washing powder etc.), Gala (makers of sausage rolls), AJ Seward's (pharmaceuticals) and African Timber and Plywood etc. Len's first job on leaving secondary school, before joining the navy, had been with Kingsway Chemists in Northern Nigeria.

The position they were interviewing for now was at Niger River Transport based on the island of Burutu in the Niger Delta. This was a deep water port used by oil exploration companies as well as by UAC who, when the River Niger flooded, towed lines of barges loaded with groundnuts from the Northern Region to

Burutu where they were loaded into ships for export. The company also had its own ship repair yard located there and Len was asked to go to Burutu for a second interview. I was already past the due date of my pregnancy and had been told that, if labour did not start by 6th July, I would be taken into hospital to be induced, but on 5th July Len had to leave to attend the interview, hundreds of miles from Lagos so it was arranged that his cousin Dan, who lived a few miles from us, would take me to the hospital the following morning. Although great efforts were made to get Len back in time he finally arrived at Lagos Island Maternity Hospital on the evening of the 6th to find that I had given birth to a second daughter. She was two pounds lighter than her sister, weighing in at birth at 6lbs 15oz; the birth was, thankfully, straightforward so that in a few hours we were home. I was very relieved as I had heard rumours that there were rats in the hospital. She was given the names Adaora Janet. Adaora in Igbo means 'a daughter for us all'. The family soon shortened that to Ada, but her friends and colleagues use her full first name now.

The UAC personnel asked if Len would bring me to their headquarters in Lagos so that they could meet me. They knew that Burutu, being a small island reached only by a daily public ferry journey of several hours or by launch, which still took two hours, was very different from Lagos and I might find the change difficult. In 1966 Niger River Transport was the main employer on the island. There was a village for the local fishermen and employees of the company and their families. This had a market and a few shops, including a chemist. The British managers of the different departments of NRT and their families lived in a secure compound which had a small general store with a cold store, and a small hospital run by an Irish doctor which served the whole community. Within the security fencing there was also a swimming pool, a managers' club house with bar etc. and a cricket pitch which doubled as a heliport for a few oil executives who served the drilling rigs in the Delta area. I must have given the right answers to their questions as a few weeks later we were on our way.

There had been one slight problem as we were told that all of the managers' houses, one of which we were to have, were fully furnished. As almost all the managers were British expatriates this was perfectly acceptable to them. Len, however, was proud of the furniture we had accumulated, including the items we had brought from the UK, so it was agreed that NRT would transport our furniture to the island. Meanwhile, Len sold our Volkswagen to friends on an instalment payment arrangement as we wouldn't need it.

At the end of 1965 there had been a lot of civil unrest around the elections in the Western Region which affected the area in which we were living but not us directly. In general, Nigerians were unhappy with their government and there was talk of widespread corruption at all levels. The 1965 Federal Election results were also disputed by many of the population. On January 15th 1966 there was a coup d'état led by mainly Igbo army officers. Major Kaduna Nzeogwu, who was born to Igbo parents in the northern town of Kaduna, was acknowledged as the ringleader. He had been a fellow student with Len at St. John's College in Kaduna in the 1950s before joining the army and training at Sandhurst Military Academy in England. The Prime Minister, Sir Abubakar Tafawa Balewa, a Hausa, and the Premiers of Northern Nigeria, Alhaji (Sir) Ahmadu Bello, the acknowledged leader of the Northern people, and the regional premier of Western Nigeria, Samuel Akintola who was a Yoruba, were all killed, as was Chief Festus Okotie-Eboh, the flamboyant Minister for Finance who was a Mid-Westerner, along with several other government ministers and army officers. The armed forces took control of the government and appointed military governors for the four regions of the country. The most senior army officer, General Aguiyi-Ironsi, became the head of the Federal Military Government. The regional governors were:

Lt. Colonel Chukwuemeka Odemegwu Ojukwu for the Eastern Region;

Lt. Colonel David Ejoor for the Mid-Western Region;

Lt. Colonel Adekunle Fajuyi for the Western Region, who died during the counter-coup in July 1966 and was replaced by Lt Colonel Robert Adeyinka Adebayo;

Lt. Colonel Hassan Usman Katsina ruled in the Northern Region.

They were all indigenous to their regions.

The President of Nigeria, Dr Nnamdi Azikiwe, an Igbo, was abroad at the time of the January 1966 events. The Premier of Eastern Nigeria, Michael Opara, also an Igbo, along with the Premier of the Mid-West, Dennis Osadebay, survived. The coup leaders were all brought to Lagos and imprisoned. The following months continued to be very unsettled with rumours flying around of Northerners taking revenge on Southerners, particularly the Igbos, for the January coup. On May 29th there were mass killings of Southerners living in Northern Nigeria. The Federal Government played down the issues and it appeared that they made no serious attempts to control the situation.

At the end of July 1966 there was a counter-coup which started with a mutiny of Northern soldiers based in Abeokuta in Western Nigeria during which General Aguiyi-Ironsi was killed as well as Lt. Col. Fajuyi. After an anxious few days, on 1st August it was announced that the new Head of State was to be Lt. Col. Yakubu Gowon, a Northerner from a minority tribe. Hoping that the national situation would now settle down we carried on with our plans to move to Burutu in the Mid–West State.

Our journey to Burutu was very interesting. We hired a Peugeot 404 taxi from Lagos to Warri via Benin City and Sapele. Uche was now two years old and Ada had inherited the carry cot and transporter we had brought from Scotland. With a plentiful supply to hand of towelling nappies, feeding bottles, snacks etc. we made reasonably good time. At Warri we were met by the NRT launch 'The Thrush'. I had never been to the Delta region before and it was a new experience to see 'water roads', channels through the river delta lined with high reeds, grasses and trees. From time to time a canoe would emerge from a small watery side-path propelled sometimes by a fisherman with his nets heaped in the boat or by a woman, often accompanied by children and sometimes with a baby tied onto her back paddling to and from a market. There seemed little in the way of navigation points but the captain deftly guided us through what seemed like a maze of mangrove swamps for several hours until we reached Burutu.

Once there we were welcomed by one of the managers' wives and shown to the bungalow which was to be our new home. Generators provided electricity to the island. An inventory was taken of the furnishings remaining in situ in the house such as the cooker, curtains etc. and for the first few days we used the furniture already in the house until our furniture and other luggage arrived. The only damage was that there was a cigarette burn on one arm of the settee. We soon settled in.

We had not brought any house help with us from Lagos since Paulina had returned home at her family's request and we had been reluctant to bring someone from Lagos so far away from their home. When word spread that we had a baby and a small child several young people from the village, which was only feet from our home on the other side of the high security fence, came to offer their services and we employed a young man called Promise who was from the East. I had thought a young chap would not want to be doing laundry and washing nappies for a family with a small baby but he was willing and said that what he really wanted was to learn how to bake so that he could teach his mother, who could then make and sell sausage rolls!

Making pastry in the Nigerian heat and high humidity was not easy until I realised it was better for me to work not in the kitchen, but in the bedroom which had the only air conditioner in the house. The children's bedroom adjoined ours but had no air conditioner so we left the connecting door open so they could share the benefit.

I loved the open-air swimming pool at Burutu which only the management staff and their families used and often during the working day I was the only one enjoying it. I used to wheel Ada in her pram, with Uche walking beside me, and it was quite a pleasant stroll from our house, which was in the School Compound (there had been a technical school there previously), past the now disused school building and dormitories to the main compound where the British managers lived along with some Americans who were working for the oil exploration companies. They were joined by their wives and children for only the cooler part of the year. We had a little game where Uche stayed with Ada while I swam a length and then she would jump in and I would catch her. One day Uche gave me a fright when she ran ahead and jumped in at the deep end of the pool while I was only half way up the pool! I managed to surface dive, grab her by her hair and pull her out coughing and spluttering. At two years old she couldn't swim; she wasn't at all upset but I was very shaken by the experience and we went straight home that day.

It was a surreal life as the managers hardly used cash. They signed a chitty at the Club House for drinks etc. and did the same at the onsite general store. At the end of the month the accounts department would deduct the total of each manager's chits from his salary. Len did not like this idea and insisted that we always paid cash. He also tended not to go to the club after work as the other managers did. Most of them lived a bachelor life for most of the year as there was little for their wives to do on the island and no suitable schools for their children and, as a teetotaller, Len said he did not want to be drawn into the expense of buying rounds of drinks. Also living near our accommodation in the school compound was a Nigerian family and a single Ghanaian man, both men working at management level.

As 1966 progressed the unrest in the country did not abate and many Southerners, who had been living and working in the Northern Region, sent their wives and children back to the South as they felt it was unsafe but they did not want to lose their employment or business. In time, as riots continued, the men too started to leave, in particular those from the East who were the main targets. Igbos and other Easterners started to leave Lagos too as rumours spread and stories were told of riots and killings although the central government tended to play down the news and the newspapers, radio, TV, etc. carried very little news of what was going on. The international community also kept very quiet in those days long before social media, satellite communication etc. In Nigeria international telephone calls had to be booked and made via an exchange and it was customary for the operator to interrupt your conversation and even tell you to 'Say bye-bye, your time is up!' We received the daily newspaper either late in the evening or the following day but the editors were constrained by the military government and were very careful about not upsetting them.

When the barge trains of produce from the North came down the River Niger that autumn there were hundreds of refugees on board. Many had disembarked further up the delta but those who reached Burutu, and the many Easterners already living there, began to make arrangements to send their wives and children home to the East. Again, the men were reluctant to leave their jobs as they were aware that in the East there would be few employment opportunities with the huge numbers of skilled and unskilled refugees who had already gone home from other parts of Nigeria. At this time most of the public services, railways, electricity power stations and waterworks were predominately staffed by Igbos, Yorubas and other Southerners. They had embraced Western education when it was offered by Christian missionaries. Many were doctors, engineers or mechanics, and had invested heavily, building businesses and homes in other parts of the country where opportunities abounded. In general, Northerners had not been too keen on Western education, which was primarily in the hands of Christian missionaries. They preferred their traditional lifestyle. The killing of the most important Northerners in the January coup by non-Moslem infidels brought home to them that these 'strangers' had the best houses, best jobs and so on and they should drive them out of the North. Many Southerners had built their homes in the North in areas called Sabon Garis (strangers' quarters), where they built schools and churches which became targets for rioters. Indeed as recently as 2015 they have again been a target for reactionaries.

In Burutu, Len was working under a Scottish engineer and, once more, tension was beginning to mount between them. Just before Christmas the General Manager hosted a drinks reception in his home to which all the managers and their wives were invited. Len took offence at something the General Manager said about the Igbo people and the current situation so it was no surprise then when a few days later Len was told his appointment was being terminated while he was still on his six months probationary period. The General Manager was in short-wave radio contact with UAC Head Office in Lagos and had probably been briefed about the real situation in the country. I believe the company could no longer guarantee the safety of the many Igbo and other Easterners in the work force although to lose them might severely affect the company's operations. The fact that Len was not fitting in to their management style was obvious to all so it was no real surprise to me. Many Easterners had also left Lagos and other areas of the south of the country in fear. Early in the New Year, arrangements were made for our furniture to be taken to Onitsha by barge. Meanwhile we packed up, returned to Warri by boat and then over the recently completed Onitsha to Asaba Bridge which spanned the River Niger and back to the Eastern

Region and on to Azigbo by road. There was no question that we could go back to Lagos so we joined the hundreds of thousands of refugees returning to the part of Nigeria they had left some decades before seeking better opportunities outside their densely populated region.

Chapter 2.

Cut off from the World we Become Biafrans

In January 1967 the president of Ghana, Joseph Ankrah, heading a military government which had overthrown Kwame Nkrumah the previous year, hosted a meeting in Aburi in Ghana to try to resolve the situation in Nigeria. It was attended by the Nigerian Head of State, General Yakubu Gowon who was a Christian Northerner not from the largest Hausa tribe, accompanied by the regional military governors, including Chukwuemeka Odemegwu Ojukwu, who was the military governor of the East, along with other government officials. At one time I owned a copy of the verbatim discussions which took place at Aburi, a lengthy document published by the Federal Government Printer but sadly I no longer have it. The summary of the Aburi Accord stated:

• Members agree that the legislative and executive authority of the Federal Military Government should remain in the Supreme Military Council, to which any decision affecting the whole country shall be referred for determination provided that where it is possible for a meeting to be held the matter requiring determination must be referred to military governors for their comment and concurrence.

• Specifically, the council agreed that appointments to senior ranks in the police, diplomatic and consular services as well as appointment to super-scale posts in the federal civil service and the equivalent posts in the statutory corporation must be approved by the Supreme Military Council.

• The regional members felt that all the decrees passed since January 15, 1966 and which detracted from previous powers and positions of regional governments, should be repealed if mutual confidence is to be restored.

(Source: Wikipedia)

When we arrived in Azigbo we found Nne's house full of refugees. It was the same all over the East. In our family the position was as follows. Before the war Len's mother (who was always addressed as Nne) lived with her youngest child Helen, then in her late teens along with two young male relatives Elias and Steven. Len's father had had three wives. He had died in 1962 and his two other wives had predeceased him. As is the custom, each wife had had her own small house separate to his, all within the walled compound but these dwellings had now completely collapsed. Meanwhile, Len's mother had moved into her late husband's house, which was more strongly built; it even had a zinc (corrugated iron) roof instead of traditional thatch. It comprised one bedroom and the 'parlour' at the front with three further small rooms behind.

She now used her own old house as a kitchen, store and home for the family goats, sheep and hens which were rounded up each evening and locked away for the night in a room in her former house. Pots and foodstuffs were also locked away each night in an inner room.

Most village homes have the kitchen separate from the main accommodation as cooking with firewood causes a lot of smoke and with most of the earlier buildings being thatched there is quite a fire risk. One of my greatest handicaps whilst living in the village was my initial inability to cook with firewood in the traditional way. The cooking pot was balanced on three rough lumps of clay and I seemed quite incapable of keeping the fire going, either forgetting to move the wood in as it burned or letting the flames die out and then not being able to revive them by blowing on the fire. I could blow all right but it resulted in clouds of smoke, ash in everything and no flame! The exasperating thing was that three-year-old children could get the fire going with a few puffs. It was something I had to master as there was no gas or electricity or even kerosene so it was with a great feeling of achievement that I finally mastered the art of 'blowing the fire'.

Len's half-brother Edmund had been living in Jos in Northern Nigeria since 1945 with his wife, Felicia, and their seven children all of whom were born and brought up there. He was a trader dealing in bicycle and sewing machine parts and had a lock-up shop in the main market. Felicia was a petty trader, selling things like soap, candles and tinned foods. She also did some sewing, all in addition to her duties as a housewife. Edmund took over Len's education towards the end of his primary school days and paid his fees right through secondary school. His own children were all younger than Len. Edmund died in 1958, the year Len was to complete his schooling at St. John's College, Kaduna. His widow, after bringing her husband's body home for burial, returned to Jos and continued to raise her children there.

In 1966 her eldest son Adolphus finished his secondary schooling and got himself a job, just a few weeks before the May 29th massacres. The rest of the family fled to the East but Adolphus, hoping things would soon settle down, decided to stay. Eventually however he too had to flee. They were all robbed of the few possessions they had tried to take with them. However, they returned unharmed physically and moved in to a room in the family house with Nne in Azigbo.

Len's oldest sister Caroline had also settled in the North. Her husband worked at the waterworks at Challowa, near Kano. They had eight children of which the two oldest were now living in the East whilst the others, including two-year-old twins, remained at home with their parents in Challowa. When the troubles started Caroline's husband, Cornelius, sent her and the children home to his people who lived in Amichi, the next village to Azigbo. As they had no house of their own there, Nne took in the twins and nine-year-old Grace while the rest of the family stayed with his family at Amichi a few miles away. Since the pogroms of May and June there had been no news of Cornelius and we had all begun to fear him to be dead when we heard that he was in hospital at Nnewi. Later we learned his story which was only too typical of many of the returnees.

Cornelius had been in his home at Challowa when a Hausa friend rushed in and told him to run for his life; a mob was coming to kill all Igbos. Cornelius dashed to get his savings and ran out of the house – right into the mob! As they started to beat him, a commotion was heard further inside the Sabon Gari. Cornelius fell into a deep ditch at the roadside and the men hurried on to the source of the noise. After some time he managed to crawl out and started to make his way through the bush to Kano (twelve miles distant by road). En-route he encountered another group of men who asked him what he had. He gave them the £57 he had on him and after a cursory beating he was allowed to go on. Just as he reached the outskirts of Kano however, a third party, fresh from Kano, set on him but he had no more to give them. They were armed with machetes and inflicted cuts all over his body. The most serious were ones from the back of the neck to just below the ear, one on each palm and two which damaged the ligaments at the back of his ankles. His back was also injured near the waist. He was barely conscious but remembered feeling the knife being wiped on his back after his ankles were cut.

He must have lapsed into unconsciousness then as he next became aware that it was night. Probably the evening dew had revived him. He started to crawl towards a lighted building and as he approached a dog barked. He was very weak but managed to get nearer until an expatriate woman appeared at a window and then came into the garden with a lamp. With her husband, she did what she could to clean and bind the wounds then the couple drove him to the hospital where he joined other wounded Igbos; it was an extremely risky act of mercy by this British couple. From there the wounded were taken to Kano Airport and flown to Enugu. He was in hospital in Enugu for two months, very seriously ill and unable to even give his name. When he was finally able to speak and say where his home village was he was transferred to a hospital in Nnewi and it was only then that he was able to send a message to his family that he was still alive. Caroline and his brother hurried to

Nnewi General Hospital where they searched the wards but did not recognise him. Weakly he called their names. As Caroline moved forward his brother stood rooted with tears coursing down his cheeks.

It is a great credit to the doctors who treated the maimed returnees that so many of their patients made amazingly good recoveries in the face of extreme shortages of equipment and drugs and the terrific pressure on the medical and nursing professions. The mental traumas they had to deal with can only be imagined. Thanks to the ministrations of the staff, after a while Cornelius learned to walk again, though for a long time it was only with a stick.

Once we arrived back from the Mid-West, there were then seventeen of us living and sleeping in that small house. I was grateful that we did not have to sleep in the parlour this time but in what had been Lens father's room which no one had occupied on our first visit to the village. Len and I shared a single bed which took up all but one foot of one side of one this room and half the width. Ada, now six months old, still fitted the carry cot and being a fairly small baby she was able to sleep there. Uche slept with us in the single bed; I discovered there was more room if Len and I lay head to feet. Nne and Helen slept in the smaller of the front rooms. Edmund's widow Felicia, her two oldest daughters and her baby girl, slept in the other bedroom. Caroline's twins, Janet and Jerome, their sister, Grace and Felicia's sons Birom, Patrick, Azubike and Adolphus all slept on the parlour floor on raffia mats. As the youngest children nearly all went to the toilet in the night there was a great deal of stepping over bodies to get out and often the youngest ones, who had started sleeping furthest from the door, would lie down again nearer the door rather than try to get back to the corner they had started the night in!

Len and I agreed that we could not manage indefinitely there and we decided to move to Onitsha, twenty miles away, to try and start a business there. We had hoped to wait till our furniture arrived but Ada became ill and the nearest doctor to Azigbo was four miles away. As we now had no transport of our own, we thought it best to move to Onitsha as soon as possible where we eventually took a flat in Oguta Road, one of the busiest thoroughfares in the town. The building was barely finished, four storeys high, and consisted of six flats and two lock-up shops. We moved into the middle floor flat at the front, and were the first tenants in the building. We had been told that our furniture would be sent by barge from Burutu to Onitsha and, expecting it 'any day', were determined to manage until it was delivered. We arrived on moving-in day with our cases, cameras, projectors and pram. The whole place was locked up so Len off-loaded the children and all the equipment from the transport to wait with me on the pavement and went to find the caretaker. A narrow road separated the side of our house from Tabansi's printing works, which were occupied on the ground floor by the office staff. Another new building at the rear housed the press which handled a lot of the jobbing work in Onitsha and at night printed a newspaper.

Within a couple of minutes two young women emerged from the Tabansi office.

"Madam," one said, "come and wait inside out of the sun."

"Dalu" (Thank you), I said and soon we were out of the fierce heat and I was given a seat with a view of the window so that I could see when Len arrived back. I did not know how long it would take for him to locate the caretaker. They must have been very curious but when they started quizzing Uche she was too shy to answer. Len eventually returned with the caretaker who let us into our new home.

Our neighbours on the other side were the Assembly of God Church. The church itself was on the upper floor of the building, level with us, while the pastor and other members of the congregation stayed on the ground floor. As their windows were opposite ours and we had no curtains, we were obliged to keep the windows on that side of the house, which were fortunately of frosted glass, closed for most of the day. The church had services every evening and it seemed the whole of Sunday. They were a very exuberant congregation, one which included a lot of rhythmic clapping, singing and testifying in their worship. Opposite us was the yard of the Tabansi 'Prince' lorry fleet, where the scarlet painted lorries were serviced and parked between trips.

When we moved into the flat the painters had only just finished and there were a few empty gallon paint tins lying around and two 'Snowcem' drums each about 20-inches high. We used the paint pots as stools and one drum served us as a temporary table while the other became the dustbin. In all there were five rooms in the flat. The sitting room ran the whole length of the front of the building and was really the size of two rooms. Our friend, Mr Okolo, loaned us a kerosene stove and we bought some raffia sleeping mats. We lived like that for two weeks before our furniture finally arrived. We made pillows from our clothes but after the first night I decided I needed more than my head cushioned and had extra padding for my shoulders and hip bones. We had one small cooking pot; Ada was still drinking a lot of milk so I used one of the empty Lactogen tins as another pot. We were determined not to buy anything we could do without as I had plenty of saucepans and kitchen equipment in the barge. We had a few plates but were very short of cutlery. Between us we had two forks, one knife and two teaspoons but I knew I had two full canteens of cutlery coming with enough for two dozen place settings.

A woman fried and sold akara balls every morning next to the church and we usually bought a shilling's worth for breakfast. Akara is made from ground beans (black eyed peas), which have first been soaked, often overnight, and the husks removed. Water, salt, chopped onion and pepper are added and mixed together then the mixture is dropped in spoonsful into hot oil and fried until golden brown. It is usually eaten with akamu, also known as 'pap', which is locally produced from cassava or corn flour with rather the appearance of a soft white cheese when sold, then, in pennyworths. It is prepared by mixing the flour with a little cold water and sugar to make a thin paste. Boiling water is then poured on it until it turns to a starch-like consistency, then it is ready to eat. It is used widely for weaning babies. So for a maximum expenditure of one and sixpence, we were able to have a fairly well-balanced breakfast.

The Tabansi girls were clearly puzzled that we seemed to have no furniture. One day I answered a knock at the door and one of the girls stood there.

"Madam, do you want a baby nurse?" she asked as she tried to look past me into the room to see if we really had any furniture.

"No thank you," I replied, and she left little wiser, but I kept her at the door so she went. However, at last the great day came when our loads arrived and everyone began to relax. We were respectable again and even though we had only four pairs of curtains and the living room alone had three walls almost completely windows, we hung curtains at either end and left the front wall free for the 'breeze' to get in.

Our nine-lamp chandelier, which Len had arranged to be brought back from Holland along with the refrigerator in the NNS Nigeria, was finally assembled. It was a good hour's job fitting the thing together and dismantling it was no easier. Seen from the road, through our curtain-less windows, we even looked prosperous. Some of our visitors could hardly talk for looking at it!

We now had two signs made for our business. Along the front of the balcony hung a long red board on which was written in white 'LENLEY FILM PRODUCTIONS' and the address. Downstairs another sign stated that we would make films on eight and sixteen millimetre, colour or black and white, silent or with sound. The evening it was erected Len spent hours beside it explaining further to a curious group of passers-by. We had business cards printed and went to introduce ourselves to the local newspapers; the only outcome of that exercise was that I was asked to write the women's page for one of them twice a week. I did so but stopped after a few weeks when there was no sign of any payment coming my way.

Having no transport of our own was a real headache and foot-ache as we were out most days walking for four or more hours canvassing for contracts and business while Len's niece Paulina once again cared for the children in the flat. Len decided to make a documentary film of Onitsha with advertisements paid for by local traders interspersed with scenes of Onitsha life. We hoped to make enough from the adverts to cover our costs and we would then show the results free to the ordinary folk, who still believed that film making was a kind of magic. We started to film local landmarks and personalities and also made a commercial for a man who built bus bodies onto imported chassis.

We travelled to Enugu to meet Mazi Ukonu who was in charge of variety programmes on radio and television. He produced and presented 'Ukonu's Club', which was a request programme on radio and a variety show on TV. It was said that many people only turned on their television sets for the news and Ukonu's Club! Certainly you could always tell the houses with TV sets by the number of people watching and crowding round the windows on Saturday nights. He also produced another TV show during the week featuring different cultural dance groups. During our conversation with him we mentioned that we were keen ballroom dancers and he invited us to appear on his show as guest artistes. Without seeing the studio we agreed and the date was set for March 25th.

On the day of the show we travelled to Enugu to have a morning rehearsal in the studio. The television division of the Eastern Nigeria Broadcasting Corporation was temporarily housed in the six-storey African Continental Bank building, pending the completion of their own new premises at Independence Layout on the outskirts of town. We climbed up several flights of stairs and eventually came to a landing with a door to the right. There was a red light above the door and a large 'Silence' notice. We opened the door and found ourselves in a narrow passage with another door on the left and a plywood cubicle ahead. We turned left and entered the studio. I nearly fainted! The whole place was the size of a small office, which was probably what it was built as, not more than fifteen by twenty feet. One corner was partitioned off and had two large windows and acted as the control room. Two cameras, booms, microphones, spotlights and a monitor set took up the rest of that side of the room. The remaining floor space was where we would dance. Mazi chalked a line two feet in front of the cameras. "Don't cross that," he said. "And remember, the club members sit here." He indicated where we were standing, about two yards inside the door.

An air conditioner rumbled in a corner. The electricians switched on the lights. It was as dazzling as constant lightning. "Let's try it," said Len, so we rehearsed a quick step to the records we had brought with us. One figure and we were up against the wall; a turn and a few steps took us over the chalk line: a 'V6' and we were right where the club members would be sitting. My feet stumbled over the uneven floor where several of the tiles were missing. The electrician switched off the spots. We had danced only half the record and perspiration was dripping off me.

"Oh, by the way, the air conditioner is switched off while we are doing the show. It makes too much noise!" said our host.

Recovering my breath I ventured to ask, "What about the changing room?" I had asked for this, as I was to change for our second dance – a cha-cha.

"Follow me."

We were taken out of the studio to the half landing where I was shown through a pair of swing doors. Two doors opened off the little square, both of which were locked. I waited to see which one our guide would open. He didn't!

"You'll have to manage here," I was told. I was fortunately too dazed to speak.

On the way back to the friends' house where we were to spend the night we talked.

"How are we going to dance in that small room? It's ridiculous! I know we need the fee but..." I was close to tears.

"We will just have to manage by taking smaller steps," said Len who didn't seem too concerned so we practised taking little steps in the quickstep. We were not too worried about the cha-cha which can be danced in a small space.

That evening we made our television debut; between dances we rested in the separate air-conditioned control room. Ukonu himself did all the announcing and in between dashed into the control room and organised things there. For our performance we were paid the top rate of £3.3.0. (£3.30) out of which our transport to and from Onitsha cost us £1.4.0 (£1.40). Fortunately, our kind friends Mr. and Mrs. Okoye, who came from Azigbo, put us up for the night and ran us to and from the studio in their car.

A few weeks later we were invited back 'by popular request' for another show. It was on this occasion that we learned that a new programme, devoted to ballroom dancing, was being planned. We joined it and started appearing every week. 'Let's Dance,' as the programme was called, was shown on Wednesdays at 8p.m. We also had rehearsals each Monday evening. The rehearsals were held in the uncompleted studios of the new TV House. These were fully up to international standard. There were about six regular couples in the show; two of the men were doctors and a third was a pharmacist. We had a lot of fun together, especially when I introduced them to the St. Bernard's Waltz, the Gay Gordons and, most popular of all, the Military Two-Step. Uche, who had watched the Ukonu programme on our TV in Onitsha, refused to go to bed afterwards. First she thought I would appear out of the TV like magic then she was sure I would soon come in. Had she not just seen me dancing?

Nationally, however, the situation was deteriorating. The people were angered by what they took to be the unsympathetic reactions of the Federal Government to their plight. Civil servants who had returned to the East from other parts of the country could not all be absorbed into their departments here. Pensioners did not receive their pensions and employed men could not get their salaries. There was no talk of compensation for lives lost or property abandoned.

Large groups of demonstrators started to parade the streets chanting war songs and calling for the implementation of Aburi, for the promises made at Aburi when all parties concerned discussed the issues in January 1967 had not been actioned. At the end of March the military government of Eastern Nigeria issued an edict instructing that all taxes collected on behalf of Eastern Nigeria be paid to the Government Treasury in the Eastern Region and not to the Federal Government as previously. This was to enable the government of Eastern Nigeria to meet the financial responsibilities of the refugees and the non-implementation of the Aburi Agreement.

The Federal Government responded by imposing a total blockade on the Eastern Region. The border between Eastern Nigeria and Cameroun was closed, the passports of civil servants who had transferred to the Eastern Nigerian Civil Service were cancelled, Nigerian Airways flights to Eastern Nigeria were suspended and ships destined for Port Harcourt and Calabar were diverted to Lagos; Federal troops set up road blocks to prevent trade between the Eastern Region and the rest of Nigeria.

By mid-May an estimated crowd of 80,000 attended a rally at Enugu Stadium and called for an independent state. Two weeks later, 100,000 attended another rally in Port Harcourt and made a similar demand. At Nsukka, Oji River, Calabar, Aba, Okigwe, Owerri, Umuahia and Onitsha – indeed it seemed everywhere – the call was echoed.

The Consultative Assembly met on May 26th in Enugu. Representatives from all over the East were addressed by Lt. Colonel Ojukwu, the Military Governor of the Eastern Region following the first coup in January 1966. After reviewing the crisis he asked them to choose, either (a) to accept the terms of the North and The Federal Military Government under Gowon and thereby submit to domination by the North; or (b) to continue the present stalemate and drift; or (c) "ensuring the survival of our people by asserting our autonomy." He went on to warn that if they chose the third alternative it would mean real sacrifice, hardship and inconvenience, a period without friends – hostilities – financial difficulties, etc.

After two days of deliberation the Consultative Assembly mandated Lt. Colonel Ojukwu to declare a free, sovereign and independent state, the Republic of Biafra. The name came from the Bight of Biafra where the Eastern Region's land met the sea. Within hours the Federal Government responded by declaring a State of Emergency in Nigeria and creating twelve states – three of them from the former Eastern Region. There are over 250 tribes in Nigeria; the three largest are the Hausa, Igbo and Yaruba and their eponymous languages are widely spoken but the other tribes all over the country have their own traditions, customs and languages. Although Igbos were the majority tribe in the former Eastern Nigeria there were several others in that region, in particular living in the southern part of the East around Calabar and Port Harcourt. Having access to the sea and having the major oil fields and refinery they were being given their own states, probably with the expectation that they would thus remain loyal to the Federal Military Government and could effectively cut the Igbos off from the sea and the oil-rich areas in that region. As no distinction had been made between them and the Igbos in all the troubled times recently experienced, many had also been killed or fled in fear of their lives so their loyalty to the Federal Government was only an assumption.

On May 30th 1967 the Republic of Biafra was created, encompassing the three newly-declared Eastern states. Most of the Biafrans still living in the rest of Nigeria now returned home by any means, sure their safety could no longer be guaranteed in Nigeria. There was initially great rejoicing throughout the new state although I was sure the ordinary people had no real idea of what this step was to entail. Thousands rushed to enlist in the Biafran forces and the actual fighting started on July 6th when Nigerian soldiers clashed with Biafrans in the northern part of our new republic. I watched as crowds of young men hurried past the housing, swaying and singing:

"We are Biafrans fighting for our nation.
In the name of Jesus we will conquer."

No one expected the fighting to last long and although it had little effect at first on some people at this stage, it killed our fledgling business at once.

Unaware of how events would rapidly unfold we had sent an order to Britain for processing equipment for 16mm films as the Government Film Unit had no facilities for reversal processing. We even sent cash with the order! At the same time we sent our savings account book to Lagos for updating but hardly had we done so when the blockade was imposed on the then Eastern Region. We lost the address of the company who advertised the processing equipment and the savings pass book had still not been received in Lagos, we were informed, three years later! The 6th July was also Ada's first birthday. International communications were also affected and I could no longer post a letter to my parents or receive from them. It was to be over a year before we had news of each other again. I found this very difficult as I had kept in close touch with my parents by airmail. Worrying about them worrying about me did not help.

Our financial situation was once again critical. Len started to look for a job and got a small contract to repair three air-conditioning plants at TV House, Aba, but we were now down to our last few shillings. We didn't even have enough money for him to travel to Aba. We were very reluctant to borrow but there seemed to be no alternative. Len got ready for the journey and, putting on a pair of trousers which he had not worn for ages, he discovered the exact amount of small change needed for the fare (£1.3.0). We took this for a good omen and he set off. Everyone was now extremely vigilant and road blocks were set up all along the way, mainly by self-appointed civil defence men. Travelling as I did for the TV show in a seven-seat Peugeot taxi four times a week on the Onitsha-Enugu road, I soon sorted them out into various classes.

European women travelling on public transport were a very unusual sight in Nigeria and I reckoned I was probably, at that time, the only one on that particular road four times a week. However, each time we were stopped at a checkpoint we were all asked to come out from the car which was then searched. Meanwhile, the passengers would all identify their luggage which was also searched. On Wednesdays I always carried my dance dress, frilly underskirts, satin shoes, Len's best suit and his dance shoes. By the time these had been handled up to twenty times on one journey, they were none too clean. After the Aba job Len was taken on under the temporary 'absorption of refugees' scheme at the Enugu TV station. Government wheels being slow to grind and a bit of indecision on what was to be his salary meant that at first he was being paid on a day-to-day basis. He was put up by various friends and we started looking for a house in Enugu.

The checkpoint men now seemed to have become increasingly suspicious of me; most of them I concluded did not have TV. Some adopted an air of 'Oh, it's you again... How are you? On you go', but the majority obviously thought *'YOU AGAIN*? There must be something suspicious going on here and if there isn't we'll make so sure first that you'll learn to stay at home more often.' Then there was a third group who had never seen me before in their lives and they would search my case and handbag and peer into my purse. A plain gold-coloured lipstick case was so often mistaken for a bullet that eventually I had to leave it at home. I had to carry my passport at all times and it was studied so often (occasionally upside down), that it began to look as if I had been around the world as a hitch-hiker.

All these road checks, some less than half a mile apart, caused terrific jams and the journey took longer every week. The sixty odd miles were taking over four hours by August. Later in the war checkpoints were manned mainly on the outskirts of big towns. We all had a lot to learn.

One day an Englishman called at our Onitsha flat. He had been asked by the British High Commission to inform all British nationals that, should the situation deteriorate, they would be repatriated if necessary, initially at the expense of the British Government. However, on arrival in Britain our passports would be held until the cost of repatriation had been repaid. Len and I talked it over. He felt a deep moral obligation to stay and we agreed that this was our home and we should remain together as a family. By the time the word to evacuate expatriates had been passed we were already in Enugu and I was not informed, although I had notified the Deputy High Commissioner's Office of our change of address.

Almost every week that I went to Enugu now we stayed with different friends of Len as we could not take advantage of one family's hospitality too often. At length one of Len's schoolmates offered us a room in his flat and we moved in with a few things. We still had to keep the Onitsha flat on as we had nowhere to store our furniture. It seemed impossible to find a vacant apartment. We walked all over Enugu even looking at nearly completed buildings. Nsukka to the north, a busy university town, was now a battle area and people from there were also desperately looking for accommodation in Enugu. Some friends of ours paid six months' advance rent to the landlord of a nearly finished house so that he could complete it and enable them to move in.

One evening a young girl called Josephine, who also worked in the BCB (Broadcasting Corporation of Biafra) offered to take us to a landlord she thought might be able to help. We met at her home opposite Queen's School and started out. We took a short cut along the railway line where were suddenly accosted by a man demanding to know who we were. When we asked why he wanted to know, he replied that he had information that this man (indicating Len) was believed to be in league with a Russian spy. Me! I offered to show him my passport and my marriage certificate but he cut me short saying, "Do you know who I am? I can kill you and throw away your bodies and no one will ask questions."

It was now becoming clear that this man had been drinking but his loud talk and accusations attracted a fine crowd, all rapidly becoming hostile. Just as they were beginning to wonder what they were waiting for and why shouldn't they just start beating us, a more cautious one sneaked away and called a policeman. When he arrived he listened to the statement of the man who had called him and then Len was given a chance to speak. He explained that we were not spies at all and, turning to the now very attentive crowd asked:

"Are you not the ones appealing to foreigners to stay with? Is this how you choose to treat the wife of a Biafran who has decided to stay and fight with us?"

At this the crowd was melting. Then Len continued to speak. "Have you not seen us dancing on television every Wednesday on 'Let's Dance'?"

In fact many of them would not have had a TV but wouldn't want to admit it publicly. At this the crowd gave a murmur of anger at the man who had disturbed the peace of such 'important people' and some actually set off after him. He, obviously perceiving what was coming, had quietly melted away. In the meantime two of Len's schoolmates arrived at the scene on a motor cycle. I was very shaken by the experience as I thought we could easily have fared very badly.

Len had also turned his attention to the direction in which our accuser had gone and had decided to hurry and follow him and find out more about him. Josephine and I followed at a slower pace. As we took a turning on the road the man could be seen some two hundred yards ahead. Len pointed him out to his two schoolmates and they gave chase on their motor cycle with Len following as fast as he could. The man quickly disappeared into a nearby building and the three pursuers stopped short of the building and waited whilst Josephine and I caught up with them. After waiting outside for some five minutes the man did not reappear. Len and the others entered the building while I waited outside with Josephine while my heart started to beat more normally.

After about an hour, during which several army officers entered the same house and I was growing progressively more worried, Len emerged with the fellow who now apologised and offered to help us find a flat. And he did! A few streets away a three-storey block was just being completed and we agreed the rental terms with the landlord. Once more we were to be the first tenants into a building. It was quite a relief to us to think that our days of commuting to Onitsha from Enugu were nearly over. Len arranged to hire a lorry to carry our furniture over.

"Why don't we take some of the furniture to Azigbo?" I asked.

"No," said Len. "We can't afford to hire a second lorry. You are being negative," I was told.

We were on the move once more.

Chapter 3
Village Life

And so at the beginning of September we moved all our property from Onitsha to Enugu. We had now also recovered our car. This was the Volkswagen which we bought second-hand in Lagos in 1966. When we heard we were going to live on Burutu, an island thirty-two sea miles from Warri and having no roads, we decided to sell the car. Some people were starting a new business, we knew one of them and, as they wanted transport and we were not then desperate for money, they paid us a deposit and promised to pay the balance later. We agreed and hardly realised that this balance had not been paid until we found ourselves back on dry land with no transport. One day Len saw the car on the road in Onitsha and stopped it. The driver took him to the company's office but after some time we realised that they were unable to pay the balance so they agreed to return the car to us. They had had the use of it for one year for the deposit of £50 which we thought wasn't a bad hire!

The day we recovered it it was in a wayside mechanic's workshop and we had to buy some spare parts at the second-hand market – including wheels – to get it mobile again! We were anxious to travel in it to Len's home village the next day as we had heard that a close relative had died. We had gone only a few miles when the engine began to knock. We pushed the car to the side of the road and locked it up. It was already late afternoon and we wanted to reach Azigbo before dark. We were able to stop a taxi and Len successfully negotiated a price with the driver to take us to the village. The following day we came back with Len's cousin Dan, who had been visiting his family nearby, intending to be dropped beside our own car but we couldn't see it. At first we thought we had mistaken the spot but soon we realised that we had actually passed it. Dan was in a hurry to get back to Enugu so he drove us to our flat in Onitsha and dropped us off there.

Len immediately went off to get a taxi to take him back to where we had left the car. I was sure we had seen the last of it. However, when Len came back he told me he had found it some yards further down the road and had pushed it into a little turning. It seemed that thieves had come along and, after forcing a window, they unlocked the car and tried to push-start it. When they realised that this wasn't possible they had pushed it off the road and started searching it. The roof upholstery was slashed; apparently some people keep money there. Our tools were scattered around and the bonnet and boot were opened .The intention was probably to strip the car of any parts which could be re-sold. To Len's amazement however, he found that though several parts had been dismantled they were all strewn around. Nothing was missing at all. In fact there were more tools than we had started out with! The thieves had obviously been scared off. With help, Len managed to get the car pushed back on to the road and to a nearby house where he asked the owner to keep an eye on it until the morning when he brought a vehicle to tow it back to Onitsha.

After it had been repaired we drove to Enugu. This car had always preferred to be driven in the towns and on our two previous attempts to drive from Lagos to Ikenne to visit friends Tai and Sheila Solarin, who had a school there, it had broken down both times so that on the first attempt we arrived so late that the family had thought we were not coming and on the second we had to stay nearly two weeks for the car to be repaired.

How those people drove it from Lagos to Onitsha – a distance of over 300 miles – we never found out. However, we got to Enugu without any major breakdown although it was in pouring rain.

The first air raid we experienced at Enugu came early one morning. We were staying with friends at New Haven, which was within sight of State House. A few yards from the house where we were visiting there was a deep valley with a stream at the bottom.

As the plane flew over there was a general panic – adults grabbed children and ran pell-mell for cover in the wooded valley. A few shotguns were fired at the plane. It took about thirty minutes for everyone to emerge and later there were moves by people to camouflage their houses by spreading palm leaves on the roofs.

Air raids soon became more frequent and as we never knew which planes were our own, we took cover from them all. Soon, however, we were able to recognise our big B26 which was around twenty years old. We also saw Ojukwu's helicopter taking off in the grounds of State House. It often took him to the fighting zones. His presence on the spot did a lot to encourage the army which was out-numbered, under-trained and ill-equipped. We heard that he often turned up by himself unannounced and would frequently drive a few miles to get to the real front. On one occasion he arrived at a camp and asked for the commanding officer. When he was told that he had gone forward Ojukwu followed and was nearly caught in an ambush set by the man for nearby Federal troops. The officers appealed to him to give them advance warning of his visits and it was rumoured that Kaduna Nzeogwu suggested that if Ojukwu wanted to be in the field, he would go and mind State House instead!

At this time it wasn't surprising for working class people in local palm wine bars to discover that the man sitting quietly in the corner was Ojukwu himself, out to see what the people were thinking. After an air raid in Enugu he was quickly on the scene, casually dressed and driving a small green car, sometimes before the victims had been taken to the hospital. The people appreciated his identifying himself with them in this way. Time and again during the war he would appear informally in a town or village which had just been raided to move among the wounded, see the damage and often be away before any official welcome could be organised.

Biafra was already experimenting with the making of weapons and there were inevitably some explosions and accidents. The noise of fighting was also getting louder though very loud explosions were passed off as 'our people testing the new weapons', and were even cheered by the innocent. Others, like us, were beginning to feel uneasy. Biafran troops had advanced right through the Mid-West, heading towards Lagos, and were apparently going well when suddenly things started to go wrong. The troops started to retreat and when a mango tree outside Broadcasting House in Enugu was split by a shell, people started to get really alarmed. There was a feeling on both sides that if Enugu fell, the war would end.

A day or so later a taxi travelling along the road outside the old Secretariat was shattered by a shell. I met the expatriate wife of an Igbo who was travelling in the car directly behind the stricken taxi. She was with her husband and children, having just left their house which they felt to be within shelling range. She said the heat of the explosion was such that all the water in their radiator boiled up. We tried to go and see the scene but the street was cordoned off.

I called at the National Council of Women's Societies' office one evening and saw there was a huge bonfire burning in the backyard of the American Consulate building nearby. I guessed they were burning files and documents and preparing to pull out. True enough, they went round one night collecting their people and assembled a convoy which drove to Port Harcourt. When they reached the port the American wives and children who had been living in Port Harcourt joined them. Later Len saw the American diplomats formally leave in a convoy of cars. The first carried the Stars and Stripes flag. There were only men in this procession. At the end were large removal lorries and another car with the American flag. The British also left, but as they didn't tell me, I don't know how they organised it; some of the families got mixed up with the Americans I heard later.

Large numbers of our own troops started to appear in the streets, many of them carrying weapons, yet we knew that there were not enough arms to go around at the front. With the news from the Mid-West becoming steadily worse, the civilians were not happy to see so many of our soldiers hanging around and at one point a delegation was sent to Ojukwu, asking him to withdraw all soldiers to barracks and let the civilians go and fight instead! There were widespread rumours of sabotage and it was said that one section of the Biafran Army had been ordered to fire on another section on the pretence that they were the enemy. Officers found that their orders were not obeyed and, while the confusion raged, the enemy entrenched itself around the town. Inside Enugu people were moving their families from one side of the town to the other. Those who tried to leave the town were turned back at the outskirts and rallies were held and appeals made for volunteers to fight the aggressors and save Enugu.

On the surface there were attempts at acting normally. We continued to dance on television every Wednesday. We even started to practise a new dance, the 'Dashing White Sergeant'. At home we had not had the chance to unpack the smaller items. However, we got the chandelier assembled and hung it up on the ceiling fan hook. We talked about what we should do and we decided that if Enugu was evacuated, we would go to Azigbo.

Word was at last given that men could evacuate their families and should then return to defend the town. Within two days the town was half empty. Shells started to fall on the General Hospital before all the patients were evacuated but we still hoped that we would not have to move out.

On the Friday morning Len said I should pack a few things just in case we had to move quickly and he went off to work. I packed some cases with our clothes and then sat down to do some sewing. The noise of the treadle machine covered the sound of the shelling and it was only when Len arrived in the middle of the morning that I rose from the machine and started to pack the car.

Uche, then three-years old and Ada, fifteen months, were quite excited. We packed as much as we could into the car but we were really thinking that it would just be a case of a fortnight at most till we were back and Len planned to return the following day anyway. We left his pot of stew in the fridge and I had another pot of soup resting between my feet in the front of the car. Paulina sat, or rather squeezed, into the back with Uche and Ada sat on my knees in front. They both had their teddies but the rest of their toys were left behind. Eventually we got started and had just reached the main road when we got caught in a traffic jam. The car was so loaded that Len couldn't see anything in his rear mirror and the first he knew anything was wrong was when Paulina shouted a second before our rear mud guard crumpled. Looking out of the windows we were amazed to see a prefabricated house looming over us! On closer examination it turned out to be a 'troop carrier' made of corrugated iron sheets mounted on caterpillar treads. After cursing us soundly the driver ordered us to clear to the side of the road while he passed.

We drove out of Enugu through Milliken Hill which meant climbing a road with a series of hairpin bends with a sheer drop on the right and notices to 'BEWARE OF LANDSLIDES' on the left. All the way up we passed a continuous stream of refugees, mostly on foot, a few pushing laden bicycles. The gradient is very steep and under the hot sun it was a real effort for the children among them to keep going. We reached the top and stopped for clearance at a checkpoint but after we had been given the all-clear the car refused to start. There was no mechanic around but after we had unloaded it completely and Len had tinkered in its innards for about an hour, some soldiers pushed us and we started again. "Don't stop the engine!" they cried, so we hastily packed everything inside and piled in and we were off. We slowed down at the checkpoints ahead but didn't dare stop again. We were barely managing to climb and as each new hill rose ahead, I prayed we would get over it. Just after Awka we chugged up to yet another checkpoint where the men refused to lift the barrier and we had to stop.

Immediately a cloud of smoke rose from the front of the car. We tumbled out and joined the men who were now twenty-five yards off waiting for the bang but nothing happened. When the smoke died down, Len sent for some mechanics. They discovered that the nearside front wheel was near red hot. The brakes had been binding right from Enugu. We followed the car as it was pushed to the mechanic's workshop where we waited for over five hours; it was well after dark when we started off again. With our single headlight on dim we crawled to Onitsha, then Nnewi and finally home to Azigbo. The noise of the car engine shattered the still of the night and ensured that the family was aware of our imminent arrival long before we stopped. We put the children to bed and Len explained the situation in Enugu. He also said he would be going back in the morning but his mother and sisters pleaded with him that, as Saturday was a half-day anyway, he should wait over the weekend and go back on Monday.

The following day he was still not happy about the car and we went to Nnewi, the nearest town, situated on the main road from Onitsha to Owerri to buy some spare parts. While we were there we suddenly became aware that there was unusually heavy traffic on the road from Onitsha. Then the market broke up in disorder and women started scurrying home with their goods unsold.

"Onitsha is burning, the Waterside is ablaze." Within minutes rumours reached us that a petrol storage tank was on fire and Nigerians were shelling from Asaba. The price of petrol in Nnewi immediately rose to fifteen shillings (£0.75) a gallon and some petrol stations stopped selling completely. The panic was total and terrible. Soon refugees on bicycles started to arrive so we decided to return to Azigbo at once. Many cars having run out of petrol were being pushed along the road while the queues at those petrol pumps still operating were so long that they must have taken hours to be served, especially as the pumps were hand operated. Len decided to go back to Enugu on the Monday to try and bring out some more of our property. The car, he felt, could be managed. He did indeed go back but he didn't realise that Federal troops were already in the town.

He got to our flat and, although hampered by not knowing where many things were and distracted by close-range shelling and gunfire, he did manage to salvage my sewing machine which he tied to the roof of the car, cushioned with bedding and a lot of other miscellaneous items. At times like these many people were not even able to think. We heard of one man who went to remove his possessions but became so confused that all he took was a local broom worth a few pence. We were glad to see Len back again but after a few days rest he had to go to Aba to report for duty at the Broadcasting Corporation. Among the things left at Enugu by the BCB was our 16mm cine camera which was on hire to the television side of the BCB.

I was now set to lead life in the village again. We had Uche's cot mattress on the floor of our little bedroom. Ada slept on this while Uche lay on a camp bed. During the day we had to put the mattress on the camp bed in order to move around the room. After they had gone to bed the door could only be opened about a foot and Len and I had to step on the cot mattress to climb into our own bed.

Soon Len had re-joined the BCB at Aba but we were very reluctant to set up home again and start buying furniture etc. All of our major household items had been left in Enugu so he shared a room with some young bachelors and tried to visit us on alternate weekends. The distance was about 100 miles.

Many Saturday nights we would be waiting for him to come and he would arrive after eleven when we had almost given him up. During the week I did very little apart from washing clothes and cooking for the children. I did not do my own marketing but told either my sisters-in-law or Nne what I wanted and gave them the money and they shopped for me. I was still weak from a bout of malaria I had had in Enugu and which had not been treated and anyway, no one thought I should go out more than necessary. Most of the young people who were confident enough of their English to speak to me were young secondary schoolboys. The educated girls were either shy, married or trading so I had few to talk to apart from the children. Often, after the adults had gone to the market or to the farm, I was the only 'grown up' in the compound with an assortment of children.

Another problem was the lack of water. It all had to be fetched from several miles away and most days the older children and young people would get up at four in the morning to go to the stream to fetch water before the sun got too hot. I probably used water more than anyone and it was to their credit that no one complained about my consumption. When Len came at weekends he would pack all the water containers into the car and would bring back enough for his mother and me for a few days.

Up until this stage Biafra and Nigeria were using the same currency. Now Nigeria announced a currency change and within a few weeks started to withdraw the existing paper money. Biafra countered by announcing that she was also changing her currency and gave a deadline of about ten days for all paper money to be handed into the banks. The money was, we assumed, sent or taken into Nigeria and deposited in banks there before the deadline expired. The new Biafran currency was being printed in Europe and came in on the arms planes. With the speed at which the transaction was put into operation there was only a very small amount of paper money available and this heralded the start of the cash crisis which was to plague Biafra for most of the remainder of the war. The banks limited withdrawals and people stopped depositing money.

For us it meant that as our bank was now in Aba, I was dependent on what Len could bring on his fortnightly visits. The adult members of the family had very small farms which yielded them some food staples and a little over for trading. This meant that they would go to the market with whatever they had to sell and when they had sold that they bought what they needed. Thus very little cash was needed, although they lived on a subsistence level. Throughout my stay there we ate meat only at Christmas when we killed a goat. Len was sometimes able to buy eggs and bread with him from Aba. As the area controlled by Biafra decreased in the course of the war, more and more people were forced into smaller and smaller land areas. Stocks of normally imported commodities finished and the larger food producing areas of Igbo land became cut off one after the other.

That December of 1967 Len spent his first Christmas in his father's compound for sixteen years. We killed one of the goats we had been given at our reception when we first arrived in 1964. We bought rice and palm wine (for the adults) and invited all the children in the family for a meal. The size of the extended family was such that more than a hundred children turned up. A lot of adults appeared too and somehow Nne managed to stretch that goat so that everyone had a little.

However, this party knocked a big hole in our budget. Len went back to Aba and by the end of the second week I had virtually no money. On the Saturday night we waited for him but he didn't appear. Very late we heard his cousin, Dan, arriving, also from Aba and in the morning I went to see him; he told me that Len wasn't able to come. "Was there any message for me?" I asked. "No." I went home and searched all through our clothes for loose change in the pockets. I found about two shillings so with what I had in my purse I had five shillings and no stock of food to feed three of us for a week. The week before, I had started eating less at each meal. There was no one to borrow from and I wasn't going to admit that I had nothing. Uche and Ada were too young to understand what hunger was about and I determined that they should have something to eat even if I had to go without. There were three women cooking in the compound and each would give a little to any of the other's children who happened to be around at meal times. I reasoned that if they hadn't had enough with what I gave them, they would likely get a little more from Nne. When times had been better I had shared the food I bought with them. As for me, when I felt hungry I drank water and ate a little food once a day. As everyone else was busy with their own work no one noticed that I wasn't eating. I had an upset stomach and used this as an excuse to spend most of the day in my room. My appetite diminished and this was a great lesson to me for the future when I dealt with cases of starvation and acute malnutrition. Even the smell of a favourite food or the sight of it can do nothing to suddenly waken a deadened appetite. Some children died after being forced to finish a large meal after weeks or months of semi-starvation.

I became weaker and as my attack of diarrhoea got worse I was using more and more of my energy just going to and from the toilet. Once or twice I fainted and I remember going out during the night once and being unable to get back. Fortunately someone had heard me go out and eventually they came to look for me and I was helped back to bed. Word somehow reached Len that I was sick for the next Saturday, although he still was not able to come himself he sent some money with Dan. There was also a message that I was to come to Aba, leaving the girls with Nne. Ada was not very well either and Nne wanted me to take her too. I felt I couldn't cope with such a small child on the journey in my present condition and after buying some medicine for her, I turned over the rest of the money to Nne to pay for the children's food while I was away. I think it must have occurred to someone that I had not been eating for that night they started to cook some rice. Rice was usually a special occasion food in the village although I ate it quite often in normal times as I preferred it to the pounded cassava or yam they ate. I took no interest in the cooking and had gone to bed before they finished. However, I was wakened and told to come and eat. I rose and went in my nightdress to the inner compound where we all sat outside around the fire and ate. All the children in the house were present as they were quite used to being wakened to eat. When a mother returned from market at dusk she usually brought the ingredients for the evening meal with her, which then had to be prepared and cooked.

In our compound the evening was usually passed thus. Water having been fetched during the morning, the children, with the babies tied to their backs, collected firewood during the day and the early evening would pass quietly. Towards dusk women started passing by on their way home from market. The children might wander to the road to see if their mother, or in our case, Nne was coming. Sometimes Irene would come in with some things which Nne had asked her to carry home. She would collect any of her children who were left with us and hurry home to start her own cooking. As it got later there would be a stir of restlessness. Although no one would have dared suggest that Nne should stop going to the more distant markets, we all got worried if she wasn't home by dark. Sometimes we would hear her give a special call which travelled some distance. Most families had this type of ululating call which seems to travel further than a normal shout. It was particularly useful for calling in the children from the farms. If we heard it when Nne was coming back from market then we sent the older children to go and help her carry her load in. Usually though she would be inside the compound before we knew it. We would help her lift down her load from her head. She would sit down and have a drink of water and unpack her purchases. When I first met her she used to carry the traditional oblong-shaped basket to market. However, with the arrival of some labour-saving devices she immediately saw possibilities in one blue plastic baby bath.

In good times there was something for those who had stayed at home on market day. Sometimes she would bring a few bananas or oranges. At other times it would be groundnuts or a small loaf of bread. The work of the evening meal would start as she set each to various tasks and while the meal was cooking all the news from the market was shared. This was the newspaper and local radio of the village, although now, with a lot of township dwellers back in the villages as returnees and refugees, there were some transistor radios. The cooking is no five minute job and the preparation of the stew and pounded food to eat with it would take up to two hours. The younger children usually fell asleep long before the meal was ready. The older ones lent a hand stoking and blowing the fire and pounding various ingredients or preparing the vegetables (another name for the green leaves which are used in most dishes). Most stews or soups contain dried fish or crayfish with fresh fish or meat where available. This supplies first class protein. Then there is palm oil which gives various vitamins and fat and vegetables of some kind. Egusi, dried melon seeds ground to a powder, is sometimes used; it thickens the soup and gives it a flavour not unlike groundnuts. Okro and/or ogbono can be added to the basic soup which is then gummy. Various leaves like bitter leaf are added to soups which then take their name. Tomato, either fresh or in paste form, is often used in more well-to-do houses to enrich the flavour and there are also local herbs and spices to be added by those who like them. There are no recipe books in the local homes, each mother teaching her children her methods. From town to town the ingredients and proportions change so that, for instance, Owerri people eat large snails with relish but in Nnewi areas no one eats them – at any rate not openly.

Anyone who arrives by chance, or design, while the household is eating is always invited to come and eat. It is a part of tradition like the host's exclamation at being seen eating, "You meet us well."

Another custom which is widely upheld in Igboland is the sharing of kola nut with visitors. This is usually a man's job. The nut is presented on a small plate, sometimes with alligator pepper or a little green fruit called 'mmimi'. The host offers it to the oldest man present who offers some prayers before breaking the nut, then he takes a piece and it is passed around among all those present as a sign of friendship. The nut itself is bitter and leaves a dry taste in the mouth; it is a stimulant and is much used by long distance lorry drivers to keep them awake.

To get back to our village evening; when the meal is ready the children are wakened. When waking anyone they are always called by name first. This, it is said, allows the sleeper's spirit which may have left the body to return. When they have been served a prayer of thanks is said, and having washed their hands, eating begins. Several people share a bowl of soup and a plate of whatever the carbohydrate dish is. This is a pounded food and is eaten by breaking off a small piece, dipping it into the soup and eating it with the minimum of chewing. Meat and fish is left to last and the most senior person takes first, the others following in order of seniority. Water is usually drunk after the meal but if there is a lot of pepper in the soup it may be taken with it instead. Only the right hand is used for eating or for receiving or giving anything. It is considered an abomination to use the left. Anyone like me, who is left-handed, has to be constantly on the lookout so as not to offend anyone. After the meal there may be storytelling or family gossip but usually within an hour the family settles for the night.

Chapter 4

The Last Rites

To leave Igbo customs and return to our story, next morning while it was barely daylight I left for Aba with Dan. We had other people in the car as there were always people going to trade in the big towns. Cars were being commandeered by the army and we travelled mainly on un-tarred back roads to avoid soldiers as much as possible. We reached Aba at mid-morning and went straight to Len's office at Ogbor Hill and I waited in the library until he closed for the day, then we went to the town centre.

Len had rented two rooms and though he had moved in on the Saturday before he had only a camp bed so we went to a street where readymade furniture was on sale and bought three dining chairs, a dining table, which had a removable top, two wooden arm chairs, two stools, a coat rail and a food cupboard, all for less than £10. Len then bought a fancy reclining canvas chair for forty-five shillings (£2.25). We bought four cushions for the chairs, a Vono metal bed frame and local mattress and then hired a truck to take them all to our new home. A truck in West Africa is a large two-wheeled hand cart mounted on the rear wheels and axle of a lorry. The body is made of wooden planks and it is pushed by a man who is probably a member of the Truck Pushers Union. Meanwhile, we left the market and drove to the Catering Rest House where we had a three-course chicken lunch for seven and sixpence (£0.75). Interestingly, nothing was done about me getting any medical treatment.

We then set out for our latest home. The house was owned by Dick Tiger, the former world champion boxer. When we got there the truck pushers were waiting so we offloaded at once. We shared the U-shaped single storey house with six other tenants. Each room connected with its neighbours on either side by doors which could be locked and they also had a door to the inner yard. It was thus easy for the landlord to rent out one, two or more rooms to a tenant. The bottom of the 'U' faced the street and on the opposite side of the yard was the kitchen area which all the tenants shared, along with two latrines and two shower rooms. An outside tap supplied water. The whole yard was walled round and a narrow passage with doors at each end led to the street. Each room was ten feet by twelve feet; the inner yard was cemented and the shared amenities were kept clean by the tenants. Our neighbours included two teachers, a nurse and an engineer. Most of them, in peace time, had had a flat each but now we were all simply glad of what we had.

One of the teachers, a young woman called Gerty, was our next door neighbour. When we found that she had not been paid for several months and that she was staying in Aba only because she didn't want to be a burden on her parents who lived near Owerri, we arranged with her that we would feed her if she would help with the cooking. On our first walk along the road that evening Gerty, Len and I were surprised when a green Morris Minor car passed us and then reversed back. We were hailed by a hearty Irish voice and so we met Fr. Owen Carton, our parish priest who apparently lived just a few hundred yards away. He was the first white person I had spoken to since we left Enugu five months before. We chatted for a few minutes and then he asked us to call and see him at the Mission some time. He told me to write a letter to my parents and he would try to have it sent out to them, giving them an address to reply to.

Now that I was eating again I began to feel a bit better so that what happened next was a great surprise. I had arrived at Aba on a Monday and by the Friday I felt well enough to accompany Gerty to the market about a mile away. After rising, dressing and having breakfast, we started to prepare to go to the market. I don't remember the rest but I am told I made a list of what I wanted to buy and we walked to the market. We had bought everything and I was apparently acting normally, by now the sun was high in the sky and I was feeling the effects of the scorching heat. The market stalls were roofed but there was no shade for the customers.

"There is something I need to buy from the other side of the market," said Gerty. "You wait here; I won't be long." We both knew that if we were seen together the prices would surely rise.

Unfortunately, while she was away I collapsed and lost consciousness. She returned to find me being helped into a car which took me to the General Hospital where I remained unconscious for three days and semi-conscious for another three.

Gerty managed to get a message to Len at his office and he rushed to the hospital to find me writhing on the floor of the casualty room, moaning and calling out. Nobody seemed to know where to start treating me. A doctor came and prescribed but when there was no change after a few hours, it proved impossible to find him. Len drove from one doctor's house to another looking for someone to treat me. They were all out except for one who refused to come because I had already been seen by the first doctor who, he said, should continue to treat me. After some persuasion he prescribed but without seeing me. By evening I was still on the same floor, the first doctor could still not be found and Len was getting frantic. Eventually, a West Indian Staff Nurse advised him to go back to one of the doctors who had been out earlier in the day. He had just got back home when Len arrived but, after hearing his story, he agreed to come to the hospital and examine me. He arranged for me to be admitted to a ward where, as I was still extremely restless, I was laid on a mattress on the floor.

The hospital was very overcrowded and understaffed. Many of the patients were air raid victims but there were also wounded soldiers. The ward I was in was divided into cubicles and I was lucky to have one to myself. This was partly because the single ward hand wash basin was in it and there was no room for a second bed. For the whole time I was unconscious, Len scarcely left my side. The overworked staff turned a blind eye as he did what he could for me. The parish priest came and administered the last rites as I lay unconscious. Bernadette, an Azigbo nurse who was on night duty at another hospital, came to relieve Len for a short while. I was under the effects of the drug Paraldehyde and eventually my brain started to function – after a fashion. I had the idea firmly fixed in my mind that Len and the nurses were floating horizontally.

"When did you learn to move like that?" I asked him.

"I have always been able to move like this," he answered.

"Well why can't I move like you?" I continued, "Everyone else seems to know how." There was a big hole right above my head and people kept floating over it effortlessly. In reality, my head was twisted back and I was seeing the open window behind the bed. To me, however, it was a hole in the roof and as I never saw their legs thought they were all floating.

Then I noticed there was a suitcase beside my bed and also a thermos flask on the bedside table.

"This isn't my bed. These things don't belong to me. The owner will come back and want this bed. I need to find my bed which will have my belongings."

As I started to get up a nurse approached.

"This is your bed and the suitcase and flask are yours," she told me. I knew she was wrong and I decided the only thing for me to do was to walk around until I recognised my belongings beside an empty bed. I took to wandering around and time after time I was returned to the same bed. I must have been a nightmare patient but as I was also the only white person I was at least easily found. I later understood that the flask and suitcase had been loaned to me.

At another time I believed I was rushing down a big shaft in the sea with wooden beams and walls towards a brighter place. Later I realised that I had been on a trolley and being taken to another part of the hospital.

When they were not available in the hospital dispensary Len was unable to buy the drugs prescribed for me in any of the local chemists. Eventually, he was advised to try the main market and there he found all the items he needed, including intravenous drips. Once I woke and grabbed at a long brown object floating in front of me. "What a big fish!" I exclaimed. Then I caught hold of it and it was warm and hairy! I realised it was Len's arm. "I must be going mad," I said. "No," said Len, "You are just getting sane."

On 8th February 1968, my sixth day in hospital, I asked what the date was. On being told I stated that the next day would be my sister's birthday and I was right. From then on I made rapid progress. The doctor had still not made a diagnosis and there were so many critically ill patients that, now that I was fully conscious having no pain and able to get about, I hardly saw him. I made friends with two young patients and we used to sing together in the evenings. In fact, when I sneaked a look at my case notes, I saw that one nurse had written in the report that I was singing from the 'Record Song Book'.

Len's cousin Vicky, who was a widow and a corporal in the CID, lived opposite the hospital, in the police barracks and she sent all my meals in for me. Incidentally, it was her husband's funeral we went to attend on the day our car was stolen near Onitsha. He was a policeman and was killed at Nsukka when his patrol was ambushed at the start of hostilities.

As I was still weak and as the doctors were still puzzled, I stayed in the hospital for another week. Meanwhile, Len got a message from home that Ada was ill and his mother wanted him to come and take her to hospital. The same week there was a big air raid on the market at Awgu. It was the worst raid up to that time and over one hundred died and the wounded taken to various hospitals. In Aba the doctors came round discharging all the patients they could but I was not. On the Saturday Len left for Azigbo as he had decided to bring Uche and Ada and Paulina back with him and keep us all at Aba.

The same afternoon lorry loads of wounded started to arrive and I went out to where they were unloading. I don't know how many were in each lorry but they seemed to be all on top of each other. Red Cross volunteers started to bring them out. The floor of the lorry was about four feet from the ground and trying to lift down 'stretcher cases' without stretchers was very difficult. Among the casualties were some babies and children and some very old people. Those of us who were patients were ordered back to bed. The few trolleys the hospital had were put to full use whilst the children were carried in the arms of Red Cross volunteers. Those who could walk were helped along and the nurses erected all the spare beds and even put mattresses on the floor between them. Even the linen cupboard had a bed set up in it and more beds and mattresses were put on the verandas.

The moans and cries of the patients were terrible to hear. From my window I could see them pass a few feet away. A young Biafran Red Cross man wheeled a trolley past. On it lay a man with his head covered in blood. A few minutes later the same trolley came back empty. Outside my window the young man stopped and wrung out the pillow. The blood ran out like water from a sponge.

The staff were all working flat out. I managed to stop one of the doctors as he hurried by.

"I can't stay here," I told him. "These people need a bed much more than me. Please discharge me," I implored him.

He was too busy to argue. "Very well he said but you will need to come back tomorrow to collect the medicines you will need to continue to take."

Fortunately, he did not ask where I was going, which was just as well as I didn't really know myself. I had been told that the police barracks were near the hospital but I didn't know exactly where, nor did I know Len's cousin's room number. I didn't know the way to our house from the hospital either, nor did I have a key. I told the houseboy who brought my next meal from Vicky that I was leaving the hospital and asked him to tell his madam that I would come with him to her rooms when he came for the empty plates. I hoped she could then take me back to the rooms we rented. I explained to some of my co-patients where I was going in case anyone came looking for me and asked the nurses to tell Len when he came back.

Len's cousin made room for me to spend two nights with her. I was unable to get my medicines until the Monday but the ward nurses gave me enough to get on with. As I was taking a barbiturate three times a day, I found myself too weak to do much. However, I did take care to find out where to take cover should there be an air raid!

I was very relieved to get out of the hospital. There had been two air raids on Aba while I was in there and we all felt very vulnerable, being in the middle of town and in a compound surrounded by a high fence. Being a hospital did not make us immune from being a target. On the Monday Len went to the hospital and was surprised to find I was not there and unfortunately he didn't meet anyone who knew where I had gone. He had just come from our house and he arrived at his cousin's in a rush. On the way home he told me he had brought Uche and Ada and Paulina. He also told me that his mother had shaved both the children's heads! This had been a long-standing issue between me and Nne who thought that all small children should have their heads shaved for hygienic purposes. All the other small children had their heads shaved and after seeing the fuss we had each day in combing their curly hair, she decided to take things into her own hands. They looked awful. What with their bald heads and the dirt on their bodies, partly due to the water shortage and partly to the dusty journey, they were a sorry sight, so I washed and washed them and they shed so much red dust they changed colour completely.

I became very nervous about leaving our rooms for any reason. The onset of my illness had been so dramatic, without any warning, that I was afraid of a repetition. Even going across the yard to the toilet was delayed as long as possible. I was still taking the barbiturates and was pretty tired most of the time. Sometimes I found myself several yards away from where I thought I was so I did no cooking at all in case I should fall over the stove. The fact that the doctors had not told me what had been wrong with me didn't help re-assure me and when I asked one on my fortnightly check-up if I had had epilepsy, he said it was possible. I went home and read all about the condition in my nursing text books, which advocated no swimming, or driving, care when cooking and that one should not get married – and there I was with two children already. I was really worked up by the time Len came home. He, however, was convinced it wasn't epilepsy and told me so. The final verdict was that it had probably been encephalitis or cerebral malaria.

I continued going for check-ups and more supplies of phenobarbitone until we left Aba in August. One morning a neighbour gave me a glass of refreshing palm wine just after I had taken my tablets. Within minutes I was fast asleep and slept for five hours! The danger of mixing alcohol with medication was well driven home.

Two days after I got back to our home on the outskirts of the town there was another big bombing raid on Aba and twenty four bombs were reported dropped. This was one of the biggest raids on a town during the war and caused considerable upheaval. We decided that Ada, whose baptism had been put off several times, should wait no longer. That same evening we went to see Fr. Carton. Bernadette, our nurse friend who had helped me so much in the last few weeks, agreed to be Godmother and the next day we went to church where Ada, then twenty months old, was baptised Adaora Janet. The others being baptised were all small babies. Uche, sitting a row behind, was quite peeved that she didn't have her head washed too! The same day I received a letter from my parents, the first news I had had from them in eleven months. The next day I ventured out alone for the first time to buy a writing pad and envelopes to write a reply.

A carpenter with a small roadside workshop across the road from us had just finished a simple double bunk frame for Uche and Ada and we had two special mattresses with waterproof covers made to fit. Len surprised me by buying me a set of jewellery, a necklace, brooch and earrings set with green stones. He also bought two buckets, two plastic plates, two plastic cups, earthenware cups and saucers and a frying pan. The people living in the town centre were becoming increasingly nervous about the air raids and many of them left for the nearest wooded land each morning, returning to their homes at night. As we were living on the outskirts of town, we stayed put.

News reached us that Len's brother-in-law had died after falling from a palm tree which he had climbed to cut palm leaves to cover the zinc roof of the house as camouflage. He left behind three young daughters and his wife, Irene, two months pregnant. At the same time Edmund's daughter was preparing to get married so Len went home to console Irene and take the place of his late brother at the bride price ceremony for Beatrice. Marriage customs vary very widely in Nigeria even within an area of a few miles. In most places a bride price is paid by the bridegroom and his family to the family of the bride. Before this each family will have looked carefully into the background of the other, checking that there was no criminal background, insanity or any black mark on their reputation. Some families were still considered as outcasts, known as Osu, descendants of slaves which would prevent them from marrying Nwadalia (sons of the soil.) The Osu caste system has since been legally ended. The amount is fixed by negotiation and such factors as the amount of education the girl has had, how pretty she is and how she rates in wifely skills are all taken into consideration. There are comings and goings between the two families with traditional gifts given and customs observed. Marriage is seen as being an alliance between two families, not just a union of husband and wife. Extended family links are very important.

Back at Aba food prices were starting to rise dramatically. I kept track from time to time in my diary. Before the war a cup of salt was two pence (there being 240 old pence to the pound), rice was four pence, beans (black-eyed peas), three pence. A cup was a metal tin which had become a unit of measurement when cigarettes were also sold in tins. Buyers were well aware that a battered cup would hold less and some unscrupulous people were believed to put in a false bottom. By the middle of March 1968 we were paying six shillings a cup for salt and seven pence for rice. Salt, being an imported commodity, became much scarcer later in the war and other prices also rose steadily. As more salt is needed in tropical climates a cup a week was our usual consumption as a family.

I started to go to work with Len. The Onitsha Library was using part of the school buildings which were now also housing the offices of the BCB, so I spent the mornings reading the few foreign papers which found their way there and then the biographies and reference books which were all that had been brought out of Onitsha. My nerves were still in pretty bad shape and I just couldn't stay at home with the children day after day. On those days when Paulina had to go to market I had to stay home but the change of atmosphere and my ability to lose myself in a book were absolute life lines. As the library was so small, borrowing was forbidden but as I could normally finish at least one book a day, that didn't worry me too much.

One drawback, however, was that our home and Len's work place were at different ends of the town. Wilcox Memorial Grammar School, now the Ministry of Information offices housing the BCB, the library and other departments, was at the top of Ogbor Hill, virtually overlooking the main town. Our car was giving us trouble again, especially in starting and fuel was becoming more precious daily. The fighting was now around the oil areas to the south of us as the Nigerian troops tried to reach Port Harcourt and its giant refinery. Those on essential services had official petrol quotas and Len started with twelve gallons a month but that was later reduced to four gallons.

People still strived to carry on with life as near to normal as possible. Our spirits were still high and we decided to enrol at a local correspondence school in GCE subjects. One of my choices was Economics but unfortunately we were unable to keep paying the fees and the whole thing lapsed after a while. We also tried to arrange a settlement for our 16mm cine camera which Len had hired to the television boys at Enugu and which had been left behind when they left there. Now they refused to pay either the accumulated hire fees or even to admit that the camera was lost. Eventually we were asked to claim for the replacement value and that was the last official word.

On 1st April we heard distant shelling which was rumoured to be from Uyo. Four days later there was an air raid on Aba and a bomb hit a petrol station in the town centre. A Biafran Army officer carrying explosives was in his car a few yards away and the car blew up. We discovered later that he had been best man at a wedding in Lagos at which Len and I were the witnesses. The total dead on the spot were thirty-three in number. We had passed the spot barely five minutes before on our way to work; it was a grim reminder of the seriousness of the situation.

There had been some re-allocation of classrooms at Wilcox and one morning a new sign was set up to acknowledge the birth of the *Biafra Time* magazine. It was to be modelled on the American *Time* magazine and the editor was the former editor of the very popular *Drum* magazine, Nelson Ottah. He had found readjusting to life in Biafra difficult and the frustrations he had with this new venture could not be underestimated. To install the printing machine a room had to be virtually rebuilt. The floor was dug up and reinforced and a wall had to come down to get the machine in. Then the surrounding ground was so soft that the low loader bringing it sank and had to be dug out. Cement had to be obtained in considerable quantities and it was almost impossible to find any to buy at all. The type and paper were also giving headaches and the production side was unable to catch up with the backlog of issues ready to be printed. Added to all this there was also a difficulty about paying for the materials and contributed articles.

Petrol rationing was getting tighter and black market fuel passed the £1 a gallon mark. At the bank there was a terrific shortage of money so that every day almost all the customers were there before opening time to try and withdraw a pound or two. It seemed that most of the town's business was being done at the bank. Withdrawals were almost always limited to less than £10 per customer and often only £1 was paid out and on several occasions no payment at all was made for some days. Needless to say, no one was depositing money and as the 'come tomorrow' days became more frequent, all prices were rising.

On 13th April people danced round the town as the news that Tanzania had recognised Biafra as a nation spread. This was a great morale booster although the recognition did not take the form of actual support of aid in any form. The Nigerian side responded by stepping up and on the 22nd Aba had its worst raid. Bombs falling on Pound Road and Okigwe Road killed over ninety. Some bombs had fallen on the police barracks where Len's cousin, Vicky and her children, stayed and first thing in the morning we went to the General Hospital, then to the mortuary. The victims were laid out for identification in front of the small mortuary building. Many people had already removed their dead but there were more than fifty bodies still there. Some were horribly mutilated while others had no visible wound at all and looked asleep. There were several children and a woman's headless body, as well as a man's head with no body attached while a five-foot high mound of pieces of human limbs and organs was set to one side. A silent crowd tried to identify the remaining corpses. The silence would be broken periodically with loud wails as a body was identified. Relatives brought speedily made coffins and took their dead away for burial. As we moved away porters brought mats to protect the remains from the sun, flies and the vultures which were already wheeling overhead.

I felt great anger against the outside world which turned away from this wanton slaughter of defenceless civilians who only asked to be left in peace having been driven out of most of Nigeria.

In front of the Outpatients Department men sluiced the blood-covered floors and even the sand in the compound was stained scarlet. A heap of charred clothing was piled against a pillar. We were numbed. We had not recognised anyone but some of the bodies were beyond recognition and others had already been removed. We crossed the road and went to the police barracks.

Vicky's quarters were locked up. As we stood outside a neighbour appeared and told us that Vicky had moved out to a friend's house a few days before, then he pointed out to us another house and told us that a couple from it had been killed. Apparently the wife had come from her home village with their baby to collect some housekeeping money from her husband. She put the child on the bed while she took a few steps outside with him and they were both killed while the baby was unharmed. We murmured something and walked on.

The following day there was another raid. The day after I was reading in the library when I heard a plane approaching. I moved quickly to the door and stood behind it against the wall. I hoped that the triangular space formed by the two walls and the wooden door would offer some protection if needed. There was a loud bang from an anti-aircraft gun nearby and almost immediately I heard the sound of metal pieces landing on the roof. My heart leapt wildly but the building held. The sound of the plane died away and I emerged to find no visible damage. However, a small crowd was making for a spot some ten yards away and in a minute or so one of them returned carrying a long metal cylinder. The anti-aircraft rocket had misfired, exploding over the library roof. The crowd followed behind as the shell was carried back to the gun crew who were already examining their missile launcher. "My brother, I think you dropped this one," said the man as he handed back the case. These home-made weapons at this stage of the war were prone either to jam or misfire and, as there was no warning system, they were sometimes unmanned at the time of attack. Overzealous lookouts mistook vultures for planes and at times the crews were asked by those around not to draw attention to their location by firing when planes did appear. After asking the gun crew to leave killing us to our enemies, everyone went back to work.

Fighting around Port Harcourt was now heavy and petrol restrictions were increased. In order to get the official quota the car owner had to take the paper stating his allowance to the Treasury and join a long queue. After checking that the paper was genuine the money was paid and a treasury receipt issued. This could take two days. The car was then taken to a petrol station which had supplies where another long queue formed. Some drivers slept at the petrol stations for two nights before being served; most of them were waiting for fewer than four gallons.

On 8th May 1968 Gabon accorded diplomatic recognition to Biafra. Although everyone rejoiced, the news of the worsening situation in Port Harcourt dampened the festivities. On 16th May, Radio Biafra announced that Biafran troops had killed twenty thousand out of twenty-seven thousand Federal troops and captured large quantities of arms, but the next day Port Harcourt was being evacuated under heavy shellfire. Everyone was very downcast now that the main port and the oil refinery were out of our grasp. Even the news on the 20th that Zambia had recognised Biafra did little to boost morale. Refugees streamed in from the South, food prices rose sharply and salt disappeared completely from the local market and was sold secretly for eighteen shillings a cup. There was no petrol or kerosene and, of course, no cooking gas. Electricity was spasmodic and we joined the masses cooking on firewood. Peace talks in Kampala yielded nothing but no one had had much hope of peace anyway.

At home Uche and Ada were now adept at 'taking cover' and learned the marching songs sung by the recruits on their morning marches through the town. There were no toys for them now and they played with old tins, mud and grass. One day we took them for a walk and they picked wild flowers. Uche gathered hers in a bunch but Ada, coming up for two years old, was occupied in taking one blossom to pieces. After throwing the stalk away she would refuse to walk on until Uche had given her a replacement. Eventually Uche tired of her sister's demands and handing her yet another flower she told her, "If you lose that one, I'll take it back!"

A few days later while eating our evening meal, Uche told me, "If this fish bone enters my tummy I will go to hospital and change my tummy."

These lighter moments of innocence were welcome. Both children were growing and I cut up one of my dresses to make two little dresses for Uche who was outgrowing hers which, in turn, were passed on to Ada. Both children were now barefoot as there were no shoes to be found.

We were still able to listen to our portable radio to the news from other countries, especially the BBC World Service, Voice of America and Vatican Radio. On 3rd June a message was broadcast for me on the BBC World Service Morning Show programme. My parents wished me a happy birthday, more than six weeks late and nearer Uche's birthday, which was two days before. Later that month Switzerland and Czechoslovakia announced they were sending aid to Biafra and the *Daily Sketch* in the UK said they were sending half a ton of dried milk.

I also noted in my diary that in June we paid for the car insurance premium and for three months' vehicle tax. Even in such times of air raids, refugees and all the associated difficulties, no one would take the risk of having their precious vehicle seized for not having the right particulars. Meanwhile, I was invited to write book reviews for the *Biafra Time* magazine, starting with the June issue. Unfortunately, although the issues up to September were compiled, only the April and May magazines were ever published.

Relief materials from the outside world were now starting to trickle in but most of the refugees were totally dependent on the local people for food and shelter. A few refugee camps opened in schools. Individuals and organisations helped and the Government appealed for those who could to offer homes to the homeless. In the camps there was no food most of the time and many refugees begged at the roadside. Although fairly common in some parts of Nigeria, begging was previously held in great contempt by the Igbos but now people were faced with a choice of that or starving and there were many cases of kwashiorkor. Life was trying hard to be normal. Law and order was, in fact, maintained right to the end of the war. Prices continued to spiral and the packet of eight candles that had been one shilling and sixpence before the war was now twelve shillings and sixpence. They were used very sparingly.

Edmund's daughter announced that she would be getting married in August, whilst all around we were walking the same road with death. One rainy Monday we were coming back from work when we came up behind a cyclist pedalling along with a corpse tied seated on the carrier. Although the head and trunk were covered with a cotton wrapper, the legs hung down lean and naked.

When Helen arrived from Azigbo a few days later she told us that Nne had contracted kwashiorkor. This is the wasting disease caused by malnutrition and in particular, protein deficiency. We went to the bank and were stunned to discover there were only 8 shillings and 4 pence in our account and we had issued cheques amounting to ten pounds which had not yet been presented. There were a few people who owed us small sums and I had still some artiste's fees from the TV programme at Enugu. Len put in his claim for official mileage allowance and we tried to speed the payment process for these. A friend, who did not know how desperate we were, suddenly repaid a loan of three pounds while another friend loaned us two pounds so we were thus able to send some money back with Helen to relieve the situation. Kwashiorkor was the real enemy in Biafra and responsible for the deaths of many thousands of civilians of all ages but particularly the old and the very young.

By 10th August we were hearing shelling every day. After about five days a decision was taken to evacuate the military hospital; panic hit the town and the people started to leave en masse in the middle of the night. We were awakened by a neighbour who was a nurse on night duty at this hospital. She came home at 1am, calling her houseboy to get up and start to pack. The whole house was roused and by the time she had gone back to work everyone was outside debating the situation. We tried to go back to sleep, thinking it was a false alarm but at 3 o'clock she came back and said the whole town was moving.

Living as we did on the outskirts of the town, it was not at first apparent what was happening. We still felt there was surely no need to run like this but although we tried to get back to sleep again everyone around us started packing, and eventually Len decided to go in to town and see for himself. A lot of people from Len's village lived at Tenant Road and it had been arranged that should any emergency arise the Azigbo Progressive Company lorries would take the Azigbo people home and they would congregate at Simon Okafor's house at No. 23 Tenant Road. When Len reached the place, the lorries were already there and being loaded. There was great confusion as those outside packed boxes, bundles and children in to the lorries.

He entered the house and got a bigger shock. Simon, on being roused by someone beating on the door shouting that Aba was running, had had a heart attack. The crowd outside didn't know that the chairman of the A.P.C. was lying dead, only feet from them. His death was a great shock as he was a man highly respected in his own village and was for years a councillor on Aba Town Council. His body was put in one of the lorries to be taken home for burial but at the outskirts of the town the vehicle was turned back by the natives of the area who accused the people of deserting the town as soon as trouble threatened. Eventually, they said that if everything except the body was offloaded, the lorry could pass.

Meanwhile back at home I told Paulina, "Cook a big pot of beans so that if we have to move we would at least have cooked food."

I packed our suitcases while trying not to wake the children and Len returned around 8am. The exodus continued all that day though there was no shelling. The following day was the same. Len went to get petrol but there was none. During the panic of the first night the few petrol stations which had any fuel finished it all and we had no money again. Our young nurse friend Bernadette asked us to put up her young brother for a night and in the morning, before they both left for home, she gave us five shillings and some garri. We had only a couple of shillings of our own and the banks had closed because of the unsettled situation. People from around Aba were also pulling out, some passed through the town and transit camps were set up at various points. One was at the Mission along the road and several hundred people were camping there. On the morning of the 20th I went there to see if I could be of any use to Fr. Carton at the camp.

"My God," he exclaimed. "Are you still here? I thought after you had been so ill you had left the country."

"No, I haven't been out very much but I am very much here," I responded. "I have come to see if I can be any help to you with the refugees you have here."

On questioning me he soon found out our situation and said he was very sorry that I had not come to him before. I was not able to endure the crowded church on Sundays as I have always found it very difficult to stay in a crowd, especially when I can't move around and so, rather than have to draw attention to myself trying to get outside during mass or, worse still, fainting (which I have done more than once), I stayed at home.

So instead of me helping him with the refugees, he gave us the first relief we were to get in the war. I did not even know then that any relief was being sent in to Missions so I was speechless and close to tears as he brought from various corners of the Mission thirty-eight cups of dried beans (we measured them later), an eight ounce jar of Marmite, an eight ounce tin of Nescafe, two bags of ground coffee, a five pound tin of beef, nine large onions, two pounds of flour, four bars of washing soap, a cake of red Lever soap, a packet of matches, sixteen candles, a tin of dried milk and a tin of cream. (Virtually none of these items could be seen at all in the local market.) He then asked how we were for money; I replied that we had none and he insisted on giving me fifteen pounds, then dipping into an enormous pocket in his soutane he brought out a handful of loose change; there was fifteen shillings and eight pence there which he also gave me.

I asked if there was anything I could do to help him, which was really why I had come in the first place. He said that there were meals to prepare for the transit refugees twice a week and if I could come and help at the next cooking he would be grateful. The only other thing he needed help with was his car battery which needed charging.

When Len came back from work that day and saw what we had been given he could hardly believe his eyes. We spent the whole evening going to look at it all, touching each item one after the other. We could not help exclaiming over and over at the great change that had occurred in such a short time. We set some aside for a poor neighbour and the next day we took some to Paul who had helped us when we had no money. We also, of course, went together to thank Fr. Carton.

Len and I took the car battery to Broadcasting House the next day to have it put on charge; we were asked to bring two bottles of distilled water and, after a considerable search, we bought them for fifteen shillings. The battery was charged and returned to our benefactor.

While we were thanking God for His blessing on us, the front line was coming nearer and nearer. The sound of shells was now very close and the situation was clearly not good. Fr. Carton had told me to write a list of the things we needed most and also told me to write a letter to my parents in case he had a chance to send news out. When I took these to him the next morning there was another priest with him. He was introduced as Fr. Donal O'Sullivan the Fr. Superior of their order, Holy Ghost Fathers, in Biafra. Little were we to know then that he was to become the really great friend we made during the war and a life-long friend to our family. At this time he was very concerned about what would happen if Aba fell. There were a few other foreign wives of Biafrans in the town and he was anxious that they should all keep in touch with him so that he could help where he could.

They asked where I would go. "To Umuahia," I replied.

"Did I know anyone there?'

"No."

"Would I not think of flying out with the children?"

"No, we were a family and we are going to stay together. We married for better or worse and if this was the 'worse' we were going to be together to face it." Len had made that very clear.

Father O'Sullivan advised, "If you get stuck at Umuahia, go to the Holy Rosary Convent and ask for Sister Mary Thomas. Tell her I sent you."

Fr. Carton offered to take a suitcase of clothes to Mbutu Ngwa where he expected to be staying if he had to leave and I could get them back when I got settled. We were still hoping that it wouldn't be necessary to leave Aba. Many of those who had taken part in the mass evacuation had come back although some were removing more of their property. We saw one man with a dog in a large cage tied on the carrier of his bicycle; he had probably evacuated everything else. No one brought anything back. On Sunday 5th there was an air raid and bombs fell on Azikiwe Road and the town started to empty again.

On Monday there was heavy shelling throughout most of the day and we decided the time had come to move. We bought what we could from the market and Paulina made a big pot of egusi soup and cooked some beans again. We loaded the car, tied the mattresses to the roof and towards evening we set out for Ogbor Hill on the outskirts of town on the road to Umuahia.

There was the usual blackout. Groups of people were coming from all sides, old and young, walking along together carrying their possessions on their heads or on bicycles. There was no talking. No sound except for the shuffling of feet and the occasional cry of a baby. As we moved on, the groups joined up and formed an ever-thickening, never stopping stream. By the time we reached the main road there was barely room for the car to pass. There was an atmosphere I will never forget: a mixture of fear and faith. Some of those people later abandoned the few things they had salvaged when they could not carry them further, rather than stop and rest. Some abandoned sewing machines and suitcases.

When we reached the Owerri Road we turned right, heading back into the town centre on our way to Ogbor Hill. We were the only vehicle going that way. As we approached Barclays Bank we found the road ahead blocked. We were at the end of a long line of cars and eventually those in front started to turn back and we learned that the bridge at the bottom of Ogbor Hill, which the Army had been preparing to mine earlier that day, was not passable at present. We too turned back and made our way to Broadcasting House in the GRA (Government Residential Area), which still had a telephone link with Umuahia. What else could we do?

Chapter 5

Family Addition

When we reached Broadcasting House we found that some BCB families and others had gathered there to wait for transport. The building was a private house which had been requisitioned and fitted out with monitoring and broadcasting equipment while the studio was in another house two streets away. The monitors listened to the news broadcasts from other nations such as Voice of America, BBC World Service and Vatican Radio and any other national radio stations they could pick up. The monitoring equipment had been moved out already and we moved into an empty room, originally a bedroom, and slept there on the floor.

Lorries came in the middle of the night and were loaded both with BCB equipment and some of the families. On the Tuesday there was no water in the taps and no markets were held in the town. A lot of noise was coming from the railway station as people struggled to get onto the few departing trains. Some people who had spent the night with us went and dug up yams from gardens nearby for food.

One of Len's responsibilities was the battery charging room (in civilian days the garage). While looking at the machinery there he noticed a heap covered with a dirty white cloth in a corner. He pulled back a corner and there lay a little girl of about four years, very sick with kwashiorkor. She whimpered and tried to cover herself. Len put the old sheet over her again and a little later he came and told me. Shortly afterwards we saw her stagger out and approach some young men roasting yams on an open fire in the garden. They shared the yam with her and she went back to her little corner. When I had finished cooking our own food I sent some down to her but knowing the terror some children have of Europeans I did not go myself. A young couple seemed to be with her most of that day. We didn't know them and there was a lot of general confusion, especially as more people left and the battle front was apparently nearer.

On Wednesday morning Len and I made a last trip back to our old home. We called at Fr. Carton's house but it was locked up. However, I pushed a note under the door. When we got back to our rooms the whole building was deserted. In fact the whole street was empty. We had now removed all our furniture except for a coffee table, the kitchen cupboard and the frame of the girls' bunks. We put the coffee table on top of the car and went to the little garden plots at the side of the house where we picked some vegetables, or rather leaves, and dug up a few yams but they were too small so we put them back in the ground again. The sound of shelling was now very near and there was also the sound of small arms and the unmistakable sound of Ferret armoured cars. I told Len, "I can hear Ferret cars and I am not waiting to see them. Let's go."

We went back to Broadcasting House where a final lorry had arrived and we loaded most of our furniture in it and all the other things that had been left behind and the few people remaining without transport of their own, got on board. The little kwashiorkor child came outside but no one seemed to be making any move to put her in the lorry. The young couple who had been looking after her had left on a motor bike that morning. I thought he might have made an arrangement with someone to bring her to Umuahia but no one seemed to be caring for her. Len stepped forward, lifted her up at the back of the lorry and asked the people inside to take her. They refused, saying that there was no one to look after her and she had better travel in the front of the lorry. The front of the lorry is the best place and mothers and children try to sit there if possible. Len carried her round to the front of the lorry.

"Please take her," he said. "There is no room. Let her go in the back," replied the driver who was clearly anxious to go.

As Len carried her towards the back of the lorry the driver started the engine and drove off. Len stood the child on her feet. She looked across at our laden car and said to Len in Igbo, "Papa nga eso na moto," that is "Papa I will go in the motor". Papa would have been how she addressed any adult man. It was 28th August 1968 and so Nnenna joined us.

Len and I looked at her carefully. She was filthy, she smelt, flies hovered all round her. Her whole body was swollen, her eyes were barely open. She had an enormous tummy and the little pink cotton dress she wore hardly covered her bottom. Interestingly, the dress had had a frill added to lengthen it which I recognised as Royal Stewart tartan. As she stood there, fluid from her swollen legs trickled out through little cracks. Her groin and buttocks were red raw, her hair was sparse, white and straight. The only strong thing about her was her voice. She had a very shrill penetrating voice, like that of an old woman. After a long pause Len spoke.

"Is it infectious?" he asked. "Not unless she has lice," I replied.

Obviously we could not abandon her. By some miracle the water tap which had been dry for several days, started to work and I led her to it and put her under it after removing the dress with difficulty. She was obviously in considerable pain as I washed her as best I could. She couldn't walk more than a couple of steps but to carry her was agony for her too. Back at the car we rearranged things, tied more possessions on the roof, stowed some smaller articles under the seats and on most of the back seat. Paulina and Uche got in the back and the little child joined them while I took Ada on my knee in the front, with the radio and soup pot sat on the floor by my feet and Len prepared to drive off. Just then a man drew up on a motor cycle. He went into the house and came out carrying the telephone. It had been agreed that the telephone link to Ogbor Hill should be maintained as long as there was any chance that we might not have to leave Aba; the removal of the phone was the last act.

We asked the child her name. She told us it was Nnenna. That was the only information she ever gave us about herself. Nne is the Igbo word for mother and Nna is for father. When she was born she had probably been given the name as she resembled a grandparent, perhaps the mother of her father. Many Nigerians believe that when someone dies they may return as a baby in the same family. As we made our way out of Aba it was clear that each movement of the car was causing her pain and she whimpered but there was nothing we could do. The town was virtually deserted. The road which we had been unable to pass on Monday was now re-opened for single line traffic. After the first few miles we started to pass refugees in transit camps set up in schools by the roadside.

We stopped to buy garri. Nnenna wanted to drink it but there was no water to prepare it so we moved on. The car was going very slowly and at first we thought it might just be overloading but eventually we had to stop. We were back to our old trouble of binding brakes. Just in front was another car in trouble and a soldier came back from it to borrow a spanner. When he saw us all crammed in the car with Nnenna he started asking questions. We all climbed out of the car and Nnenna announced that she was hungry. Just beside us was a heap of coconuts for sale. She wanted one but the owner was not around.

"Why is she crying?" asked the soldier. "Because she is hungry and ill," we explained. He took two coconuts and smashed them against each other just as the owner arrived.

Water was brought for Nnenna to have her garri and the coconut was shared among us all. She sat down in the sand to eat.

After some work on the car we set out again for Umuahia. A Nigerian plane crossed the road ahead of us and as we bundled out of the car and took cover at the road side, we heard the bombs explode. When we reached the place where they had landed we saw a large tree, a few feet away from the road, had been uprooted but fortunately it had not blocked the road. Nnenna started to cry again. We were worried about the effect the car journey was having on her but we had to push on. The car started giving trouble once more and we were forced to stop again. It was now more than three hours since we had set out from Aba although the distance between the two towns is only about 40 miles.

Once more we all got out of the car. The road was almost deserted except for a local eating house or 'hotel' in a thatched hut a few feet away. We asked Nnenna if she would like to eat garri. She said, "Yes," so Len gave Paulina a shilling to go and buy her some garri with soup. Once inside the hotel however the child saw other people eating meat and at once demanded the same, so Paulina ordered sixpence-worth of meat for her, along with the garri. She only ate the meat and asked for more. Paulina came out but Nnenna refused to leave so Len paid for another shilling's worth of meat which she also finished. She still didn't eat the garri nor would she leave. Paulina said she would leave her if she didn't come but she was unconcerned. We eventually got her to leave after the hotel owner gave her one more piece of meat on that condition she left before finishing it. By this time a mechanic had almost finished working on the car. Uche and Ada behaved well, apart from having some trouble about where to go to the toilet. To them it was all a great game and the fact that it was already after six, we didn't know where we would sleep and, if we didn't reach Umuahia by curfew at seven, we might not even get into the town of course had no effect on their exuberance.

By the time we did reach the check-point at the outskirts of Umuahia it was well after seven. However, after answering some questions we were allowed to enter the town. We didn't know the way to the Holy Rosary Convent and to ask at that time would have labelled us saboteurs (anyone who had to ask his way had no right to be where he was). As we crossed the town, without lights as blackout was in force, we saw hundreds of people sleeping on the veranda of the Post Office. The market area too was a huge mass of people lying down, talking quietly. Okigwe had also been evacuated and it seemed everyone had made for Umuahia. Eventually, we had to ask and as we were so obviously refugees and, with a child like Nnenna, hardly likely to be spies, they gave us directions. We pushed on and eventually we had crossed the town to the checkpoint at the other side.

Fifty yards beyond was the drive leading to the Holy Rosary Convent and College. The soldiers guarding the entrance let us pass and we drove up the drive and stopped at the front door of the convent. Two very large dogs started barking before we stopped. In a minute a tall white-robed European nun came out.

"Who do you want?" she asked. "We would like to see Sister Mary Thomas," I replied and she went to call her.

By this time I had come out of the car and the children wanted to get out too. Sister Mary Thomas then appeared. Less than five feet tall, she was packed full of dynamism, had a heart of gold and a complete lack of fear of any man. All were combined in this Irish woman who had every one who met her shaking his head over her. She soon got over her initial surprise at seeing a strange family on her doorstep. We explained our position and she thought for a minute. Then she put us in the picture.

"I am a refugee too," she explained. "I moved out from Port Harcourt earlier in the year. The Holy Rosary College dormitories have been taken for the nurses at Queen Elizabeth Hospital which has been moved here. The classrooms are being used by the Red Cross as a store and even the staff houses have been commandeered. There is nowhere for a family to stay."

We looked at each other. What were we going to do? Then Sister Thomas remembered something. One of the classrooms happened to be temporarily empty and she might just be able to get a duplicate key. She went inside to speak to the other nun, Sister Mary Raymond, who was in fact her elder sister. Soon she reappeared with a hurricane lamp and walked over with us to the classroom.

"What are you going to do with her?" she asked, referring to Nnenna.

"We will take her to the hospital in the morning and see if they can help," we answered.

"The hospital is so over-crowded that she will probably die there. I will give you what I can find for her but what she really needs is food and looking after."

After letting us into the classroom she went off and soon returned with some thin mattresses and all sorts of foodstuffs. She had even found some high protein baby food but she warned us that the child was already very sick and might even die before morning.

"Don't cook tonight,'" she advised. "I'll bring you some tins." We explained that we would have to boil our soup pot to save the soup from spoiling but she came back again with Ovaltine and two unlabelled tins.

"One is meat, the other is fish – I think," she said. "Put one in your soup now."

I opened the first tin. It contained butter. Butter! Here we were, we who had not seen butter for over a year and a half, who hadn't even seen bread for months. And now we had an open tin of butter. There was no place to keep it, no fridge, and it would spoil in hours so we had to give it back to Sister Thomas. We opened the other tin which did contain meat and added the contents to our soup pot. We enjoyed a good meal and soon settled for the night.

We were pretty exhausted and lay down to sleep. Len and I never discussed what we should do with Nnenna. We saw that her only chance lay in staying with us but she was going to need a lot of help before she could become a normal child. We didn't know then that it would take a good six months. That night she cried out in her sleep for her mother but never referred to her again after that. We tried to find out more about her but every approach drew a blank and we know no more about her today than we did the first day we teamed up. We feel that her mind had probably refused to register the horrors she had seen and experienced.

She had a very strong will and that probably kept her alive. She refused to eat the high protein food or to drink the milk; she just wanted to eat garri or, more often, to drink it. Garri was what she had probably been used to eating. It is the staple food of the people and is made from the roots of the manioc or cassava plant. After washing, drying, grating and frying, a sawdust-like powder is obtained. This is garri. It can be drunk by adding cold water and as such is very refreshing and temporarily satisfies hunger. It is more usually added to boiling water and allowed to thicken into an almost solid form. It is then eaten with a local stew or soup by dipping a piece broken off in the hand and moulded into a lump, into a separate dish of soup. Nutritionally it is almost pure carbohydrate and though it has the advantage of satisfying hunger, its only other merit is that it is usually cheaper than rice or yam.

We woke several times each night to take Nnenna out to the toilet as she was incontinent.

On our first morning at Umuahia I went over to the convent to wash. On my way back I saw a heavily loaded car had arrived and was parked near ours. From it emerged another white wife, a Welsh woman, with her Igbo husband, two young sons, brother-in-law and three very large white hens which were all travelling in the car with her. They too were refugees from Aba but they had not come to Umuahia direct. As we stood talking a Peugeot pick-up drew up and out stepped Fr. O'Sullivan and I was very relieved to see him. Just then Nnenna appeared round the corner of the building. Fr. O'Sullivan could hardly believe his eyes. She was quite a sight to behold. As she had been complaining of cold, Sister Thomas had looked for some warm clothing for her but all she could find was a red school blazer made of wool and of a size that would fit a teenager. On Nnenna it barely skimmed the ground. I went to meet her as she tottered slowly towards us and we introduced her to the Irish priest.

Fr. O'Sullivan, murmuring, "I must find something for her," rummaged in the back of the pick-up. Deep down and well to the back he found a box of men's singlets. He brought one out and we removed the blazer and the skimpy little dress. As a result of her illness, where the skin had become sodden in the big fold under her tummy and on her thighs, she was mottled pink and brown. Fluid glistened on the cracks on her legs and a multitude of flies descended upon her. There was no point in attempting to put pants on her. Fr. O'Sullivan stepped forward and slipped the singlet over her head; the armholes came down to her buttocks while the hem trailed on the ground. Father looked at her apologetically then he smiled, raised the shoulder straps high about her head and tied them in a knot behind her neck. Nnenna raised her head and looked at him solemnly. She had no fear of white people but she was still too weak to make any overtures of thanks or friendship.

Our number one problem was now going to be accommodation. Fr. O'Sullivan left, promising to keep his eyes open. The Scandinavian representative of the International Red Cross arrived and was horrified to find two families camping in 'his' store, for the other family had moved in to the classroom next door which had a lot of desks and chairs stacked in it but hadn't been needed yet as a store. Sister Thomas drove us to the administrator's office, to the Catholic Boys' Secondary School and back to the convent. No luck. Everywhere was full and even overfull.

At the convent there was no water and Paulina had to walk a mile to fetch a bucketful. That morning she had written a letter to us asking to be sent back to her family in the village and let her suffer with them. We refused as we simply could not manage without her.

The next day, Friday, we went out with Sister Thomas again and visited the Housing Directorate but once more there was no luck. While we were out a Swedish Red Cross worker told our neighbour that we all might have to move out at very short notice.

On Saturday I went with Len to his office. All our furniture, which had been in the lorry from Aba, had been left outside for two rainy days, including the mattresses. The exception seemed to be the dining chairs which had disappeared completely and the legs of our dining table had been substituted for another set which didn't fit the top. We gathered what was left into one corner. So much for our staying at Aba, loading other people's furniture, while they went ahead and secured accommodation for themselves! Meanwhile, another visit was made to the Housing Directorate and the Provincial Office but again we had no luck.

On Sunday we stayed in and Nnenna seemed a little better. I had suggested taking her to the Queen Elizabeth Hospital but Sister Thomas said again they were so busy there that she felt that the food and individual attention we were giving her were the best we could do for her. Beside us the Red Cross were unloading stockfish, the first dried fish to enter the country in bulk since the blockade. These dried Icelandic cod are so hard that they have to be broken with an axe or machete. Small chips can be eaten dry but the fish is usually soaked and boiled. It is a popular source of protein in this area where there is little fresh meat or fish. The fish can keep almost indefinitely in its dry state. Nnenna was fascinated by the sight of the men cutting the fish into small rations and, of course, the characteristic aroma soon drew her nearer. Eventually, the men gave her a small piece which she started to eat at once.

The day before, I was astonished on coming back from the convent to see her making her way down the drive.

"Where are you going?" I asked.

"Away," (in Igbo).

"Where to?"

"Away!"

I turned her round and helped her back; she could scarcely reach the classroom. We wondered if this was how she had been living. Begging a meal here, a place to sleep there and moving on as soon as she felt stronger. It was a grim picture of life for a child who looked no more than three or four years old.

Gradually, as she grew stronger she picked up a few words of English. Uche and Ada were very helpful talking to her in Igbo, explaining things and fetching things for her. Nnenna had an exceptionally strong shrill voice and as she improved we heard a lot more of it. It was a couple of days before I realised that she was responsible for the banana skins I kept finding in odd corners and the trails of garri across the floor. If we offered them to her she would not accept them but later we would see that they had gone.

The discovery came on the Tuesday. That morning Len had left to do a job away from Umuahia involving the setting up of a radio transmission station. He expected to be away for only a few days but it was essential that the radio link with the outside world should be secure – Radio Biafra was a very important feature of the people's lives and there was near panic if it went off the air. So we were early to bed. It was a very dark night and though there were windows all along the sides of the classroom, no moonlight shone in. About an hour after we had settled I was startled by a loud clatter.

"Paulina?" I whispered, thinking either she had tripped looking for the candle or we had thieves.

"Mama Uche!" she quavered.

I groped about and found the matches and candle. The flickering light revealed Nnenna surrounded by cutlery, clasping a cup. She had decided to drink garri and had managed to find a cup, water and garri in the dark but when she reached for a spoon the tin of cutlery fell over. Although she would ask for a certain food, when it was cooked she would not eat. She would ignore it for hours but if we threw it away she would scavenge it out of the rubbish heap. We tried leaving her alone with the plate of food but still she didn't respond. She had another habit of going to the soup pot and helping herself to the meat with her fingers.

Our greatest problem at this time, and indeed for the next six months, was her inability to control her bowels. No matter how many times we took her to the makeshift toilet she messed herself up about a dozen times a day. One of her pastimes was to cover everything in reach with the mess. Every day we had to wash the mattress and mat she slept on and, quite understandably, Paulina got very fed up with this.

When we returned to the Housing Directorate the next day, my Welsh neighbour and I were both getting desperate. Our policy of hiding from the Red Cross or rushing by when one of them approached was quite a strain. The man in charge at the Directorate was just going out to a meeting when we arrived so we said we would wait and we did, for three long hours. He then allocated us a house at Umudike, some miles from the town centre. It was a house of two rooms which we were expected to share but when we got to it, we found that someone else had just moved in and had no intention of moving out!

The Swedish Red Cross representative cornered me and told me that I must move out that day as he was expecting a consignment of stockfish that night which was to go in the room we occupied. Sister Thomas was very busy with emergency feeding at kitchens that had been especially set up but Fr. O'Sullivan arrived and I told him of the latest development. He mentioned that a priest in a rural parish had offered the room his steward slept in to anyone desperate for accommodation. The steward, it appeared, had a house in the village and would not mind moving. However, Fr. O'Sullivan went to see the Red Cross leader first but couldn't find him. He went to the town but there was no one at the Divisional Office or the Housing Authority who could help. We had, it seemed, no choice in the matter.

Chapter 6

Off the Beaten Track

I decided that I had had enough and before Fr. O'Sullivan came back I had started to pack, although Len was not due back for another two days. I loaded what we would not need at once into our car and gave the keys and a note for Len to Sister Thomas. We packed the rest into Fr. O'Sullivan's car, piled the remaining furniture we had salvaged into one corner of the room and said goodbye to our neighbours. They had decided that the wife and boys would fly home to Britain. There were about eighty wives planning to leave at that time and once they had gone there were fewer than twenty of us left. Efforts were made to persuade me to go too with Uche and Ada but I refused. I would have worried much more had Len and I been separated like that and I knew Nnenna would probably not have survived either.

It was early evening when we left Umuahia and the children had not had supper. My usual policy of running with cooked food had not succeeded so they ate three packets of biscuits which Fr. gave them. He decided we should stop at Uboma for the night and continue in the morning on to Ugiri.

Although our arrival was unexpected at the convent at Uboma we were welcomed by Sister Joseph Therese. Hers was an indigenous order of nuns and they showed us wonderful hospitality. The English missionary doctor who normally lived with them was visiting some out- stations and we were put up for the night in her room. In a few minutes two girls arrived with buckets of hot water for us to bathe with and plates heaped with boiled yam, eggs and meat – a real feast. Paulina set up our kerosene stove and half cooked some Biafra beans. These beans were locally grown and had to be soaked for a day, part cooked, left overnight and cooked again for hours the following day. We expected the next day would be a busy one so she rose early in the morning to complete the cooking.

Fr. O'Sullivan had spent the night with some other Irish priests at a mission a few miles away. After eating breakfast he drove up, still with our old striped cotton mattress tied on top of his car, and we loaded everything in and moved on.

As we travelled down the main road, Father remembered that he had a message for Fr. Sweeney at Ehime so we turned off the main road and along an untarred track bordering a football pitch. As we approached the house we saw a large group of young girls around it. They had formed a long line and we remembered that it was the first Thursday of September and that the Legion of Mary had assembled for confession. All eyes were upon us as the laden car drew up. Father climbed out and the car was immediately surrounded by the girls. They gazed at us, pushing so close we could hardly breathe. Back through the crush came Fr. O'Sullivan with Fr. Tom Sweeney. He was the nearest priest to Fr. Michael Wasser in Umuahia diocese, living about seven miles apart. He was a very jovial and practical man who was trying to do much more than his health would permit and he was clearly in the midst of a very busy morning.

We soon said goodbye to Fr. Sweeney and re-joined the tarred road for another two miles before branching off to the left at Mbano on to an untarred road for the last few miles to Ogbor. About halfway we crossed a stream which was from where all our water would be fetched. Although Ogbor was where the priest lived, the parish was known as Ugiri and consisted of twelve villages covering an area approximately twelve miles by five, each with their own church and primary school.

There had been no time to let Fr. Wasser know we were coming and he too was busy hearing confessions when we arrived. However, he soon made us feel at home and had his cook make us coffee while he explained to his deaf and dumb steward, Martin, that he should move out of the old Father's house to his family home at the market a few hundred yards away. Martin was a tall young man whom Fr. Wasser had 'inherited' from the previous parish priest.

Although he had no formal education, he had a quick brain and by a series of grunts and gestures he was very well able to make himself understood. He served Mass and took great pride in ringing the church bell. To do this he climbed the tower and stood inches away from the bell while he summoned the faithful. The noise was terrific from ground level and I doubt if anyone with hearing could have stood as near the bell as he did!

He understood what was happening and packed up his few bits and pieces, the car was unloaded and we moved in. It was so much better than I had expected; a well-built bungalow about twenty yards from the Father's two-storey house. We learned it had been put up, in the days of the District Officer, for the visiting priest who needed somewhere to spend a night once in a while or the DO who had stayed over if there was a need for a legal decision in the days before Nigeria became an independent nation. Two small rooms flanked the parlour and little verandas connected them. Later, two more rooms had been added at the rear of these. To pass between them one had to come outside. After the erection of a modern 'upstairs' house for the resident parish priest, the bungalow became the parish office and store. Later, Martin had been asked to sleep there as a night watchman. The parish responsibilities included the maintenance and running of the local Catholic schools and churches so there had been some building materials stored there too.

The room Martin had used, the one behind that and the central room known as the parlour were cleared for us by the Uma Marys (Legion of Mary). There were four large tables and lots of shelves, some full of old books which I saw had been donated by the Library of Thurles in Ireland many years before. Fr. Wasser sent us over four armchairs and four dining chairs from the house and he also sent his spare single bed which we used with our own mattress. The journey had exhausted Nnenna and she curled up on the floor while we got things straight. Fr. Wasser then called us over and gave us some foodstuffs. He was very pleased at the thought of having some company as he was rather isolated, especially now that there was an acute shortage of fuel; his Volkswagen Beetle car was grounded and his electric generator had broken down. He now visited his parishioners on a light motor bike.

By the following morning, however, we all had mild dysentery. Fortunately, a barrister dropping in to see Fr. Wasser offered to take me to the hospital at Mbano to collect some medicines and by Saturday we were feeling a bit better though I had a temperature which I correctly diagnosed as being the start of malaria. On Sunday I was too weak to attend morning mass which caused a misunderstanding. Fr. Wasser had been touched apparently by our taking in Nnenna so he mentioned it in his sermon. He had never asked if we were Catholics or not and so, not seeing me in the congregation, he referred to me as "this woman, not even a Catholic". I knew nothing about this for several days until a young girl stopped and asked me:

"Madam, why are you not a Christian?"

"But I am," I said.

"But you are not one of us," she replied.

"How do you mean?"

"A Catholic."

"Of course I am a Catholic."

"Were you married in a church?"

"Yes."

"Well, Father said you are not!"

The next Sunday the priest had to put things straight while I tried to keep Uche and Ada quiet in the front pew.

In the intervening week I helped at the local food kitchen. Relief materials, supplemented by local palm oil and vegetables, were cooked by a committee of women and distributed to the villagers who assembled in the primary school. The proceedings took the whole of the morning. Immediately after mass the villagers, whose turn it was that day (for there was a rota system so that each village had a turn twice a week), arrived to collect the raw materials.

I usually went over to Father's house to help share out bags of cornmeal, rice, salt, dried fish, tinned meat, yams, sometimes a few jars of baby food, high protein baby cereal and some dried milk powder. The milk was to be mixed in buckets and shared amongst the children while everything else was cooked. The villagers were asked to bring what they could – vegetables, oil, pepper or even firewood. The teenage girls brought water and everyone brought their own plates. Most of those who came were children with a fair sprinkling of pregnant women and the very old. The majority were still too proud and not yet too desperate but more and more adults came each time as conditions worsened.

Nnenna, in spite of the improved living conditions and regular feeding, grew steadily worse. She became more and more swollen, weaker and less inclined to eat. She never gave any sign that she was pining for anyone and we could not understand it. She gave no information at all about herself and we wondered if the travelling had been too much. I was very worried about her and also that we had now been here over a week with no news of Len.

The catechist visited us and, noticing that the children had no beds, he gave us a bamboo bed for Nnenna. Later we bought two more for Uche and Ada. By the Saturday I was so worried about Nnenna that I asked Fr. Wasser to help me take her to hospital. When we arrived there was a great crowd awaiting treatment. I got out and carried Nnenna while Father went to get a treatment card and to see if there was a doctor around. We were lucky to see one quite quickly but there was not much he could do other than prescribe worm medicine and vitamins and ask us to continue trying to give her a high protein diet. The dispensary stocks were negligible but a Biafran Sister took me inside while Father waited in the car with Nnenna. Eventually we got some of the medicine and left but I was very low in spirit as we drove back to Ogbor.

That evening Len arrived from Umuahia with the car laden with what I had stacked in it plus some cloth and provisions from Sister Thomas. He told me she had been very upset when he finally turned up eight days after we had left for Ogbor. She berated him soundly for abandoning his young wife and children and a very sick child for days in a strange town without money or food or permanent accommodation. Before he had time to explain she thrust the car key and my note at him and disappeared inside the convent. Len was surprised and decided to wait for an opportunity to explain himself. After over an hour Sister reappeared and he was able to tell her that I had access to all we had. He explained why his return had been so delayed and she understood and apologised and even thanked him for coming back to explain. She then gave him some relief materials and cloth for us and told him to keep in touch with her.

He then explained that the car was not roadworthy and he could not move it until it had been repaired. Also he had no money. She asked him how much he thought it would cost and he told her so she said 'go and pray in the chapel' and a few minutes later she came and pressed into his hands the money he needed. She then insisted on accompanying him to the mechanics' shed where she astonished the man by telling him that this car had to be ready by five o'clock that day. In fact, the car wasn't ready until after six but Len determined to set out for Ugiri that night although he did not know the place at all. He arrived about 10pm and very relieved and pleased we were to see him. However, he wasn't at all well and complained of backache and fever and by the next morning it was clear he had malaria, so we didn't attend Sunday mass again. We had gone over the previous night to introduce Len to Fr. Wasser who left on the Sunday afternoon to spend the night at Umuahia and see what he could get for his parishioners.

By Monday Len was well enough to drive Nnenna and me to Mbano Joint Hospital. After prescribing treatment for Len and ordering him nine days sick leave, the doctor decided that Nnenna should be admitted to the ward. The custom, in many Nigerian hospitals, was for an attendant from home to stay with the child in the ward, usually the mother. We had no one to leave. Paulina was needed at home to look after the children, fetch water and go to the market so we explained the situation to the Reverend Sister in charge of the Children's Ward. We were on the point of leaving with Nnenna when she called us back. The ward was very overcrowded and such a patient would clearly be a big problem to the already overworked staff but it seemed there was no choice. We had done all we could at home and her condition was steadily deteriorating; she had to stay in the hospital.

We came home feeling downhearted. Len was suffering the after effects of his nights in the bush trying to install a radio transmitter but the malaria he now had was probably the only thing which had forced him to rest and I was only glad he had reached me before the fever got too bad. However, with his mind at ease regarding our accommodation and with the relief supplies and medication, he soon started to recover.

The strain of looking after Nnenna and trying to keep her clean had tired all of us. We expected that we could have a rest before she was discharged but that evening Fr. Wasser came back from Umuahia with two large bottles of vitamin pills, some diuretic tablets, eye-drops, aspirin and bandages.

"You're a nurse," he said. "Give these out to the worst ones at the feeding centres." I had never completed my training before I got married but reckoning that a little knowledge was better than none I agreed, little knowing what I was starting.

The following day there was no feeding centre so I cut out five dresses, two blouses and two skirts from the cloth Sister Thomas had sent. The dresses were for the children, the others for me. After cutting them all out I sewed one skirt by hand and arranged for someone to bring a sewing machine. The following day Len took the car and brought a girl and her treadle machine. I paid her one pound ten for the use of it for one day plus the thread I used. I sewed all the dresses and both tops while she helped with the hems and hand sewing.

112

At the feeding centres I now walked round the people as they waited; most of them were there a good hour before the food was ready. As I went I singled out the obviously sick, gave them little tokens and then gave them more intensive medical care. At this time I still only had the multi-vitamins and aspirins and for complaints not covered by these, I ordered what I knew they could get – plenty of fruit for the constipated and anaemic, boiled water only for those with diarrhoea, starch poultices and clean dressings for those with boils and open wounds and so on. The food kitchen was usually finished by early afternoon and I would then walk back home for lunch. I only attended the kitchen at Ogbor to supervise and my duties mainly consisted in ensuring that all the food was cooked and that those doing the actual cooking did not take an unfair share of the food home with them.

The afternoon was spent quietly at home. Often we would all have a siesta. At about 5 o'clock, when we would hear people passing going down to the local evening market a few hundred yards away, Fr. Wasser would walk over and we would stroll together down to the market and then about a mile further along the road. This we termed 'the constitutional' and it was enjoyed by all. The children would be either way ahead or running round us.

By the time we got back, which varied according to how many people with whom we stopped to chat, it was time for the children to have their supper and prepare for bed. With no electricity, candles or paraffin (kerosene), we did not keep late nights and it was dark around 7pm. We did have a transistor radio which we tuned in to, particularly for the BBC World News. Fr. Wasser had a portable record player running off batteries and as his sitting room was upstairs and got plenty of evening breeze, he would ask us over to spend an hour or so listening to records or chatting. By nine o'clock we were usually home and soon after would be in bed.

Len's malaria ran its course and he began to get ready to go back to Umuahia. He hoped to spend every second weekend with us if he could get petrol for the car or transport. The following Saturday

Len, Father and I were just going out for our evening stroll when a lorry stopped near the school. To my surprise two Sisters in ground-length white habits jumped down from the cab and started on foot towards us. The back of the lorry seemed alive and the canvas cover heaved and bulged to a growing crescendo of sound.

"It looks like Mother John," muttered Father. "I wonder what she wants." He looked around as if to take cover. "She always gets her way," he added reluctantly.

Meanwhile the two figures were obviously making for us. The younger one was limping and obviously struggling to keep up with her stouter companion. Mother John soon came to the point.

"We've been asked to leave our orphanage by the Air Force. We didn't think they were serious but they moved in this morning and I've got two lorries on the road behind me with the rest of the orphans, including about fifty babies. The older ones are with us in the lorry."

Looking back down the road we saw that already nearly a dozen children had clambered or were in the act of clambering out of the lorry. It was 6pm; in less than an hour it would be totally dark. I could almost hear Fr.'s brain churning as he wondered what to do with them.

The old primary school had a corrugated iron roof but only half walls and no doors. The new school was loaded to the roof with palm kernels which would normally have been turned into palm oil but due to the situation had had to be stored. Meanwhile, I was gazing at the other Sister. She was a beautiful girl, clearly not African but with an olive complexion and dark eyes. There was an aura of peace but also of sorrow around her. She didn't seem at all disturbed at the problem facing us, to her it was obvious that God would find somewhere for them to spend the night.

"The school at Umuozu is better," stated Father, "and there are better teachers' quarters. Let's go and see Mr. Okoroji there."

Mother John turned, "Sister Dolores had better stay with the children till I see the place."

Father brought out his Volkswagen which had just been repaired and Mother John climbed in. "Come on Leslie!" he shouted, so I got in too while Len went back to help Sister Dolores cope with the children who were now spilling out of the lorry.

As we bounced down the drive I looked back. She looked very tired and I hoped Len would be able to get her a cup of tea and a chair before we returned. We learned later that she had broken both legs in a car crash and that she was actually Lebanese although brought up in Nigeria. Dolores, Our Lady of Sorrows. She was well-named and although she loved the children and they her and the babies clung to her skirts while she played and taught them, there were times when her eyes were on the horizon and she knew nothing of the noise around her.

"It will do," was Mother's verdict when she saw the school, "but we cannot move tonight. They must stay at Ogbor tonight and move in the morning."

"But there are no toilets in the school at Ogbor. The pits have fallen in and there's no water," responded Fr. Wasser.

"Then we move tonight."

By the time we got back to Ogbor it was already dark; the children had lit fires and swept the classrooms and Len had just got Sister Dolores into our house and the kettle on the fire. Everything was put back into the lorry and the children rounded up and hoisted inside. Sister Dolores and Mother John and their driver climbed back into the cab, having refused the Ovaltine already prepared.

"We must get the children settled," said Mother and with a roar of the engine and a lot of rattling of loose buckets, they heaved down the drive, round the corner and out of sight. As we listened to them in the distance, Father turned to us.

"She'll want mass every morning, and how am I to get over there for Mother John and her chicks?"

The name stuck and she was always known as 'Mother John and her chicks' or 'Mother John and her brood' for she fussed protectively over her charges just like a broody hen.

"Don't forget the other two lorries and the fifty babies," I said. "They were told to come here!" Fortunately they had stopped elsewhere for the night.

They soon established themselves at Umuozu, about two miles from us. They had to share the school there with the World Council of Churches' store of relief supplies for Owerri Province, which had been evacuated from Egbu-Owerri. The store was being beautifully run by Bob Burke, a very sprightly elderly Irishman, aided by his charming wife Anne. They were scrupulously honest and set a great example of Christian love. With their only daughter married and living in Sweden, they had decided to stay on in Biafra where they had lived for many years as Protestant missionaries.

News of Nnenna from the hospital was not good.

"She doesn't want to get up," we were told.

She was sleeping in the duty room. I wasn't able to make the nine-mile round trip on foot to see her but Len always looked in on his way home and other people whose business took them in that direction brought us reports. It was thought it would be better if she didn't see me too much in case she refused to stay in hospital after the visit. We were very relieved when, after a few weeks, she was discharged and from then on she had no setback in her recovery.

On the Feast Day of St. Michael, Fr. Wasser gave me a Sunday missal. Although I had been a Catholic for five years, I had never owned my own missal. He was also saying the daily mass more slowly so that I could follow it.

Apart from the food kitchen, transport and supplies for the clinics in other villages were the big headache for me. I had bartered for an old bicycle with a carrier on the back. Accommodation was not too bad. The church or school in most of the villages were used for the feeding centres but medicines were virtually impossible to find. There were plenty of volunteers to help, even a few nurses from refugee camps who would give an occasional morning's work.

We knew that there was an International Red Cross store not too far away and Fr. Wasser and I went with his car to see if they would help. By providence we found the only European woman based there who also happened to be in charge. She was feeling isolated and rather lonely and made us very welcome. While she led me through the store, she explained that most of the supplies on the shelves were for hospitals but there were some UNICEF boxes of assorted drugs for sickbays. Would we mind taking them? She could give us five. We were delighted. Anything at all would have made our trip worthwhile. We expected small packages but she indicated a stack of large boxes in one corner and asked a man to put five outside for us. To our astonishment each box contained around twenty-seven kilos of assorted medicines. She added to these some disinfectant powder. We thanked her and I drew a map of how she could reach us if she could spare time and transport for a visit.

We started heaving the load into the car. We could hardly believe our good fortune. Fr Wasser's Volkswagen Beetle sank down on its springs as we loaded up; however, we persevered. Fortunately, we were not too far from the tarred road and we toddled along, barely scraping the tarmac, until we came to Ehime where Fr. Wasser couldn't resist showing Fr. Sweeney what we had been given.

Our good fortune continued as Fr. Sweeney had 'inherited' some pigs which the priest at Uboma had been keeping until he got caught behind enemy lines and was deported. Being born in a country area of Ireland, Fr. Sweeney had no qualms about 'liberating' these abandoned animals, bringing them back to his mission and 'sticking a pig' and Fr. Wasser had been offered some pork. Fr. Sweeney had just finished slaughtering when we crawled to a halt at his door. Seeing the car so laden he could hardly talk for a minute.

"We'll give him a box," said Fr. Wasser under his breath.

Fr. Sweeney had to hear the whole story and sat enthralled. At the end he shouted, "Man, that's grand! Can I borrow her?" (meaning me).

However, he settled for a box instead and then went off to look for something to wrap the meat in. He came back in a few minutes with a big towelling bundle. Lacking any kind of paper, he had wrapped the pork in a bath towel!

"Here you are then. I put in a bit of the liver. Mind you cook it well." As we drove home we debated on whether it would be safe to eat it at all but when the smell of freshly cooked liver drifted over from the kitchen shed, we hesitated no more.

This was the only fresh meat any of our family had tasted for nearly two years apart from the Christmas goat. We did, however, receive meat in gold-coloured unlabelled tins. The origin and age was much speculated upon and it was known as 'bully beef', 'anonymous meat' and so on. After the war ended I learned it came from Bavaria. Millions of tins must have reached Biafra for every child seemed to have an empty tin. Being fairly shallow they were used as plates at feeding centres and were still deep enough to hold milk if necessary. Filled with a mixture of earth and palm oil and with a rag wick, they became Biafran lamps when other types of lights could not be found or fuelled.

The English lady doctor, Anne Seymour, who lived near Amaimo Hospital, went further and used them as receivers in the sickbays and she also used the cartons, which had contained two dozen tins, for cribs for the premature babies. Even the metal bands round the cartons were cut into improvised forceps. She had been a lay missionary doctor in a hospital in Eastern Nigeria for some time before the war. During her time there she one day stopped a man from begging around the hospital compound. He was an epileptic and had mental health problems and he was generally making a nuisance of himself. However, Dr. Anne realised that by stopping him from begging she was depriving him of his means of livelihood so she 'employed' him as a night-watchman. Thus she ensured that he was fed and he proved to be quite effective as most people were scared stiff of him and not without reason. 'Mr. John', as he was known, tended during his fits to attack anyone or anything handy and Dr. Anne frequently ended up with bruises through trying to save him from injuring himself. He also had a rather disturbing habit of reciting parts of the mass at the top of his voice in the middle of the night or saying fifteen 'Hail Marys' to the decade during the evening rosary to the utter confusion of the rest of the household. When her hospital was evacuated, she became Provincial Medical Officer for refugees in Okigwe and was based about four miles from Ogbor. For furniture she had two school benches and a table until Father Sweeney loaned her a spare bed and mattress.

There was no car for her. She had left hers jacked up and the Ministry couldn't help. All they could offer was an old bicycle so she took it and went to another Irish priest and 'exchanged' it for a new Caritas bike (Caritas was a leading RC charity now sending in relief supplies). On this she would set off each morning visiting refugee camps and sickbays, treating the sick and inspecting the amenities. She travelled sometimes over twenty miles a day, seeing up to five hundred people, taking no food other than fresh fruit and a small flask of coffee until she reached home. Twice a week she came to Ogbor in the afternoon. We would watch out for her and have the kettle boiling and some snack ready. She would come in and browse through the books in our library. Then after her 'cuppa' we'd go down and start a clinic in the school. At six o'clock she would leave and start cycling the four miles home as she liked to be back before dark as it was each night by seven o'clock.

She had now added a mother with a child who had become weakened by polio to her family in addition to 'Mr. John' and Elizabeth, her housemaid, who had come with her from Awgu. There was talk of her getting a car from time to time but she never had much time to go and press for it. However, one day she rattled up in an old Volkswagen Beetle. She had finally managed to squeeze a car from the Ministry but with a petrol ration of two gallons a month, she couldn't do much in it. In addition to having the inevitable complaint of a broken exhaust, the gear stick had to be held in position at all times. That first day she took advantage of having extra room to shop at one of the markets some miles away and she bought some plantains for us. A few weeks afterwards she drove up with two one-eyed 'grannies' she had taken from refugee camps to join her family.

"What on earth?" we asked. "I didn't mean to have the two," she explained. "I have been watching this one for weeks and thought I could look after her better at home as she doesn't seem to have anyone to help her. So I put her in the car. At the next camp the other one saw her and she wanted to come too. They will be company for each other and with one having a left eye and the other a right, they should get on fine together!"

We said nothing but couldn't help wondering how many more would find a home with the madam doctor. But now her family was complete except for a little kitten she got some weeks later.

With the UNICEF medicines, mainly pain relief, anti-malaria drugs, vitamins etc., I was able to set up more little clinics in the surrounding villages. I could also advise those who needed to see the doctor to come to one of the twice weekly Ogbor clinics. We had to do whatever we could for each other in these times of fear and want.

Chapter 7
Room for More

While the good lady doctor's household was growing, so was mine. Mrs. Burke had suggested I should accompany her and her husband to Umuahia when they attended the fortnightly World Council of Churches meeting. While they kept their appointment at the Queen Elizabeth Hospital, I could wait at Dr. Middlekoop's house in the grounds of the hospital, talking to other wives, foreign journalists and visitors while waiting for Len, who was based nearby with BCB, to come and see me. Sometimes we spent only an hour together but at other times he was able to join us in the Burke's minibus and come back for a weekend.

Late in October at Dr. Middlekoop's I got talking to an English girl who had just arrived the previous night. Elizabeth Ihebom was married to an Igbo and had three children, the youngest born just at the start of the war. They were living in Port Harcourt then and, having found it increasingly difficult to buy powdered milk for the baby, she and her husband agreed she should go back to England with the infant, leaving the two little girls with him. She left Port Harcourt when the British and American evacuations were in progress in 1967. Once in England, having been repatriated by the British High Commission, she had her passport taken until she could repay the fare as was the custom. However, she was so worried about the members of the family in Biafra, especially when Port Harcourt fell into Nigerian hands and later Owerri (her husband was from a village near Owerri), she determined to come back to at least know if they were alive. She had no idea where they might be but felt that if she contacted her husband's employers, a Government department, she might be able to trace him. It was six months since she had heard from them.

When I met her she just didn't know where to start. One of her cases had been lost en-route and she had lost the keys to the one she had with her. Her nervous state was such that she had been under sedation and was just recovering from the flight from São Tomé the previous night. She had approached a relief organisation in Europe who, because she was a State Enrolled Nurse, had arranged for her to be brought to Biafra on one of the relief planes bringing in food and sometimes evacuating very sick children to São Tomé for treatment. Her little boy was left with friends in London.

The air raids in Umuahia were nerve-wracking. Now that the area held by Biafran troops was reduced in size the air raids were concentrated on a smaller area and towns were being bombed frequently.

I felt sure that Fr. O'Sullivan, who had already come to the rescue of my family, would be the most likely person to be able to help trace her family on his constant rounds of the missions. Mixed-race children were not that common. After a quiet word with Mr. and Mrs. Burke I suggested that she come back to Ogbor with me. She agreed and the Burke's managed to squeeze her into the minibus.

Back at Ogbor, Fr. Wasser rose to the occasion and speedily sent over another spare mattress for Elizabeth and she bedded down on our living room floor. As we were not sure when Fr. O'Sullivan would call again she volunteered to help me with the clinics in the meantime. So the following morning we borrowed a second bike and set off for Ugiri-ama. Those waiting were delighted to see I had a 'helper' although the helper was in fact more qualified than I was.

The very next afternoon Fr. O'Sullivan arrived and we went over to the 'big house' and told him the story. He promised to help look for Elizabeth's family and set off the following morning. Doctor Anne visited that afternoon, as it was a Thursday, and we held a clinic which ended in a near riot with a crowd rushing us.

Next morning, Friday 1st November, Fr. O'Sullivan returned. We were both afraid to go over to the other house but at the same time we wanted to run there. When we arrived and were seated, Fr.

O'Sullivan told us he had not seen Elizabeth's husband but he knew where he was and he believed the children were safe with him. He would take Elizabeth to where they were. Elizabeth wept with sheer relief and the rest of us had misty eyes too. Hurriedly she packed. Fr. Wasser told her that if conditions where her husband was staying were very bad, she should bring the children back here and he would find somewhere for them.

Within minutes she had left and I prepared for the clinic at Oka and cycled off. Deep down I felt we hadn't seen the last of Elizabeth and when I cycled home that afternoon a little ginger-haired girl peeped over the wall of the veranda at me. Olive and her elder sister Stella had arrived with their mother and so our family swelled again. After consultations with Fr. Wasser we called Father's cook, Martin the steward and the catechist to help clear out another room in the bungalow and, after sleeping on the floor of the 'parlour' for one night, the following day they moved in just before our two husbands arrived.

We attended Sunday mass together and then relaxed. Elizabeth and I shared the rest of the house and the cooking just keeping our bedrooms a bit private. Throughout the five months we were together we never even had 'words' let alone a quarrel. On 5th November I had the unique opportunity of being godmother to Elizabeth, her two daughters and our Nnenna at a baptism held in the small oratory, part of the priest's house. Although Elizabeth had gone to a convent school she was not a Catholic but had married one. Her experience however had made her realise the powers of God and the following evening, just before dusk, she stood with her husband Francis to receive God's blessing on their marriage.

Life then settled into a new routine. Elizabeth and I went out most weekday mornings to clinics. In the evening we would stroll with Father about a mile down the road and back, sometimes with Fr. Sweeney too or Fr. O'Sullivan if they were visiting, and later, once the children were settled for the night, we would sometimes go over to the big house and listen to records and chat until about nine o'clock. There was no electric light although Fr. Wasser did have a generator but he refused to buy black market fuel. He was proud of his local 'fridge' which consisted of a large earthenware water pot resting on a block; inside another block surrounded by water acted as a shelf for the opened tin of evaporated milk and bottle of drinking water which were all he needed to keep cool.

Elizabeth and I cooked on three large stones in the middle of the kitchen floor. We bartered for firewood and water. By this time I had mastered the art of keeping the cooking fire alight aided by a small raffia hand fan. While I had Paulina to help me Elizabeth's husband's niece Abigail came to help her after the local girl she had previously employed left to enter a convent.

A typical day would start with breakfast for everyone. I would then go over to Fr.'s house and give a hand with the morning hand-out of relief supplies and food for various kitchens throughout the parish. We had a big cupboard built for medicines which we stored in Fr. Wasser's spare bedroom. We generally had a shopping bag and a carton for our medicines which we would count out from our stock. We would then strap the bags on to the carriers of our bicycles and, having made sure we had a notebook and biro each, we would give instructions for lunch to Paulina and Abigail then Elizabeth and I would wobble off down the sandy drive on to the market and from there to whichever village we were visiting.

We would aim to be at the village by 9am. The roads were sandy and rutted and sometimes the sand was so thick that we had to get off and push for some yards. We then often travelled by bush paths and saw little or no wheeled traffic. Women coming back from the stream with clay pots of water balanced on their head, girls and women walking to market to trade, again with their goods usually carried on their head in a basket or container of some kind, exchanged greetings. We also encountered men on bicycles, usually with some load tied behind. Schools had been closed for over a year and most school buildings had been pressed into other use. Children played in the sand by their homes and we would all call a greeting as we passed. Sometimes we would be hailed by a man when no one was in sight. This was usually a palm wine tapper who was able to climb a tree with a rope looped around the trunk. With a knife and a small calabash at his waist from his lofty perch he had a fine view of the paths and compounds beneath him. I had learned while living at Azigbo to look up at the top of the palm trees before going to our makeshift roofless latrine, just in case. Chickens would scurry across in front of our wheels and a few times we had to carry our bikes over a felled tree which had crashed across the path. Some roads had been deliberately blocked by a series of fallen trees but there were many bush paths and minor roads we could use. The sun would invariably be shining – there was no point in us trying to go to clinics on bikes in the rain. Then paths quickly became a quagmire and no one would have come to the clinic in such downpours. Unseen birds would be calling to each other, plumes of smoke rose from wood fires and there would be the rustling of twigs and branches as firewood was collected. We tried to get to the clinics by a shady route if possible and before the sun rose too high.

We were now out at clinics three or four mornings and one afternoon each week. We soon discovered that each village had a different personality. At one or two we would arrive to find no one waiting but people would turn up within five minutes and we would be hard pressed to get finished by lunch time. The people of Ugiriama on the other hand could be heard at the top of the hill which we had to descend to reach the church. This hill was steep, sandy and deeply rutted with a little market at the bottom. I had quite a fear about cycling down it, especially after I fell off just before the last bend one morning. However, I couldn't bring myself to walk down so I always freewheeled with my hands on the brakes, my eyes fixed dead ahead and my mouth firmly shut. There was no 'good morning' to those I passed then.

As we approached the church we usually had to dismount and push the bikes through thick sand for the last couple of hundred yards. As we came into sight those lingering around the door would hurry inside and spread the word that the 'sisters' had arrived. To those village folk, who had only seen Europeans who were priests or nuns, all white people were 'Father' or 'Sister'. We did also wear white or navy and white clothes which we had made ourselves, shirt blouses and slightly flared skirts. At this time in the 1960s no women or girls wore trousers or shorts.

Ugiriama church was in bad shape structurally. The steps leading to the front door were all broken down and inside the floor had had its veneer of cement swept off long ago. In fact the church and its condition had resulted in a big parish 'palaver' before the war and a new building had been started on the top of the opposite hill. We used to line up the pews in front of the old altar, now only a raised dais with a rickety table. We thus tried to channel the patients into some semblance of two queues rather like the sheep being prepared for dipping at home. We followed, or tried to, our usual procedure of children first, then pregnant and nursing mothers, old people and then the rest.

It didn't always work out very well what with the shouting and shoving. Elizabeth and I would halve the table between us and we then opened our tins. One of us would use the lid and the other the container or the accompanying leaflet and we would arrange our medicines before us. A few feet away a couple of volunteers manned the 'dressing table' with a tin bowl of water, bandages, antiseptic, sticking plaster and whatever else we had with us. Elizabeth and I each had an interpreter and there were others to keep order. We originally used to give out a card to each patient but we soon ran out of paper and for some time kept no records at all.

Proceedings would open by me appealing to everyone, through the interpreter, to keep quiet and orderly. Then we would start: "Kedu afagi?" ("What is your name?"), "Gini na me gi?" ("What is wrong with you?") and so on. Mothers often said they did not know how old their children were. This, however, was common in rural Nigeria where birth registration and the celebration of birthdays were unknown to most of the population, even in the 1960s.

"How do they know when a child should start school?" I asked Len.

"Ask the children to put their hand over the top of their head. If they can cover the opposite ear they are old enough. A younger child's arm is not long enough!"

"My belly is biting me," a young man would confide. Into my mind snapped a picture of sets of false teeth gnashing in his stomach but further enquiries revealed that he felt he had worms. This turned out to be a very common complaint but the literal translation from Igbo never failed to amuse me. Not so funny was the statement that a child was 'growing lean and swelling' for this was the description of kwashiorkor. Lack of protein coupled with general malnutrition reduced children and babies to skeletons or bloated balloons of creatures or a mixture of the two. Usual early symptoms were lack of appetite, listlessness, and weakness. We only needed to look at these children to know the whole story. A cursory glance inside the lower eyelid would indicate anaemia. Often the weakened body had also fallen to scabies, malaria, worms or cough. Their immune system was severely affected.

We prescribed vitamins and urged parents to bring or send the children to feeding centres and we recommended some foods. Several times I spoke to the entire waiting mass about which of the local foods had most food value. Elizabeth and I would refer the very bad cases to the nearest hospital but we never knew if they were taken there for if one child in a family has kwashiorkor, you may be sure the rest of the family isn't all that healthy either and even a loving mother may not be able to literally carry her child of perhaps eight years on her back, five miles to hospital and be prepared to stay there if the child is admitted, for such is the custom, or carry the child home again if there was no bed.

From time to time order had to be restored in the clinic and the people appealed to, to be quiet so that we might at least hear if an enemy plane was coming. This was a very real fear as there was a very widespread belief that Nigerian planes went for crowded places, markets, schools, hospitals and churches which might be conceivably mistaken for army training grounds or anyway, were more economical targets. In several cases we had air raid scares and to see several hundred people of all ages trying to get out of a church in a panic is a sight not to be forgotten. Many dived out of windows, others almost fought to reach doors, all were shouting and shoving, children were crying and being pushed about while Elizabeth and I stood our ground as best we could and tried to prevent our table being overturned and the precious tablets from being scattered. After all who wanted to had 'scarpered', I was all for locking the doors and treating the few who remained on the grounds that they were the only genuinely sick and sensible ones for it was sheer folly to race into the open. If there had been a plane passing the pilot would have surely seen the scurrying mass pouring from the building whereas if we had remained quietly inside, there was less to give away. Anyway, we were lucky in that we only had false alarms and the planes continued on their way.

At Oka, one of the smaller villages, the volunteers never failed to provide us with some local fruits for 'elevenses'. Oka was extremely well-organised with a big hall for waiting patients and a small 'consulting room' leading off it which had another door leading outside. Before our arrival the patients had all been given numbers and were seated in order. They were admitted two at a time and Elizabeth and I usually diagnosed and dispensed the medicines as we found we could do both quicker than telling another volunteer what treatment to give. On our way back from Oka, which was about three miles from Ogbor, we sometimes turned right to Ibeme and continued downhill to Amaimo where the Irish Sisters used to give us iced water and we never failed to use their flush system toilet. These were both great luxuries as were the tea and biscuits. Elizabeth and I were sometimes quite reluctant to face the road after a taste of near civilisation.

To our intense disappointment Fr. Donal O'Sullivan had to leave Biafra. He had been elected for a five-year term as a Counsellor to the Superior General of the Holy Ghost order and had to leave for Rome to take up his new post. We were all very sorry to see him go as his visits had been a great treat for us. He had also been one of those who would deliver occasional letters from my family at home and see that replies were taken out on the empty relief planes. Soon after his departure, Fr. Sweeney suffered two minor heart attacks and spent more and more time at Ogbor in order to try and rest more as his own mission was often besieged by relief seekers. He had a larger parish and was also on the main road while we were off the tarred road and pretty quiet.

The relief action was speeding up now and Elizabeth and I were seeing over four hundred patients daily. Because their signs and symptoms were so obvious, we did no in-depth consultations. In addition I found myself increasingly called on to help share out the rations to the feeding centres and sign for the incoming supplies, which arrived piecemeal by lorry, if Fr. Wasser wasn't available. One lorry bore the apt slogan 'No Telephone to Heaven' and its noisy arrival was usually accompanied by some children who hastened up from the market to try and see what we were getting. The priest had so many calls to visit the dying that he took to allocating a day for sick calls to certain villages. However, this didn't prevent him being called out up to twenty times a day. It was usual for the cook hearing the auto-cycle, which Fr. Wasser used, from half a mile away to serve the priest's lunch, only to find that he had been met at the door with another request to visit a dying parishioner and had gone straight off.

Elizabeth and I also ran a milk kitchen in the evenings. We had discovered that giving out dry powdered milk was futile as the hungry ate it straight away without mixing it with water and, having taken the equivalent of several pints of milk, they soon had diarrhoea, so we mixed the milk in buckets of water and filled the jars, bottles and bowls which people brought. The water came from the mission water tanks which in turn were supplied by the young people of the parish who brought a bucketful each regularly. We usually made up around fifteen gallons per evening and Pauline and Abigail carried it on their heads in big buckets to the school. Sometimes they were mobbed and returned home soaked in milk themselves.

We tried to keep people away from the house as much as possible, otherwise we would never have rested. Even then I was frequently brought out by a voice saying "Madam, good afternoon. Madam, I beg you, consider me." When it reached the stage that I fell over a woman lying across my bedroom door at 5am we had to have local civil defenders mount a barrier at the end of the drive. People were now really hungry. Children came out every morning with homemade swats trying to kill grasshoppers for food. We stopped our own children joining in the hunt when the village children started offering to barter their grasshoppers for stockfish.

A young Igbo priest came to stay at the mission with Fr. Wasser. Fr. Matthew offered to teach our children their catechism. He started off telling them how God made everything but when four-year old Uche asked him "Who made God?" he realised it wasn't going to be easy with this class.

From our own rations Elizabeth and I both sent supplies to our in-laws. In addition Elizabeth was helping a widowed neighbour with twin sons and I helped a Sierra Leonean woman, married to a local man, and with six children. I was very glad of the help of my Sierra Leonean friend, Lilian. She had lived mainly in Lagos with her Igbo husband and it was only when the crisis came that she left her job at an Adult Education Centre and came to his village with him and their children. They had to turn to farming a small portion of land and things got progressively worse. The two youngest children got weaker and weaker as kwashiorkor advanced. In desperation she sold the last item of value, her sewing machine, in order to buy food. It was too late; the children both died. The next youngest, a girl, was also very weak and when children were being selected to go to Gabon for treatment (on one of the empty relief planes), Ngozi was among them but there was delay and confusion about the arrangements. I had not been in Ogbor very long when Lilian came to me one Saturday afternoon with Ngozi carried on her back.

I was terribly shocked to see this small, obviously well-educated woman in such a situation. The child was already unable to walk. I think she may have been about five or six years old. Lilian too was clearly not strong and how she carried this child for three miles to bring her to me I did not know. I prepared something for them as she told me her situation. I think I gave them a drink of Ovaltine first then I made up a parcel of food and medicines and they set off for home. They still hoped the Gabon trip would come off but I asked them to let me know in a week if nothing had happened in that direction.

The following week they were back. There was little change but the child was no worse so I brought out supplies again and asked her to come or send someone each week to collect more. There was no need to bring Ngozi to me every week. The journey to and fro on her mother's back was doing her no good and her treatment really consisted of food and rest. Lilian was anxious to do something in return; could she take my washing or bring firewood or water she asked? Whatever she could manage we would be grateful for I told her but only what could be done without too much inconvenience to herself and her family. I guessed that none of them were in very good health and I did not want them becoming worse out of a feeling of obligation to me. Lilian and I soon became friends and Eddison, her son, even stayed with us for some time as a house help. Lilian's oldest daughter was working in an orphanage at Amauzari on the far side of our parish which was a help.

At the end of November Fr. Sweeney left on health grounds and Fr. Wasser, who was overdue leave himself, accompanied him. The evening before they left, Elizabeth, her husband and I went over for a meal with them; Len had not managed to come. It was a very sad occasion as we did not know who would be the new parish priest or if we would be allowed to continue with our relief work. We came back early and went to bed but I was awakened around midnight by moans coming from the sitting room where Paulina and her friend Maria were sleeping. I went in to find Paulina unconscious. I couldn't make out what had happened, she had apparently started moaning in her sleep and we couldn't wake her. There was still a light on in the Fathers' house where the young Igbo priest, Fr. Matthew, was preparing his sermon for the morrow so I went over and knocked on the front door; he let me in and then called Fr. Wasser and they came over with me. After seeing her condition Fr. Wasser said we must take her to hospital and meanwhile she should be given the last rites. Although both Fr. Wasser and Fr. Sweeney had Volkswagen Beetles, Fr. Wasser's had a 'knocked' engine and Fr. Sweeney's had no headlights. All attempts to loosen the headlamp covers from Fr. Wasser's car to put light in Fr. Sweeney's car failed. The fact that our tools were the kitchen knives probably didn't help our attempt.

Fr. Sweeney by now was also awake and insisted, despite our protests, on driving his car to the hospital for us. Paulina was lifted into the back seat and I got in beside her; Fr. Wasser climbed in in front and with his hand out of the window, directed a torch to light our way while Fr. Sweeney drove. It was a dark moonless night and very misty down by the river so that at some points Fr. Wasser walked ahead with the torch to guide us. At one point both priests, who had lived in the area for several years, were convinced we had lost the way but eventually we reached Mbano Hospital where Paulina was admitted and we set out for an uneventful return trip and we got back around 3am. Fr. Wasser then remembered a sovereign had fallen out of his case when he shook it over the balcony that morning and was all set to look for it but we eventually persuaded him to leave it till the morning.

Fr. Wasser had kept the news of his going secret as he didn't want any emotional farewells but it leaked out just before he left the following day, having said his usual Sunday mass. People were terribly upset that he was going, for his unobtrusive helping hand had aided many of his parishioners through the embarrassment of acute poverty. They feared that another priest might not be so sympathetic. I too missed his cheerful companionship.

For days afterwards people came to see for themselves that he had really gone and many told me of how he had helped them in the past. However, for us, life had to continue. Barrister Egbuziem brought Paulina back from the hospital in his car, and Elizabeth gave her the injections that had been prescribed. We 'carried on'.

Chapter 8

Comings and Goings

For a couple of weeks we were in suspense as to who was to be our new parish priest. Fr. Matthew was very young and had been ordained only about a year before and Ugiri was a senior parish. Then, during Advent, the new priest arrived. He was Fr. Bernard Onwumere, an Igbo man who, though young in the priesthood, had been a Reverend Brother for many years and a trader before that.

One of the first things he did was to have locks put on the doors of the Mission House which had never been thought necessary. The garage was converted to a store and a carport-cum-potting shed into a garage. A very high local palm leaf thatch fence went up around the house and surrounding area and guards were set at the gate. Elizabeth and I were a bit nervous of all the changes. Overnight we had no access to the drugs cupboard in the priest's house and we did not even have basic medicine for our own children. There was no warning or announcement that the village clinics would be stopped. The new man decided it would be better to set up two sick bays instead so he went ahead with converting two schools on opposite sides of the parish into these facilities. One was in Ogbor. When they were ready an announcement was made in church that all seeking admission should be brought to the site on a certain day.

There were hundreds there when Dr. Anne, Elizabeth and I walked down to do the selection for Ogbor. We tried to get everyone arranged in lines and the doctor then walked down each row selecting the cases for admission. Elizabeth and I also brought forward a few from whom the final choice was made. It was a heart-breaking job as mothers thrust forward babies and children. Adults and old people were also seeking admission; the majority of those selected were children with a few adults, mainly men. In the case of a sick child the mother and any other children of the same parents, who were almost guaranteed to be in the same or similar condition, were admitted – all counting as on one bed. This often meant we had thirty beds and many more mouths to feed.

Many of our patients had coughs or fevers as well as kwashiorkor. The men we had selected were a great problem as most were convinced they could not get better and some had to be sent home to die. They were very apathetic and had to be forced to get up so that they wouldn't get pressure sores. The children lay or sat around, sometimes scantily clad, more often naked. Many had 'craw-craw', an infectious skin disease. They usually took the high protein diet quite readily although we had to start them on it gradually.

Every day more and more people came but we were full up and could only open a waiting list, knowing full well that by the time we had a vacancy, it might be too late. The recovery was slow, a matter of weeks and even after discharge many came back after a week or two looking worse than when we first took them in. The weakest died. They just slipped away quietly. To see the little rib cage faltering in its movements, the body so wasted, skin looking several sizes too large, veins on the head standing out and to hear the wheeze of pneumonia was a chilling experience which became only too familiar to us. There was nothing we could do when there was no hope of feeding the overly weakened body. We had no drips or gastric tubes and sometimes we had to console ourselves with the fact that with one less to feed, the family might be that little bit better able to feed the others. For these bodies there were no coffins. If there was money for a coffin it would have been spent on food. Sometimes we used the cartons which had held the 24 tins of mystery beef as makeshift coffins. Later, at the orphanage, I stood helpless as three small children of the same family died one after the other.

Those who died were primarily babies, young children and the aged. Refugees with no means of earning a living, especially those who had managed small farms and had never had enough to eat in their lives, soon followed. The healthiest were the teenagers and young adults.

Those who had been educated and could get some kind of employment or trade were generally all right. These were the ones who survived and came back to Lagos and other towns. It was from the fittest group that most of the army recruitment came and many of them were then killed or wounded at the battle front. The luckiest ones were those in any way connected with the relief organisations. They had at least food for themselves and their immediate families. Even a car was no asset as the chances were there would either be no petrol or that it would be commandeered and there was also a dearth of spare parts of any kind.

By having sick bays the parish priest was entitled to a qualified Biafran nurse for each of them and, when they arrived, Elizabeth and I retired quietly although our Ogbor clinic struggled on up to May 1969 when drugs finally gave out. As no announcements were made publicly about the clinics stopping we still had a lot of people seeking us out to ask what had happened. I was now going on Wednesdays with Mrs. Burke to visit the refugee camps which were being supplied by the World Council of Churches store run by her husband and herself, as we were now freer to do as we wished. Mrs. Burke had a five-ton lorry at her disposal for delivering relief supplies to the refugee camps in her area. She arrived the first morning as arranged and I was amused to see two local armchairs in the back of the lorry; one for Mrs. Burke and one for me. On the rough roads they were certainly an improvement on the usual wooden seats beside the driver. The lorry had the sides built up with slats of wood with spaces between so that we could view the countryside and get some breeze as we went along.

We visited up to five camps a day where relief was distributed to the camp officials. We were always greeted by a large turnout of the refugees, the more desperate making appeals directly. Most of the camps had a resident nurse and we usually called on her with some medical supplies. We arrived at one camp to be told that the nurse had delivered a baby on the football field the week before. The classrooms of the school, which had been turned into the camp, were on one side of the football field and nurse had her quarters in the teachers' house row on the opposite side of the field. The mum-to-be had miscalculated the stage of her labour and was unable to get to the nurse's quarters in time.

During an air raid on another converted school (this one an orphanage), a Biafran nun in full white robes fell heavily while running across the football field during the raid. The plane circled and came back but some enterprising individual threw a blanket over her as camouflage.

Sometimes Mrs. Burke had second-hand clothing to distribute. This was received with great jubilation and any man lucky enough to be given a shirt had to try it on at once for everyone to admire. Occasionally we had machetes which might be used to cultivate a little land for growing vegetables. Some did basket making or made bamboo beds but for many there was nothing to do from morning till night.

At lunch time the driver would be told to look for a suitable place to stop. A suitable place meant somewhere on a quiet road, preferably away from all houses as a lorry stopping near people or houses would mean we would soon have visitors wondering who we were and what we wanted. Mrs. Burke had a flask of tea or coffee and often emergency rations. These were from aluminium packs which, when opened, revealed solid blocks about matchbox size of 'Kek', 'brod', a few crispbread type biscuits, a tiny serving of coffee, sugar, matches and a short length of toilet roll! The aluminium container could be used as a cooking pot and there was also fuel cake in the kit. One of the solid Kek blocks was a meal in itself.

Just as I had been dubbed a 'sister' in the Catholic clinics, I was now assumed to be Mrs. Burke's daughter and was often taken aside and asked to use my influence to ask my mother to bring some particular items on the next visit. As we drove away from each camp we would often still be handing out small items of relief. From time to time the Burkes gave me medicines for the clinic and we also received assorted medicines from Caritas. There was once a very large carton of medication left for me but when I opened the box I found that they were all samples of different preparations and all the writing was in German. We got the whole lot spread out one day when Dr. Anne was there and she sorted out a lot of single injections, tablets for various heart and liver complaints, etc. There were even a few packets of one month courses of different brands of contraceptive pills. Eventually we had set on one side less than 10% of the consignment which would be suitable for our clinic and the doctor took the rest. Similar consignments arrived at São Tomé and a German-speaking chemist had to be flown out to try and make sense of them all and sort them out. So much was not relevant to our needs that I heard later a quantity was burned, which was a shocking waste.

Fr. Sweeney had been replaced at Ehime by Fr. Owen Carton whom I had known at Aba. An extremely jovial man, he dropped in as often as he could and invited the two of us, along with Dr. Anne Seymour to dinner on a few occasions. These were dinners with a difference, for how many hosts arrive to collect their guests with a list of cutlery and crockery which has to be brought along if the meal is to be had at all?

Armed with our equipment we would all pile into the little green Morris Minor and roar off into the night. Rarely had we passed the first corner when Fr. Owen would say, "Right, girls, let's have a song," and we would sing along all five miles of jolting, pot-holed, untarred roads to Mbano, then along the two miles of tarred roads to Ehime and right up the rutted lane to the parish house. Being a Dublin man, Father always sang a few Irish songs; 'The Rose of Tralee' was a favourite. He was also very fond of two-part singing and this led into an embarrassing situation on the way home one night – but more of that later.

Picture us then arriving at Ehime parish house, a very strangely-designed bungalow which seemed to irk the priest, so much so that he usually had the armchairs carried outside and we sat there for an hour or more while the finishing touches were put to the meal. From time to time the perspiring cook would appear at Father's elbow and he would excuse himself and trot off to the kitchen or the house. Usually I would be coerced to go and "See what that lad's doing in the kitchen. He's never used potato flakes before". Neither had I but in the light from the blazing cast iron wood stove, sometimes supplemented by a hurricane lamp or a Biafran lamp, I would read out the directions and try to create some order.

Fr. Carton always invited us to "come over and we'll stab a few tins" so we knew what to expect. We couldn't have had more fun at a society 'do'. The Irish have boundless humour and with his jokes the good Father soon made us forget just how long it was taking to get the food on the table and then change the course. I didn't mention that the kitchen was a good twenty-five yards away from the house and we usually had to wait till the dishes were washed and brought back so we could proceed to the next course.

Around eleven o'clock we'd start talking about getting back, for the priest and doctor were always up early. She always asked us to stop singing as we approached her house near Mbano as she didn't want her neighbours getting a bad impression. However, as soon as we'd dropped her off we'd start again. The occasional person on the road at that hour would give us a wide berth as we rattled by. We sometimes had to remind Father that he was driving as he was quite liable to applaud at the end of a good number or conduct for a few bars but we never came to any harm.

One night, however, our enthusiasm got us into a wee spot while we were singing that oldie 'I Hear Music' in two parts; Father versus Elizabeth and me. We were just nicely into the harmony when we reached a check point where civil defenders had stretched a bamboo pole across the road to halt all the traffic. This was just at the market place in Ogbor – only a hundred yards from the mission. We halted but kept on singing. The men outside looked at us but didn't raise the barrier. We kept singing. It had never sounded so well! We were in Ogbor, surely these men recognised Elizabeth and me? Still the barrier was across the road. The time was around midnight. He could stand no more.

"For God's sake, can't you see it's a Father and the two Sisters?" he called.

"Sorry, Father," they said and we passed through.

"Goodnight!" they shouted after us as we moved past and continued to our house as he started the melody again. There was a big moon shining as we drew up.

"One more, girls," said Father and we started 'Mama's Little Baby Loves Shortnin' Bread' so we sang that too before calling it a day. Next morning the whole village had it that we'd come home drunk although I think our total alcoholic consumption of the evening was one bottle of palm wine between the four of us.

On 1st January 1969 we opened a tin of corned beef we had been saving. As the tin was a catering size, about 6lb, it was as well that Len was there too as Uche, Ada, Nnenna, Pauline and Elizabeth, her husband, Stella, Olive, their maid and I all ate our fill and even so we knew we couldn't finish it. We had to make a stew with some in the hope that it would keep for a few days if boiled regularly. Fr. Carton arrived towards evening and invited Elizabeth, her husband, Len and I to join the doctor and himself for a meal that night.

"I've got something special tonight for you," he said. Imagine our faces when the cook proudly bore in a huge plate of corned beef. Fr. Carton had also been saving his tin for an 'occasion'.

By now Nnenna was fairly recovered and was attending the newly re-opened school with Uche and Elizabeth's daughters Stella and Olive. As the school buildings were now the sickbay, lessons were held in the church. We had reports that they spent a large part of their school day looking for palm kernels to chew as we forbade them from having the special food prepared for the school children as kwashiorkor prevention, on the grounds that they were eating much more than those children at home. We did however give them a chewable multivitamin daily.

Exercise books were very scarce and we had 'slates' (small squares of wood painted black on which they could write with chalk), made for them but they all lost them and we made a second set. Chalk too was expensive and later on the children wrote and drew in the sand.

One day in March 1969 we had a visit from a young man, Robert Ezims, who had persuaded the young people in his area to form the De Gaulle Charitable Orphanage. Robert's main problem had been how to get regular supplies. More relief planes were coming in now but distribution was mainly through Joint Church Aid as The Catholic and Protestant churches were now pooling their relief operations, which made good sense. The planes coming in for JCA were known to us as 'Jesus Christ Airline'.

The following day, once Elizabeth and I were ready, we set off with an armed escort for Awomama where there was a large hospital for casualties of the war. The French team from Médecins Sans Frontières of course had no idea that we were coming but they welcomed us, invited us to join them for lunch and showed us round the hospital. We were surprised after the meal to see several of their team leave for the hospital building nearby carrying torches. They explained that they were going to the operating theatre and would not return until late in the night. Before we left they gave us cigarettes, cheese, Maggi sauce and a promise that some of them would come to visit the orphanage two days later on a Sunday. We were very impressed with their set-up. They had better equipment and more drugs than any of the other hospitals. They were very committed and dedicated to doing their best in a situation very close to the frontline.

That Sunday, Len accompanied Elizabeth and I to the orphanage for the inspection visit. The visitors were impressed enough to advise that a letter be written to Madame De Gaulle, seeking the patronage of herself and her husband. My three years of school French were inadequate for such a formal letter and I was very relieved on visiting the convent at Amaimo to find a French woman visiting Biafra who not only agreed to translate the letter but undertook to ensure that the letter did reach Mme De Gaulle. She played her part well and not long after an envoy arrived from France to visit the orphanage and soon Robert was receiving the aid he needed – officially. Later, two more orphanages were set up under the same organisation and great plans were afoot before the war ended, all the foreign aid was stopped and foreign aid personnel were deported. I lost touch with Robert after the end of the war but I am sure that such an enterprising young man became a success in whatever field he pursued.

In the early part of 1969 Elizabeth became pregnant again and she and her husband decided that she should take the girls and go home to England where their little boy was being cared for by a nanny. Around this time Dr. Anne became ill with infective hepatitis and was also preparing to go home. On 2nd April we said goodbye and they all left together, Elizabeth and her girls with the doctor on the same flight to São Tomé. Francis came back from seeing them off and we made him promise to keep coming to see us regularly although he was working about twenty miles away.

Just at this time Owerri was re-taken by Biafrans and we were all very optimistic, thinking the tide was turning. We acquired a little kitten too. The kitten was a gift from a Holy Ghost Father at Amaimo and, on being assured it was a male, we called him Kimmage after the Holy Ghost Seminary in Dublin. The name was soon shortened to Kim and he grew into a very good-natured cat, except when later he developed an aversion to chickens.

The house was quiet for a few days and then Umuahia became a battle front. Bob and Anne Burke were long overdue for leave too and they finally left on April 14th.

Chapter 9

DIY Petrol

Things had not been going smoothly for Len. The final straw came when he was blamed for the negligence of a man in another section. It was this chap's duty to obtain and hold a supply of fuel for the broadcasting machinery. Len was to draw this as required. Several times Len was compelled to do the running around to get fuel to the store which the other man had failed to do. However, one day the radio was forced to go off the air because the fuel ran out and Len was suspended without being given any opportunity to explain the circumstances. That there was no fuel in the store for him to draw, that he had taken all steps to inform the store-keeper that stocks were getting low and that Len himself was too busy to do the store-keeper's job in addition to his own. When he found himself suspended without pay and was asked to make himself available for an investigation without date, he felt he had done enough and resigned.

Len came home with the car and some of his belongings and decided we should stay on in Ogbor. Soon after, the Mercy Orphanage at Uboma, a few miles from Umuahia, was evacuated to Ogbor and the orphans moved in to the remaining school classroom as the more substantial ones had already become the sickbay. The Sisters who were with them had to be housed too and we were asked to move out of the bungalow to two small rooms in the teachers' quarters at the other side of the mission compound. This block of six rooms, each 10 feet by 12, was built before the civil war and had not been painted, nor had it any ceilings. It was divided into three sets of quarters, each with two rooms, the inner one being reached through the outer one. The outer room had two more doors, one to the front and the other to a small back yard surrounded by a fence of palm fronds. A thatched kitchen, toilet and bathroom took up most of the back yard. A road and what had been the football field now separated us from the priest's house and our former home.

We moved in with the three heavy tables we had been using in the other house. The first night we found that to set up the children's beds we had to move our three dining chairs outside and take the top off our dining table. It was now just possible to pass but not to open the doors fully. In the morning Len and I discovered that the single bed we were sharing had sunk through the thin coating of cement on the floor and we were two inches lower. We solved this by standing the legs of the bed in empty tins. Shortly after we discovered that we were in the direct line of attack from several armies of soldier ants. Anyone who has never witnessed the determination of these creatures and the pain of their bites or stings cannot imagine the frenzied counter-attack on our side with blazing paper and kerosene to try and divert them.

Len, ever resourceful, started to build an extension to our part of the building. It ran the whole length of our frontage. The width was curtailed by the height of the existing roof as the new roof had to continue at the same angle. We had nothing but local materials. Len first of all had wooden corner posts erected then others were set between them. A dwarf wall, three feet six inches high, was put up using old cement blocks bought from a neighbour and these were plastered with mud. Bamboo slats were then fixed horizontally at about four-inch intervals. Local mats were now stretched on the inside and tied top and bottom to the bamboo. The door was made from the wooden lintel which had marked the limit of the original three-foot high veranda. We had knocked down the veranda wall too and that gave us three feet of cement floor.

The roof was made of palm thatch two layers thick and overlapping. It was never completely watertight but was habitable. The floor was mud-plastered and once a week was washed and the cracks filled in by our two house girls. (We had taken on a teenage refugee as a housemaid and fed and clothed her; she slept with a family nearby.) We had some local mats on the floor though they got

144

eaten by white ants periodically. For furniture, we had two bamboo benches, one of which I covered with a blanket, while the other was 'upholstered' with three cushions. We also had a bamboo coffee table and the children ate at this, seated on one of the benches. We had three dining chairs and two wooden tables. The door had no lock so we took our radio and clock in to our bedroom each evening. This extension room made life much easier and some of the locals, who had personal refugee problems in their homes, visited us and went home deep in thought.

In the middle of May I became unwell and after being sick seven times in one morning I was taken to hospital, diagnosed with malaria, informed I was pregnant, that the baby was due in December, and sent home the next day. This was a total surprise.

We had become friendly with a lawyer and his wife, local to the village. One day, soon after he had come back from Umuahia. Len was speaking to Nick.

"I am having great difficulty getting distilled water for the car battery," he said.

"It is quite easy to make," replied Len, "In fact it is the same principle as refining petrol." They both saw the viability of starting a small refinery as they knew there was crude oil in the area. The lawyer volunteered land for the project and also the finance to buy the materials. To their great surprise, they were able to find all the pipes and equipment necessary for the construction within five miles of the site. An unusual feature of the refinery design was that the boiler was in a big hole underground. This meant that heat loss was minimised, the production was quick and the quality of the petrol, diesel oil and kerosene produced was very high. Another man from nearby who had worked in a refinery made some useful suggestions to the construction, local men were employed to do the labouring and the only problem was to get a regular supply of crude oil. The residue after refining was channelled out and used as fuel for the boiler. Altogether it was a very satisfying project for Len who designed, built and saw the project work so well.

We put up, or rather, put down two more buildings; these were two bunkers. The first one Len built for our neighbour. In the headmaster's house was another refugee, Justice Gabriel Onyuike. 'Gab' had moved his comprehensive law library to Ogbor sometime before when Port Harcourt fell and found himself sharing his house with it for several months. The books filled two rooms while Gab had another for a bedroom and a fourth as his parlour. We had some good times together. Len and he often had deep discussions, especially on philosophy and we used to share anything special that came our way. When he bought a chicken, I think for £8, he called us over and we had him in to share some big tins of meat and supplied him with coffee for a time.

He decided he should have a bunker, partly as an example to the rest of the place and partly as a retreat. The Army was to supply the labour and Gab chose a site right outside his back door. The first attempt to dig a hole to his suggested size ended in failure when one side collapsed, nearly pulling the side of the house with it. The soldiers were sent away. Len then chose a fresh site, a little further from the house, and laboured along with two men until Gab had a fine shelter over six feet deep, with two zig-zag entrances and a ceiling of palm tree trunks with almost a foot of packed earth on top and a roof of palm leaves on six-foot poles above to direct the rains off. Gab was delighted with it and had a comfortable chair carried down to finish it off.

However, that was not the end of it. After he had had his made, he badgered us into having one of our own and Len started again on another, which we constructed at the side of our house. The children played in it and our chickens sheltered under the roof from the heat of the sun. The only day a plane did raid near us (about a mile away), only Ada was at home and I seem to remember that was before we even had the bunker. The bunker was another 'tourist' attraction and our visitors always went to inspect it.

When the orphans had moved in, the Reverend Sister in charge asked me to work there. I agreed and soon we started a pitched battle for the health of over two hundred children. When they arrived they had no allocated toilets and with many of the children suffering from kwashiorkor and its allied complaints, we had a terrific sanitation problem as the orphanage building was at right angles and adjacent to the one used by the sick bay. The toilet block previously built for the school had been used by the sick bay patients and, when the orphans started using it, no one would own up to the mess it had become until eventually Fr. Onwumere had a fence erected to stop anyone using it.

As no alternative arrangement was made the result was chaotic so Len organised the digging of twelve pit latrines; seven for the orphans and five for the sick bay. A fence was built between them so there was no blame-passing. Separate kitchens were also constructed and a stout fence erected to keep the two factions apart. Girls with shovels were sent out to clear the compound and the children were ordered to use the latrines.

Lack of water made even the most basic hygiene near impossible. The two hundred children were housed in a six classroom block. The entrance was by two doorways on opposite sides of the third room in the line. The walls did not reach the roof which was ceiling-less. Ventilation was through grilled window spaces which also let in the rain. The end room at one side was used as a store at first and later as a sick bay for the more seriously ill orphans. The teenage maids who looked after the children slept in the next room at first but were later moved to a tiny place adjoining the local council hall as demand grew. Next to them were the babies. They were too young to feed themselves and we had between fifteen and thirty as more came when space was available. Each shared a bamboo bed with an older girl who looked after it. These girls, aged between nine and fourteen, needed a lot of supervision as they were apt to eat some of the baby's special diet as well as their own.

Next there were three rooms for girls and boys under five years old. Some of these slept three or four to a bed. We had neither enough beds nor space and most slept on mats on the floor. About a quarter of a mile away and adjacent to our own quarters four rooms of another more substantial school were cleared for the older boys. Under the direction of a man, who was also a barber, they were soon organised and I had an inter-house competition going with marks for tidiness, cleanliness of premises, compound and toilets and extra marks for enterprise. We had a local chap in to teach them basket weaving.

The lorry bringing relief supplies was sometimes sent to the stream loaded with empty drums, boys, girls and the laundry. At the stream all would bathe then the boys helped fill the drums while the girls started washing the laundry and the lorry would return with enough water for cooking and baby bathing for at most two days.

In the orphanage we had all the childhood illnesses, one after the other, each a mini-epidemic, for although the children had comparatively good food and were clothed, they had little resistance to infection. Illness presented quite a problem as we had no drugs most of the time and no reliable transport. On one occasion I took the worst cases to hospital in a friend's four-seater Peugeot 204 car. There were thirteen of us inside it, and one boy lay on the back window ledge the whole way. At the hospital two were admitted while one, who had been there for some time, was discharged and we all had to pile in and get back home again. On another occasion, Phoebe, who was the orphanage nurse, a young, pregnant woman and I took eleven babies and toddlers in a car, with a driver, to Amaigbo Joint Hospital. When we got there we found we had to leave the car some way away from the department we needed. Seven of the children couldn't walk and only one of the older children was above five years so we carried two babies each while the older ones held on to our skirts. Then I went back for the three remaining babies. I took two and the driver carried one and we staggered along through a crowd of the outpatients who were agog at seeing a pregnant European woman with so many children. I knew that I had not become pregnant earlier in the war because I had stopped menstruating while we were in Enugu in 1968. The condition is known as 'war amenorrhea' and is linked to stress and malnutrition, which I felt was nature's way of halting reproduction. It had been very common among women during World War 2 .While this had some advantages it also caused us some anxiety as I was never sure if I might be pregnant again. Significantly, when my diet improved sufficiently I had two periods at the beginning of 1969 and fell pregnant.

We were fortunate that we received enough relief supplies to be able to send some to Len's mother and family every month or so, when we knew someone was travelling there. We also surreptitiously passed on some to others living around us. We had to be very discrete about it as we did not want to be besieged. The mini-refinery went into production towards the end of June having been tested first with water and producing a stock of distilled water.

My health was still not good, so-called 'morning sickness' affected me all day and when another Reverend Sister was sent to Ogbor I withdrew from the orphanage a bit but also helped at the sickbay when I could. Even when a child was very poorly we couldn't always get to a hospital. On one occasion I took a very sick little girl called Lola to Mbano Hospital where she was admitted but died that night. A few days later little orphan baby Mercy Monica became very unwell and Fr. Onwumere took her with me to Amaimo where she was put on an intravenous drip. The next day I rode the bicycle over to Amaimo and was told she had taken a little milk but sadly the next day she died.

The following day I got up from an afternoon siesta fully awakened by a cock crowing as I stepped outside. The heat was going out of the African sun, shadows lengthening and I could hear the chatter of the children released from school and on their way home. Along the road dividing the mission compound from the school area women passed with baskets and basins balanced on their heads as they went to and from the little market a few hundred yards away. There was no sound of any motorised vehicle on the road and the sky was cloudless and silent. No bombers to indiscriminately defile and destroy.

Looking to my right I could make out, at the far end of the school football field now planted with cassava and with the goalposts still in situ, a small group walking down the path from the road. In front walked a man carrying a spade, then a woman carrying a bundle in her arms and holding on to her wrapper a child, maybe six or seven years old sobbing loudly. My three little daughters Uche, Ada and our 'acquired' daughter Nnenna, saw me and smiled, then they resumed playing their clapping singing game, stamping their feet, raising little puffs of dust.

"Where are you going mummy?" Uche asked.

"Just to the orphanage," I replied.

"Can we come too?

"No, not this time," I answered.

They turned back to the game again.

I caught my breath and hurried as swiftly as my swollen body would let me. Before I reached them they had stopped. The man stuck the blade of the spade into the soil and the woman laid down her load and I could see she was trying to prise the little girl's hand off her wrapper and pointing that she should go back. The child's sobs lessened but she stayed put.

As I reached them we exchanged greetings. They did not have to explain. I knew them all. Only this morning I had visited the refugees in the makeshift orphanage across the road, and where I knew that many of the children were ill; some critically so. Biafra in 1969 was shrinking and people fleeing from the front line were retreating into an ever smaller area before the gunfire reached their homes. Hundreds of small children and babies became separated from their families when bombs and strafing planes struck and people fled in panic. Others, whose parents had died of kwashiorkor in refugee camps, had been admitted while some parents abandoned their children at the orphanages in the hope that they would have food and better protection there. A number of children were traumatised by what they had experienced. The weaker ones lay on mats on the floor or on rough beds with bamboo slats. Their chests rose and fell on their shrunken bodies, all their ribs standing out, their cheeks sunken, bellies and legs swollen. Record keeping was scanty. Paper was very scarce.

Unusually, the little girl, Sarah had arrived at the orphanage with a younger brother and sister. The baby, a boy called Ezra, spent most of his time carried on Sarah's back, secured there with a long piece of cloth. Sarah was very diligent, feeding him and keeping him clean whilst keeping a close watch too on Ruth, who was about three-years old, making sure that she did not wander away and that she received her ration of food.

All the children in the orphanage were so susceptible to any infection and measles had resulted in several deaths. Pneumonia was also a real concern and it was that which had caused Ezra's death earlier that month. No wonder young Sarah was so distressed.

Earlier, on my almost daily visit to the orphanage, I saw that Ruth was one of several small children with pneumonia, her breathing shallow, her little ribs fluttering as she lay on her back with Sarah sitting beside her, watching every movement. It was heart-breaking. There was no transport to take her and the other very sick ones to hospital that day. We did what we could with the little we had. Now she too had died and the burial must take place as soon as possible in the tropical climate. I held Sarah close to me and tried to soothe her. She was exhausted. The shallow grave was soon dug and Ruth's little body wrapped in a piece of cloth was placed in it and covered. There was no coffin, no priest and no ceremony. I started to say the Lord's Prayer quietly and the others joined in. A rough wooden cross was stuck in to the red soil. Yet another cross to mark another grave surrounded by other crosses in other mounds.

"Thank you Ma," the woman said to me. She was a local woman who helped out with the children. I nodded and repeated the words to her. She took Sarah's hand and they walked back to the orphanage. I skirted the goal post, and walked slowly, retracing my steps by the side of the field of cassava to my temporary home, my husband and our three children who would soon be joined by another as my pregnancy was advanced. It was no real surprise when shortly after Sarah also died. Without her role as surrogate mother she retreated into a world of her own. Her eyes were blank, nothing I or any of the staff could do or say would give her the spark of hope to keep her going. I knew this scenario was being repeated daily all over Biafra but that did not make it any easier to accept.

I went to Amaimo a few days later and had a check-up. My haemoglobin was very low, I had a kidney infection and my weight was recorded as 9 stone 7lbs. I know that the weight gain was due to a better diet as, when I was in Azigbo before going to Aba in early 1968, I could balance a tray on my pelvic bones when lying down and my ribs were clearly visible. I had no way of being weighed then which was probably as well.

A Swedish Red Cross DC6 relief plane was shot down at Eke, which was a blow as we feared the airlift might be stopped. However, the planes kept coming, bringing food, medicine, second-hand clothing and sometimes a letter for me.

Chapter 10

Keeping in Touch

The Burkes had returned to Biafra but were now in their former home near Owerri. Sam and Wendy Ijioma were now our main links with the secular world. Sam was in charge of the World Council of Churches store in Etiti, which included our area. We saw them when he was able to keep on the road. Of course there was no way of knowing if my expected baby would be a girl or boy but I managed to make a few small items of clothing while we waited.

Wendy, who was English, came back during the war to marry Sam with whom she had worked in Port Harcourt. We were both pregnant together and she had a little girl, Uluoma, in September. In the last few weeks at the end of the war they moved to a village very near us and helped us a lot both with their cheerful company and the material supplies they were able to give us.

Sister Gabriel Mary at Amaimo sent a little home-baked bread over every week. She did everything in her power to make life easier for us and will always have a special place in our hearts. Sister Mary Thomas who had harboured us at Umuahia, when we fled from Aba, was now once more a refugee and was living at Nguru, or more accurately, she was sleeping there for she lived in her little red Volkswagen Beetle which she loaded with relief which she dispersed to the handful of foreign wives who had remained and others she knew who were in special need.

In this time of constant shortages, breakdowns, lack of fuel and spare parts she was uncannily punctual, always arriving on the same day of the month at the same hour. Having spent the night at Amaimo she would drive up and almost before we had time to welcome her, she had unloaded our ration, tried second-hand dresses on the children, taken note of urgent needs and departed. She was a very determined woman and never hesitated to speak her mind no matter to whom. She usually left us in a flat spin, half our questions unanswered and requests forgotten. The children loved her and we all tried to get her to slow down but to no avail. There were many stories of her clashes with authority. Once, at the end of the war, during the confusion in January 1970 she was in the convent at Emekuku when she noticed some strange soldiers in the grounds. She was a small woman but, undaunted, she marched up to one and said, "Excuse me son, are you a Biafran or a Nigerian?"

He looked a bit taken aback but replied, "A Nigerian."

"Huh! I thought so," she said and turned round and went back to the convent. This, at a time when the whole population was in fear of their lives, typifies this Irish woman with a huge heart who more than anyone had saved Nnenna for us. On an earlier occasion when she was stopped by a soldier at a checkpoint who refused to lift the barrier, as she expected, she was said to have seized his gun and after a few choice words struck him with it! Many years later I heard she was living in a convent in Dublin but was in very poor health and sadly I was not able to visit her.

Some of the orphanage boys learned how to make raffia mats, hats etc. Stephen, the thorn carver's wife, came to see me and told me that her husband had been conscripted into the army. She brought the beautiful little carved nativity set I had ordered and we paid her in relief supplies

We had a measles epidemic and baby Ike from the orphanage became very sick. I eventually managed to get him to a hospital where he was diagnosed with bronchopneumonia and enteritis as well. Three days later I was back at the hospital with eight more children when I heard that baby Ike had died. A parcel addressed to Elizabeth had arrived (three months after she had gone back to UK) so I took it to give to her husband, Francis when he next visited. There was also a letter for me from my mother and a parcel for me from Fr. Wasser. A soldier came with five children to be admitted to the orphanage and we kept going somehow. On 21st July we heard on the radio news that a man had walked on the moon for the first time. There was still another world outside this trouble-torn area we lived in. A world with different priorities.

In September two more epidemics hit Biafra: one was flu and the other infective hepatitis. Len was spending quite a lot of time at the mini-refinery where supplies of crude oil were increasingly difficult to get. It was now the rainy season and the constant soakings from the heavy rains soon made him succumb to the flu and he was forced to stay in bed for several days with a very high fever. Our bed was only single size and in my condition it was almost impossible for us to sleep. We had no transport and no means of reaching a doctor. After about the third day of his illness I too began feeling unwell and, by the time Gab drove in from Ogbor after a few days away, we were both quite ill. He readily volunteered his car to take us to Amaimo where we arrived at dusk. Sister Gabriel Mary took one look at me and sent me to a spare bedroom with the order to get into bed at once. Len's case wasn't so easy, as she couldn't have a man staying in the convent, so she gave him a variety of medicines and sent him back with the driver, Patrick, to Ogbor.

The following day a doctor came from Emekuku on a routine visit and, as she thought I looked jaundiced, she suggested she should go back and see if there was a bed available at Emekuku for me. Early the next morning Sister Gabriel and her driver got me into a car and took me to Owerri. Sister stopped at the Bank in Owerri while the driver and I continued to Emekuku Hospital where I was admitted and put into a side ward.

At this time there was no electricity in Owerri and candles and kerosene were very scarce so after dark, around 7pm, there was nothing to do but sleep. The night nurse had one hurricane lamp for the whole of the maternity ward and the private rooms. In all there were over fifty patients, not counting the infants, in this wing alone. Night emergencies were managed as best possible, sometimes with caesarean operations having to be carried out by candle and torchlight. Later they got Safari lamps which resembled short fluorescent tubes set in a box; these had their own rechargeable batteries.

Emekuku was over twenty miles from our home and I had few visitors but one, who was most welcome, was Mrs. Burke who had now gone back to her home at Egbu, two miles from Emekuku. She came as soon as she could and we had a fine chat. I hadn't seen her since the previous April when she and her husband went on leave. There was so much to talk about; their trip to Sweden to visit Pat their daughter and her husband Kent and the little granddaughter took us a good few minutes. Pat had given her mother a cotton nightdress for me and Mrs. Burke had also found a lovely shawl for the baby and a bright red maternity dress.

After a few days I was transferred back to the convent at Amaimo to convalesce for two weeks. I was visited twice daily there by a midwife who gave me my treatment. The convent at Amaimo was, in peace time, two duplex bungalows, each side having two bedrooms, a sitting-dining room, a kitchen, store and bathroom/toilet. One duplex was now used only for sleeping accommodation. Of the other the first half was the living room and day part of the house and the sitting-dining room had been converted into a chapel; the bedrooms on that side were empty most of the time and it was here that I had a room. The bedroom had a common window with the chapel through which room I was obliged to pass in order to visit the bathroom. Bishop Whelan, or one of the other priests, came down to say mass for the Sisters early each morning but I was ordered not to get up for mass as I was supposed to be there for rest. Unfortunately, I always awoke just as mass started and I was supremely conscious of the creaking of my bed as I tentatively turned over, while at the same time suppressing urgent messages to go to the bathroom. If I came out I would appear right behind the altar and the thought of the bishop's face if I suddenly shot out right under his nose while he was in the middle of mass forced me to lie as still as possible. Afterwards I would wait a decent interval for the priest to go and then hurry to the toilet. The

Sisters were always telling me to stay in bed for breakfast but after all my exertions to keep still I was more than glad to dress and join them.

Len was able to come almost every day so I had news from the home front. Uche was still coming out with her words of wisdom and while I was away in hospital she was heard to complain:

"If Mummy was here, she wouldn't ask someone to eat cornmeal without sugar!" Cornmeal, something we had never heard of before the war, was sent in as relief supplies. It was served like porridge as a breakfast dish. Sugar was very precious, also only seen as relief.

The Sisters proved to be wonderful company and full of fun; at nights we played Scrabble or listened to classical records. A few days after I arrived, the Sisters were invited to spend the Holy Rosary Feast Day at Nguru Convent and I was urged to join them if I felt up to it so I had my scarlet maternity dress washed the day before in preparation.

First thing in the morning Bishop Whelan walked down to say mass and afterwards stayed for breakfast. All the staff in the compound, along with the nurses, came to sing for the Sisters, present flowers and wish them a happy feast day. Sister Gabriel Mary had been baking and making up parcels for other convents while Sister Dorothea looked after the little twins, Peter and Paul, who lived in the boys' quarters with their older brother and sister. They were orphans and had been brought from the sick bay when they had recovered a little. We mounted cakes on boards covered with foil and cellophaned them, sticking down the ends with the last of the Sellotape, a great luxury. We also had little decorated cakes made into small parcels, some for priests, others for children on the compound and some for Len and my little ones at home. With so many people coming to say 'Happy Feast Day', we were lucky to leave Amaimo around eleven o'clock. We made a few calls first and distributed the gifts and after we had left Emekuku Hospital and Convent we only had one box of cakes left for Fr. Fullen, another of the Irish Holy Ghost priests. The Nguru Sisters were waiting for us and Sister Thomas, who had gone out on some emergency work shortly before.

She was soon back and we sat down at a gaily decorated table to a meal which started with tiny sausages on sticks embedded in pawpaw circles and ended with the 'Nguru' cake. It was very obvious that a lot of savings and putting aside had been done to permit such a beautiful meal and we were asked to come back for supper.

"Sure now, you don't expect us to eat all this you left!"

After lunch Sister Thomas and the Reverend Mother insisted we should all lie down for siesta. I had eaten so much I seriously doubted if I could climb the stairs but I did and was shown into the 'Princess's bedroom', for that is where one had stayed when she visited. A European princess, Cecilia de Bourbon-Parma, Patron of the French Red Cross, had flown her own relief plane in on several occasions and when she did she spent a little time in the convent at Nguru. Surprisingly, I did sleep after leafing through some novels thoughtfully provided then we rose at four o'clock and went to visit the 'returned children'. These were children who had been sent to São Tomé with kwashiorkor and, having recovered, were flown back so that others might go out for treatment. Before they left São Tomé they were fully kitted out and each left with a suitcase of clothes and parcels containing foodstuffs and toys. They were taken to Nguru and most of them stayed there as their parents did not know their whereabouts.

It was a very moving experience to cross the road and pass painfully thin women with sick children and then enter the white gates to be rushed by a mob of healthy looking children who only wanted someone to take interest in them. The first to reach us grabbed our hands, later arrivals held on to our skirts and others called out:

"Good afternoon," repeatedly.

"Come and see this."

"See our room."

"My name is Cecilia," etc.

All clamoured for attention and the few who hung back lit up like little lamps when brought forward. We were conducted through the place and they let us go only when they saw we could really stay no longer. I came out wondering who was better off – those inside hungry for love, not knowing where their parents were or those outside, starving but part of a family.

We were already due at Fr. Fullen's for tea and Sister Gabriel Mary was to negotiate for a second-hand car nearby, so she dropped Sister Dorothea and me off with the promise to be back in half an hour. Fr. Fred, as he was affectionately known, was getting on in years and had been in this parish for so long that he was really at home with his people. They thought the world of him and were convinced that if he hadn't been on leave at the time that the Pope (then a cardinal), visited Nigeria, he would have stayed with them instead of at nearby Emekuku on his African tour.

With great humour he told us of his early days in the priesthood in the poorer areas of Dublin and soon, with one joke straight after another, he had us nearly crying with laughter. Afterwards the Sisters told me he always told the same jokes but told so fast that you could never remember them and laughed heartily each time! He had had his houseboy make pancakes for us and we sat on his balcony looking over miles of greenery with palm trees silhouetted against the horizon. He had a truly wonderful view and said he often sat alone on the balcony in the evening listening to music in the rapidly advancing dusk and velvet night. After about six attempts, thwarted by "Have you heard this one my daughters?" we were eventually able to get away, back to Nguru to another fine spread and then home in the dark to Amaimo. Poor Len had not realised that I was going out and had walked from Ogbor to visit me and then had to walk home again. A few days later the children came to visit me and they enjoyed themselves immensely, especially with the flush toilets.

As I started to get better I went to visit my namesake at the little maternity home. Mrs Ofoegbu was the nurse in charge and Sister found that more mothers were coming to have their babies there when word got round that a baby born there got a new dress and some soap, while the mothers each had something for themselves to take home like a 'relief' dress or blouse.

Meanwhile, more and more tuberculosis cases were coming into their sick bay and more classrooms were taken over to accommodate the increasing number of in-patients. Feeding was the main problem. Without food there was no point in admitting them as that was the greatest part of the treatment. Food supplies were spasmodic and usually inadequate with drugs, too, just arriving on a take-what-you-get-no-orders-entertained basis. The whole life was a great strain on the Sisters and indeed on all those connected with relief work.

Sister Gabriel Mary had been having terrible headaches for some time and now attributed them to a bad tooth. Len also had toothache and I was ordered to go for tests at Amaigbo Hospital so, as the only dentists operational in Biafra that we knew of were in Amaigbo, we decided that Sister and I should go for Len one morning and we should all travel to Amaigbo together. This meant putting about two and a half miles on our journey as we were now to by-pass Ibeme and journey through Ogbor instead. About a quarter of a mile from the house at Ogbor a large plane suddenly passed at tree top level in front of us. We just had time to stop the car and run for the shade of some palm trees while it circled back. It crossed my mind that the priest's house at Ogbor was a whitewashed building and I was sure it was an excellent landmark and target. Again the plane turned, passing almost directly over us and then we heard the explosions as bombs detonated. By this time Sister Gabriel Mary and I were badly shaken to say the least. We had stopped just where a family was preparing mounds to plant cassava and they stood nearly as petrified as us. The driver had reversed the white Peugeot car under a shady tree before running for shelter. I was terribly afraid for the children and Len. Just how near had the raid been? In a second the plane was heard screeching above the tree tops. This must be it, I thought, as I clung to the palm tree, expecting to see a rocket cleave it and me, any moment. However, it passed a few yards away and, rising fast, soon disappeared.

We waited a few minutes to see if it would return but it had gone and we drove the last stretch to the house. As we skirted the football field farm I saw Len hurrying along the other path to the house. A few hundred yards behind were Uche and Nnenna. Only Ada had been at home with Paulina. She seemed undisturbed but Uche was crying because she had lost her 'slate' in the scramble to get out of the school and also because she couldn't see Nnenna in the rush. We soon all calmed down and reports came that the plane had visited Ibeme less than a mile from us where they had made for the military camp there. We would probably have been in Ibeme at the time if not for Len's toothache! That particular day almost all the women of that village had gathered a few yards from the camp for some community task. From the air they could have been taken for troops but fortunately there were no serious casualties, although a piece of shrapnel went through the roof of a young officer's room and pierced his bed and the suitcase under it.

We eventually set out for Amaigbo where Sister Gabriel Mary had a wisdom tooth extracted, Len had a tooth filled and I had some blood tests. We got back safely but I couldn't help remembering that if we had set out via Ibeme we should have been at best just yards away from the raid at the material time.

A week or so later I was decreed fit to go home. The Sisters gave us a double bed size interior sprung mattress from the teachers' quarters and I had asked Len to have a bed made for it. I was also given a fairly old hand-operated sewing machine and an assortment of tinned food, cakes, sweets, etc. At first we had wondered if we could get a double bed into our home as the bedroom, being a mere 10' x 12' and already containing a dining table and numerous boxes, cartons and a tin trunk, was already pretty full. Then I suddenly remembered how, in my parents' home, the favourite hiding place for hide and seek was under the big double bed. Len had already given the orders to the carpenter but I told him the next day that we must have the bed legs at least a foot longer than he had designed. So, after the bed with its two-piece planked base had been manoeuvred into the room and the little wooden pegs hammered into place to hold it together (there were no nails), we got the mattress on top and almost everything else in the room under it. I had been secretly wondering how we would get the baby's bed in for, although there was a lot under the bed, there was also a lot of bed and the door now only half opened.

One of our other new acquisitions was a water filter. We had never got into the habit of boiling all our drinking water though we did keep a special clay pot in the kitchen specifically for drinking water. However, if it was allowed to get near empty there was quite a lot of animal life jumping around in it. In all we had about four of these pots, each holding around eight gallons of water. They were of dubious quality, locally made and sun-baked. They were round bottomed and were either placed on a small heap of earth against a corner or wall or a hollow was made in the ground for them to sit in. I remember once when Elizabeth was still with us, we decided to cook 'meat pies' in the frying pan one day, a real treat. I had just got the fat hot in the frying pan and a merry little fire under it when, with a whoosh, a pot full of water burst and the water streamed across the floor. Most of our firewood was wet in the first flood, which gradually picked up speed and doused the fire before I had time to think. All the wood was now wet and the floor completely awash so we took the opportunity to give the floor the luxury of a good wash and fortunately the place soon dried out in the sun and enough wood dried for us to light a fire in the evening for cooking. Looking back I think we must have cooked the meat pies later that night for we couldn't afford to throw anything away!

The children were very glad to have me back again and so, of course, was Len. I was, however, still weak and with the baby due in a few weeks I stayed at home most of the time. Len was now busy, having got his little refinery into production and although our car was still off the road, we were glad to be able to help a few others to keep mobile. We also made friends with some other young couples and found ourselves acting as marriage counsellors.

Somehow we managed to keep our transistor radio going. Len once wheedled a cup of precious salt from me on the pretext that he was going to use it to recharge the torch type batteries. He assured me that I could have the salt back afterwards. With the aid of an old tin, a few bits of wire and eight batteries instead of six, he managed to generate enough electricity out of this saline mixture to enable us to hear the news. However the batteries soon ran down and I declined to take back the now black slush which had been over £5 worth of salt, or to give out any more salt for further experiments.

Although we were producing diesel, petrol and kerosene there was, it seemed, no way of making engine oil or hydraulic brake fluid. Len experimented using tin cans and baby food jars and mixing petroleum products with things like red palm oil to try and produce an engine oil substitute. Almost every day people came begging for a little to top up their oil and eventually Len agreed on condition that they understood it was not a substitute for the real stuff and while he suggested it might be alright to top up with it, he didn't recommend a complete oil change or give any kind of guarantee. Needless to say, there were some who did change over completely and, surprisingly, no one ever came back to complain!

He also made a crude black shoe polish which he gave free to those willing to risk it! He used it himself and as it did keep the rain out, didn't burn up the leather and gave a bit of a shine, he was happy with it. Another bit of experimenting gave us home-made creosote with which we stained the bamboo walls of the living room.

We were still plagued from time to time by armies of soldier ants coming out in the night and marching in columns right through the house and around it. One night, soon after we started keeping a few chickens, we woke to a terrible racket coming from the chicken run. Thinking there might he thieves around, Len dashed out to discover that an army of these ants had set on the chickens. One was already bleeding as she struggled to free herself of the little creatures with a sting or bite which is used with impunity. The poor hen was nearly demented as Len searched through her feathers and pulled ants off her entire body along with a few feathers. Not long after we heard Paulina jumping about and squealing at the dead of night and found her tackling an invasion force around her bed. The only way to stop their progress is to burn them or scorch the earth in front of them. Before they took on a new war-time value, old bicycle and motor tyres were usually burned to divert them. We found they were equally averse to kerosene and used quite a lot of that to keep them at bay. Old car tyres, we knew, were cut up and made into sandals. As there was no hope of any new shoes to buy they were better than nothing. My three girls had no shoes as new ones were impossible to find and they had joined the other children all going barefoot. I was lucky as I was still managing with the sandals I had bought in Lagos in1966.

Another great nuisance was the jiggers, which everyone seemed to get in their feet. The first that you knew about it was a slightly itchy foot. On close examination a little spot was seen. This grew and the itching intensified until you realised what was the cause or someone told you. The locals used a piece of broom twig or a razor blade to remove the top layer of skin and expose the little white jigger worm, which is usually, by this time, a mum worm with a lot of eggs around her. Great care must be taken to remove the whole worm without breaking it as doing so may cause immediate re-infestation. The eggs also have to be removed. The operation is nearly painless and even small children can endure the removal without tears. After the hole is clean a little kerosene is applied (as a disinfectant) and an attempt is made to keep the area dust-free until the hole heals. It was a basic treatment which, however, worked well. Sometimes we took six out of the children's feet in one day. They were caused by walking barefoot in sandy or dusty areas.

Cassava is one of the mainstays of the peoples' diet in Nigeria. The tuberous roots are prepared in many ways but it was only during the Biafran war that the leaves were considered as a food. It was already known that after eating certain types of cassava leaves goats and sheep died in agony. However, someone discovered that if the leaves were boiled for ten minutes with the lid off the pot, the poisonous vapours were driven off and the leaves were quite palatable. After this became known at the relief workers' meetings, they started to spread the word and to set an example we tried it and attempted to introduce it to our friends. Some people planted a little cassava horizontally in order to get more leaves. The taste was rather like spinach and, eaten with boiled yams and a palm oil sauce, it made a change in our restricted diet. No part of the cassava plant, tuber or leaves should ever be eaten raw.

Letters took a long time to come and I noted in my diary that the photos we took on Ada's birthday in July only arrived in late October. The film had been 'posted' out for processing. We were very lucky to get any mail at all as there was of course no regular overseas or domestic mail service. The few British wives of Biafrans still 'inside' were at times able to send notes or, rarely, visit each other when I heard news about Pat Kanu, Rose Umelo, Elsie Odumodu and some others. Like them, I had letters brought in on relief planes. Mine were from my parents, an aunt and later from missionary priests who had gone home from Biafra and were very worried about what might be happening to the people they had left here. It was Fr. O'Sullivan writing from Rome who urged me, even then, to start writing it all down so that I might write a book about our experiences afterwards. A year after the war when we met for a few minutes at an airport, he gave me photostat copies of all my wartime letters to him for reference. When writing to my parents I had to bear in mind that they knew nothing of life in Africa and only saw the British papers and television, which naturally showed the sensational side of the war and as Britain was supporting the Nigerian side there was a bias in the reporting. Fr. O'Sullivan, however, had spent eighteen years in Eastern Nigeria and I could tell him in my letters a bit of the situation as I saw it knowing that he understood what I was talking about. My letters to my parents were mostly 'not to worry, we are managing alright'. Although my correspondence with friends who had been through part of the war could be freer I still had to be cautious, especially with any military news. After all, I didn't want to fall foul of the authorities and get deported.

We were all of course looking forward to the birth of the new baby and everybody was silently praying for a boy. With three girls now we couldn't go on having more children if this was not the long-awaited son. At that time under Igbo custom daughters could not inherit land and if a man had no son then his land would be reallocated to male family members on his death. Wives who had no sons, or worse had no child at all, were driven to all sorts of doctors and superstitious practices to get a male issue and her husband's family would try to influence their son to get a new wife who could give them a boy. Incidentally, traditionally a wife was also seen as 'property' and could be inherited on her husband's death. Tradition varied a little in different Igbo areas. The law was changed in 2014 to end this discrimination against women. Along with the thanks we usually got from grateful people, there was often a wish that we would get a boy as 'only God could repay us'. My weight had shot up to over 11stone thanks to the better diet we were all getting so I made myself some new bras from soft cotton I had been given as my others no longer fitted me.

The Sisters at Amaimo were still doing everything possible for us and turned up one day with a swing-type hospital cot and a wooden stand for it. They also brought a piece of mosquito net for me to sew to cover the cot. I hemmed it round and threaded some elastic I had received in a parcel from home through the hem and it fitted very snugly. I had my case all packed now, ready to go to

166

Emekuku, and Len had two gallons of petrol reserved in case things started to happen. Petrol was by now virtually unobtainable and it was with the greatest difficulty that he was able to resist the pleas of those who came begging for some. Our crude oil supply had now also stopped and our car was still off the road. However, we were on four wheels of a sort, having bought a very old bicycle with worn out tyres for one hundred pounds!

At nights we sat out in clear moonlight and quite clearly saw the Federal planes cruising round while relief planes tried to land. Just before, the Americans had landed on the moon for the second time – how far away? In the same week our neighbour, Gab, bought a second-hand lady's bike for two hundred and fifty pounds but after paying the money over he learnt that the carrier and the key to lock the back wheel were not included in the deal.

Fresh meat and fish were very scarce for us but occasionally some meat was flown in for the priests and nuns. December 1st was marked by the arrival of an Irish priest walking into our house with a massive 'T' bone steak in his hand for us. There was no wrapping on it at all so we fried part of it and put the rest into our stew. It was part of his own ration, flown in the previous night on a relief plane. A wonderful generous gesture.

We now had about a dozen chickens which we were hoping would provide us with eggs. They were local birds and we spent a lot of time chasing them home in the evenings. Two disappeared for several days before we found they had decided to sleep with the boys at the orphanage. One or two laid eggs in the kitchen and one laid hers in our neighbour's kitchen. A teacher and her husband lived there now. Yet another made her nest in the corner of the bathroom and sat on it quite unperturbed while we bathed. This last one was stolen the day her eggs started to hatch. We kept her four chicks in a basket by the fire for a time but they all died eventually. Our cat, Kim, was always chasing the hens and the children would be chasing after the cat so that everyone was racing round the kitchen and back yard!

We had a little thatch-roofed corridor to link the kitchen with the house and along it we strung our washing. Big items like sheets were spread on the kitchen roof which ended a bare four feet from the ground. We also had a line stretched diagonally across the garden over part of the kitchen roof. I think at its highest the roof was six feet. In the kitchen I had bamboo slatted shelves along two sides. The fire was at the far end, with the water pot beside it and a little bamboo bench on the other side. The fourth side was half open to form an entrance and we rolled a mat down in the front of it at night. Our light was a 'Biafra lamp' or a kerosene lamp. It was luxurious by local standards.

By 2nd December I had almost everything ready for the baby except nappies. The next morning a car drew up at breakfast time and a stranger handed me a parcel from the priest at Ehime. Inside was enough muslin for two dozen nappies so I set to work cutting it up into two feet squares and started hemming them. While I was thus engaged, Wendy Ijioma arrived with baby Uluoma and some foodstuff for us. She was on her way to have Uluoma's second triple vaccination done. Uche and Nnenna were at school but Len, Ada and I decided to go for the trip and we set out together. We reached the place after taking several wrong roads and met some old friends, among them a fellow Scot, and made some new ones too. Professor Ogun invited us to his quarters where we spent a pleasant hour. We had lunch with a lady doctor and a young Dutchman who was very new to the country but eager to learn Igbo.

The next day we received some relief from two different sources. When we got relief in this manner we knew it could mean a long time till the next lot. However, we were always able to share some with friends. I continued with my nappy making and also cut a sheet into three for the expected baby. We were almost ready now.

Chapter 11

Preparing for a Son and for Christmas

On Sunday 7th December our neighbour Eric said he was going to the village next to Azigbo, Len's village and Len decided the opportunity was too good to refuse and he would go with him to visit his mother and take her a few things for Christmas. They left at 7am and expected to be back on Tuesday. My due date was December 15th and as both my previous babies had been late we felt this pregnancy would be the same. A few hours after Len and Eric had gone I got a message that a car would be taking Dr. Anne Seymour, who had returned from the UK, from Amaimo to Emekuku early the next day and it could take me to Emekuku Hospital at the same time on the Monday. This would save a car having to make a special trip for me as petrol was really at a high premium now. Because there was a possibility the baby would need a blood transfusion it was safer for the birth to be at Holy Rosary Hospital rather than in Amaimo. There was no way of letting Len know that I would be in hospital before his return so I left a note for him and told the girls I was going to get the new baby. Fortunately, my sister-in-law Caroline was convalescing with us at this time and with her daughter, Paulina, she kept the house while I was away. I was of course ready long before the car came and it was after 4pm when we got to Amaimo. I just had time for a cup of tea with Sister Gabriel Mary and the American wife of a soldier when they announced it was time to go.

We took all the back roads as most people were unwilling to drive along the straight, unsheltered tarred roads and risk being chased by enemy planes. In distance it was probably shorter too but as the road was not well maintained, and there were two very dangerous bridges, we made slow time. At one point I was amazed to see a herd of English cows being driven towards us. There must have been about twenty of them, some with calves. Most Nigerian cows are long horned and have humps but these were a real English breed.

"I often see them," said the driver.

"They're refugees from Obudu!"

Before the war there was a cattle ranch there at a hilly area near the Cameroon border. It was found that the climate suited dairy cattle and tourists staying at the ranch had the luxury of fresh milk, etc. Apparently, during the early part of the war the area was threatened and the cows were driven down from the hills. I think they were later walked to Oguta and certainly, when I saw them, they were near Owerri. It was to me quite astonishing that in spite of the desperate hunger of the people who were even eating lizards for meat that these cows survived. After the war I believe they were walked back to Obudu, where no doubt they took up their normal residence. They set me wondering about what had happened to the little baby elephant I used to see at Enugu Zoo. Was it evacuated or abandoned? Did it become a white elephant? Maybe someday I will find out.

Just before dusk we emerged on to the tarred road and, turning right, were soon at Emekuku. Evening mass was just about to start in the chapel and I attended. I seem to remember I sat on the men's side of the chapel by mistake but I didn't move. It was very beautiful with the sun's rays shining through the windows. Before the end of the service the lights had been switched on, as by now Emekuku had had its electricity restored.

Immediately after mass I was taken to a little single room in the Maternity Ward where I undressed and got into bed. I settled down with a book, then Sister Doctor came and examined me and said she would see me in the morning, and when she did she decided to induce labour; I have Rhesus Negative blood and Len has Rhesus Positive which sometimes leads to birth complications. Certainly I was told I should always have my babies in hospital just in case a complete blood change for the baby is necessary, though how one would be managed under the present circumstances had not been debated.

Now, all through my pregnancy I had longed, in vain, for curry. People had promised to send me some curry powder. My mother did but the parcel didn't reach me. However, that day while I was in labour my lunch was brought to me and it was curry. I couldn't face it and asked them to keep it for me until evening. I could have wept with frustration. Just before half past four I knew the time was approaching for the birth. All mothers are familiar with the bearing down feeling that comes just beforehand.

"It is coming," I cried.

"Wait till we get Sister," answered the nurse.

"Where is she?"

"At the convent." The convent was a good four minutes' walk away.

"You had better run then."

"Don't do anything till she comes. They told us to call her when it was time."

I honestly thought I was going to burst before the two Irish nursing sisters arrived, although to be fair I think they did run all the way. Within a minute the baby was born.

"What is it?" I asked.

"It's fine," answered the nurse.

"What *is* it?" I repeated.

"A fine big boy," Sister answered.

"Thank God!"

She held him up for me to see a very indignant black-haired baby boy.

"I thought you said this was going to be a small baby?" I remarked.

"Nine pounds," exclaimed the nurse as she weighed him.

"Thank God!" I repeated.

I was still in the labour room when the curry was brought back but I still couldn't face it. Before sleeping I wrote to my parents and to Mrs. Burke. There was no way to get a letter to Len but I wrote to him anyway just in case I heard of someone going to Amaimo.

On the following day, Wednesday, Mrs. Burke came to see us. She gave me a length of cotton which she had brought back from leave for me. On the Thursday, Chukwuemeka Leonard (soon shortened to Emeka as we had agreed to call him) was circumcised. This is usually done when the baby is a little older but I wanted it done under hygienic conditions and not with a razor blade as I had heard was common practice. Len had still not arrived but a doctor took letters for Len and Sister Gabriel Mary to Amaimo. On Friday, Mrs. Burke came again so did Immaculata who had been my midwife at Amaimo. While they were there the doctor came in with some baby clothes from Sister Gabriel Mary and the news that Len was on his way. There was no room in their car and he was coming on his bike, a journey of over seventeen miles! A few minutes later he arrived and like magic the room cleared to let the father see his son. He had brought a camp bed with him as it was already almost dark but Mrs. Burke offered to put him up for the night, and after an hour or so he left with her. He told me the next day how he slept in the medicine store surrounded by tablets and bottles of all descriptions.

"I thought I was going to be drugged by the smell!" he remarked.

By eight fifteen in the morning he was back and stayed the whole day, sharing my meals unofficially. In the afternoon Sister Dorothea arrived from Amaimo en-route to Nguru and she agreed to take us all back in her car and so we left the hospital at 7pm. I forget how many of us there were, but I know there were a man and two children who had come to visit their mother as well as Sister and her driver, Len, the baby and me. How we got the bicycle back I don't remember.

Sister Gabriel Mary was surprised and delighted to see us and after exclaiming over the baby, insisted we should eat before setting out on the last two miles. When we finally reached home the children had already gone to bed but the commotion woke Uche and Nnenna, who staggered out looking very sleepy. They each held the baby for a few seconds before going back to bed. Ada wakened just as we were going to bed when the baby started to cry.

"What is making that noise?" she asked, so we told her to come and see. She did and once convinced that it was 'our own baby', she too went back to bed. They were all thrilled to have this long-awaited infant and so was the rest of the village. We had an endless stream of visitors, most lamenting that they had nothing to give the new child. Many brought buckets of water or bottles of palm oil or other local produce. Those who couldn't come because of fear of conscription sent emissaries with little notes. They claimed the child as 'theirs' as I had been resident in their village for the whole of the pregnancy. I had now written twice to my parents to tell them they now had a grandson but there was to be no reply for several weeks.

While we were rejoicing, the war situation was getting more and more serious. BBC World radio carried the news that long-range Russian armaments were seen on the road to the East. On my arrival back from the hospital I found that another of Len's nieces, Chinyelu, had come to stay. We also had a teenage orphan girl from a nearby village and a former maid from the orphanage, a refugee, and who had nowhere to go when she left there. We had never had so much help. Fortunately, we only had to feed and board them and I managed occasional dresses for them. I wasn't able to breastfeed Emeka which was not a surprise as I hadn't managed to breastfeed the girls for more than a few days. In preparation I had been saving odd tins of baby formula. I had heard that a brand I had never heard of called Camelpo was available but many babies, who had previously had sweeter-tasting milk, wouldn't drink it. So I exchanged my variety of tins for Camelpo and, knowing no different, he accepted it readily!

Next door our teacher neighbour, Edna, was having trouble over exam leakages. However, she straightened things out before term ended and her husband Eric came with a car and took Paulina with them back to their home town for Christmas.

I had managed to get all the girls in the house a new dress for Christmas. Some were 'new' second hand but everyone was quite content to have anything different. Meanwhile, a week before Christmas, yet another set of peace talks broke down when the Biafran delegation which had gone to Addis Ababa arrived to find that the Nigerian delegation had been 'indefinitely delayed'. We heard much later that the delay was actually due to a relapse in the health of one of the Nigerian delegates who was newly out of hospital, but at the time we saw it as another avoidance of the issue and that while arms were building up there was no need to pretend that a negotiated peace was desirable.

On the home front a man in the village, who had married years ago by native law and custom and already had teenage children, decided to marry in church. The reception was an occasion for the whole village and the Biafran notes, now already much reduced in value, flowed freely when 'donations' were called for. People were very surprised that I briefly attended the reception as the baby was not yet three weeks old and by tradition a mother stays at home with a new baby for six weeks at least.

Wendy Ijioma and I had been talking for some time about circulating a newsletter among the remaining foreign wives such as ourselves. It was almost impossible for us to meet but we were in touch remotely through the relief personnel. We managed to produce only one issue.

I was also talked into marking the elementary school leaving examination papers. However, as there was difficulty in exchanging papers between the provinces, the whole thing was temporarily shelved. I never knew what happened to them after that.

On Christmas Eve, Sister Gabriel Mary sent us a cake and a box of chocolate biscuits among other food stuffs. We, in turn, gave out the ingredients for Christmas lunch of rice and tinned meat to some families we knew who would otherwise have had a very poor day.

Christmas Eve came with very heavy shelling from all directions. The mud walls shook and a loose stone fell on our bed during the night. We had arranged to have Christmas lunch with Wendy, Sam and baby Uluoma but the atmosphere was very gloomy. Sam came alone and told us that villages near them were evacuating. Shells were falling over the Imo River Bridge, the last barrier to the heart of Biafra and they might have to evacuate their store. In any case no one felt like celebrating and he left without even entering the house. At first we did not feel like eating at all but later we opened a tin of bully beef and made a stew with it and a tin of tomato juice and some onion which we had with rice.

Refugee movement increased and one evening, a little later, thirteen people from Mbawsi moved in next door to us. They were apparently all known to each other; they had with them a young mother and her two-week-old baby. After seeing me use my sewing machine they asked me to sew a dress from a damask tablecloth for one of the children, which I agreed to do, making a straight shift dress. They stayed for a few days before moving on again. The last Sunday of the year Gab and Len went to mass at Umuozu, the next village and later we had lunch together.

One of our frequent visitors at this time was a woman from Umuozu with large chronic ulcers on her foot and leg. Her home was almost equidistant from our house and Amaimo and I tried to get her to go to Amaimo where I felt she could be admitted to the sick bay. The walking to and from our house to have her dressing changed taxed her little energy; however, she was obstinate and, in spite of letters for her to give to Sister explaining her position and other assurances, she kept coming to me two or three times a week. I would wash and put a dry dressing on the wound and a bandage, give her some aspirin and, most important of all, a cooked meal and some food to take home with her. When she first started coming, she had been putting some kind of clay mixture on her wounds and it took a few visits before she accepted that I would rather she did not take off the bandage when it was dirty or put clay on instead. The mixing of native and Onyeacha (white man) medicine was something I dreaded for the results could be dramatic and disastrous. On their own the local herbs, native medicines and Juju charms all had a value. There are some illnesses for which none but a herbal cure is known. The main factor is, of course, faith in the person treating and the method of treatment. There were many Nigerians who felt they have not been treated if they didn't have injections! Unscrupulous people could make a lot of money by charging for injections of water. I used to refuse to treat anyone with my medicine if I knew he was already using native cures.

"If you want to use native medicine, it's all right by me but if you want me to treat you with my medicine you must not use any native 'cures' while you are using mine. And you must take mine us I tell you. It will not work if you do not listen and do as you are told."

I made that speech almost every day at least a dozen times when I was doing the clinics. Deep down I knew that what most of them needed was meat not medicine or indeed enough of any food to eat at least two meals a day. Medical supplies in late December were very low and relief supplies were hardly reaching anyone.

The whole population seemed to be on the move but there was no longer anywhere to go to. On the last night of the year I hadn't the heart to stay up and see the New Year in. The year before, Elizabeth, Len and I had stood on the front porch with a tot of whisky each to toast in 1969.

On New Year's Day we had Gab over for lunch. Sister Gabriel Mary had sent us some frozen meat which we used to make a stew. We had invited Wendy and Sam Ijioma and their baby daughter Uluoma, but since the cancellation of our Christmas with them we weren't sure if they were coming or not. We had just finished eating when they arrived. However, it was mere coincidence as the events of the last week had driven from their minds the fact that they were expected. They brought us two new tubes and tyres for one of our second-hand bicycles. We were very happy to get them as they were worth a lot more than the bikes themselves. A new tyre was ninety pounds then.

In the evening we went with Gab to an army-sponsored party. A very determined effort had been made to make it enjoyable. A specially made hall of palm leaves sheltered us and there was, probably for the first time in months, plenty of food. The only light was from two hurricane lamps. Too much light would have been visible from the air for it seemed the patrol planes were not taking a night off. A battery-powered record player was coaxed into life for a while and there was dancing on the hard mud floor. We enjoyed ourselves while secretly wondering where all the food had come from. It seemed that everyone was doing his best to forget the war for a few hours. We came back late but Gab had promised to call on some neighbours that night and he and Len drove there after dropping me at home but they soon came back, having found the compound in darkness. We settled down to sleep but were awakened about 3am by a car which went to Gab's house. A few minutes later it left. In the morning Gab came over to us.

"It looks like I'm travelling," he said. "I have been told to report at State House today with all my particulars and ready to travel."

"Where do you think it will be to?"

"Maybe Ghana, there is a peace conference coming up there soon."

Soon afterwards he left. We little thought that we wouldn't see him in Biafra again. He had agreed the day before to be godfather to Emeka. Later we had the ceremony and his part was taken by a proxy although Gab's name was registered.

On 2nd January the shelling seemed louder than ever – rumours had it that the people from Mile 7½ (to Umuahia), were moving out. This meant that the people had withdrawn one and a half miles from the Imo Bridge – the last real barrier to the Federal advance. Mile 7 marked the junction of the Umuahia, Owerri and Okigwe roads. During the next few days the northern front at Onitsha was still holding though under pressure. Okigwe sector was extremely noisy and refugees from Mbaise were streaming out; many of them camped in Ogbor and the surrounding villages. As our parish priest was an Mbaise man they hoped for sympathetic treatment. Ogbor was still trying to be normal but on the Saturday we discussed our plans if the situation deteriorated. However, we came to no conclusion.

On the Sunday we attended a local 'society' wedding. The Bishop of Owerri presided at the nuptial mass. The road outside the groom's house was camouflaged over to hide the guests' cars. Len and I nearly went on a bike but friends gave us a lift in their car. Len was a bit disappointed as he was rather looking forward to seeing the look on the big men's faces as he pedalled up with me on the carrier! I, however, was relieved and readily called someone to take back the bicycle and the pillow on which I had been going to perch.

On the Monday we had an early call from a friend, Pat, whose wife Kate was seriously sick. He managed to get a car and a gallon of petrol and Len and I went with them to Amaimo. There was no doctor there that day and Sister advised us to go to Amaigbo Joint Hospital. We hadn't enough fuel to get there and were afraid that it was even too late to go now as outpatients' cards were generally given out before 9am. The Sister gave us two gallons of petrol and a letter to the Sister in the pharmacy to help us. We were lucky to get to Amaigbo in time. We had stopped on the way to collect the baby, Emeka, and took him along too.

Using a little bit of 'long leg' (a euphemism for using undue influence to overcome obstacles), we were able to get a doctor to see Kate and treatment was prescribed. Seeing how tired she was I took the card with the prescription to the dispensary. The hospital had long outgrown its buildings so that a long thatched shed was erected as waiting hall, office and dispensary. I had just handed the prescription to the dispensary assistant when I turned and saw a jet plane coming straight at us. It was approaching from the back of the hospital and most people had not yet seen it. My mind whirred round. I must not run across the open ground to where Len and the baby stood with Pat and Kate. They couldn't see the plane which was coming up from behind them. If I panicked, the whole mass of people in this makeshift building would scatter outside, thus drawing the attention of the pilot to the number of people. If anything hit this building nothing could save it. There were only a couple of layers of dry palm leaves between us and the sky. In this second the plane drew nearer and we could all now hear the engine. A burst of firing set our hearts pounding. The anti-aircraft gun in the compound burst into life but at that moment we didn't know if it was the plane firing or the anti-aircraft gun. The plane flew right over the hospital and as soon as it passed I ran across the few yards of open ground to the main outpatients. In the same instant we heard bombs exploding. I had hoped the iron-roofed cement-built building would give more protection and dived into a small consulting room and stood in the corner behind the door.

A nurse in a blue uniform was weeping. She was sure the nearby market had been attacked and she had sent her child there to buy something. I tried to calm her, telling her if the patients saw her so upset it would make them all worse. I really wanted to get to Len and Emeka but the corridor was full of people and we half expected the plane to come back. The noise of the plane died away and I managed to force my way along the veranda to where I had left Len, Emeka, Kate and Pat, her husband, but they had moved away from the building to a steep embankment overhung by trees a few yards away. While I was still making my way through the crowd, a cyclist rode up with a casualty sitting on the carrier being held on by someone running behind. A Peugeot car also arrived with badly wounded men; the bomb had fallen in the market. Most of the outpatients immediately left the hospital, whether treated or not. Meanwhile, I went back to the dispensary but couldn't at first see the man to whom I had given the prescription card. Eventually he came out from where he had been taking cover and I collected the medicines. More casualties were arriving, some in a Red Cross car which had been in the thick of the raid, some on bicycles and a few on foot. We left as soon as possible, still feeling shaky. The next day we went to negotiate with our parish priest for the purchase of his spare second-hand engine for our Volkswagen. We could not get any money from the bank but we agreed to pay two hundred and fifty pounds (in Biafran currency) and he let us take it away. The banks now had not been open for business for some time.

I received a letter from my mother posted in October 1968, telling me that Fr. Wasser had written to acknowledge receipt of the parcel she had sent to him for me. She also told me that she had sold three of the raffia bags, made by the orphans, which I had sent her through him when he left.

On Wednesday, which was the following day, Len, Chinyelu, Emeka, Ada and I went with Wendy and Uluoma to the Queen Elizabeth Hospital which had moved from Umuahia the previous April and was now in the bush near Owerri, where we were treated and returned without incident. Uche and Nnenna were peeved at having been left at home but they had been at school when Wendy came.

The car engine was installed by that evening. We were given some brake fluid and work continued on the car for a few days. Meanwhile, refugees were pouring in from all sides and Mbaise was reported to have 'run'. On the 9th we had a visitor who told us, confidentially, that things were very serious and that night we heard Owerri was evacuating. By Saturday 10th refugees were everywhere around us. Those coming from Mbaise passed those moving in the opposite direction from Etiti. Having passed each other they turned back, confused. There was no way out; the net was tightening all the time. Many stopped and spent the night, exhausted, in the church, its grounds and the market square. The local people met and decided not to run. Really they had no place to run to! Rumours reached us that Federal soldiers had been seen six miles away at Amaraku.

Although we didn't know it then, that night all the expatriate World Council of Churches workers were flown out of Biafra while a planeload of kwashiorkor children with French doctors were left stranded at the airport. This was the last night planes landed at Uli Airport. The same night the Biafran leader Ojukwu flew out. One tiny happy spot on this dark day was driving our car from its resting place of the last nine months using a battery borrowed for the operation.

Chapter 12

Biafra Surrenders

On the morning of 11th January, General Ojukwu's broadcast to the nation was heard. In it he explained that he left in search of a peace settlement. We knew then that the war was virtually over. There was no feeling of anger about his leaving or that he was running away. Rather there was a great sorrow and the murmured comments were that 'We had let him down', 'We did not live up to his expectations'. When I say 'we' here, I mean the general feeling of the people. There was also a very real fear of genocide and persecution when the Federal soldiers did come. As soon as the news spread, all the refugees started to shoulder their loads and go back to their home villages. If they had to die better that it might be in their own homes and not in a strange place.

We heard that Uli airstrip was destroyed (which in fact was not true). Two Irish priests had recently arrived at the mission in our village and I went to see one of them that evening. They did not quite know what was going to happen to them. The Federal Government had made it very clear that they believed the relief being flown in had prolonged the course of the war.

On Monday morning, 12th January, Wendy, Sam and Uluoma visited us. Sam went on to the next village to visit someone while Wendy and I chatted. Len bought a second-hand battery for the car but we couldn't get it charged. Sam came back within an hour announcing, "I have been to Nigeria!"

"What do you mean?" we asked.

"I have been to Nigeria. I have seen the Federal soldiers in the next village."

They decided to leave at once and go back to their temporary home about three miles away. They felt it would be better to be 'at home' when the visitors came and as home to them included the

W.C.C. Relief Store for Umuahia Province, they had more than their own property to account for.

Just after 2pm we heard heavy firing a few miles away; there were machine guns and other arms. We were all just starting to have lunch so I told everyone to take their plates and drinking water and go into the bunker while I packed some napkins, boiled water, baby's milk and a few other things into a bag and took them down to the bunker to join them. We carried Emeka in his cot as I was prepared to keep them there until nightfall if necessary. Meanwhile, Len was out at the front of the house working on the car. The firing ceased for a few minutes and then started again – I judged less than two miles away. The children now suddenly wanted to go to the toilet so I let them out of the bunker to go. Len was still working under the car when the children came back and I got them all back into the bunker once more. We had chairs and a bench in our little underground shelter and they sat down to finish their meal while I stood half in, half out of the entrance.

Again the firing sounded, very near now so I called to Len to join us. It lasted about five minutes. Len got out from under the car and, as he stood up, a car came along the road. Seated on the roof and bonnet and standing on the running boards were soldiers with guns. A second car, a Volkswagen also overflowing with armed soldiers, followed closely behind. As we stood I heard people shouting:

"One Nigeria! One Nigeria!"

The orphan boys, fifty yards away, screamed as if they were facing death – which they probably believed they were. The second car stopped just opposite us on the other side of the football field farm and as the soldiers looked down towards us I ducked into the bunker but they soon moved on. As soon as they reached the village market crossroad there was terrific firing (into the air we learned later). To my amazement villagers were coming running from all directions calling "One Nigeria!" Many wore palm fronds tied round their heads or arms and they all headed for the market square to see these Nigerians they had heard so much about. They had been told in advance to kill a goat and cook it and provide palm wine to welcome them. A welcome address was read. The highest ranking among them, a corporal, addressed the people in broken English, telling them not to be afraid and that they were all brothers. After a few minutes they moved on to the next village. We were now 'behind the lines', on the Federal side, cut off from Len's family and what remained of Biafra. We decided it was safe to return to the house but not to go out for a couple of days.

There was a lot of confusion; from every side people were walking, resting every few miles and then trudging on, most not knowing where to but just following the others. All along the roads they were just like fallen leaves in autumn; half dead, blown about and utterly helpless.

We heard so many rumours: Mbaise has run; they are at Nguru (where Sister Thomas, and others who were there, are now nobody knows); Emekuku has evacuated; shells are landing at Egbu; Owerri has run. Everyone seems to be congregating at Ugiri or going to Orlu. All in all it is a grim picture.

Fr. John S. (Irish) arrived at Ogbor, also over 250 orphans from Owerrinta. But still the determination to survive persisted. They ask, "Where are we running to from here?" But no one asks, "Why don't we give up?"

Our own household grew as we took in another refugee to our household. This time a teenage girl from the Rivers area called Florence, who was working at the orphanage but was sent away when the food situation became bad at the end of the year. She was in secondary school Class 3 before the war and became a great asset to me. I could quite trust her to look after Emeka and the girls and everyone was very fond of her already though she had been with us less than a fortnight. We also had a young niece, from Azigbo, who was rather sickly.

Emeka kept them all busy with his laundry and of course the water situation, which had never been ideal here, sent them out most of the day to the stream.

Fighting between the armies continued nearby but with the acoustics of Ogbor, (which makes Umuahia seem next door), we didn't know where the fighting was taking place. We prayed that we were not embarking on a worse kind of suffering.

I looked around .The children's only concern was to try and wangle extra sugar for the tea we left at breakfast time. Emeka was investigating the possibility of pulling the bottom sheet, on which he was lying, into his mouth. Innocence is bliss. To them 'after the war' is when they will go to see their grandparents in Scotland and when the news of the end is official and we tell them they'll be wanting to know when they are going. To them, there was only 'today' and 'tomorrow' and a 'long time'.

The invaders turned out to be semi-literate Hausas. They fired several rounds of machine-gun fire and some other guns. The amazing thing was that the local people were literally racing to see them but because of the shooting I hid the children in the bunker and kept low myself.

They had camped at Ibeme; I believe the infantry came there direct from Amaimo. All day we were hearing shooting as they showed their strength. I am sure they used more ammunition than most of our soldiers had handled in the last two and a half years.

In the evening they returned to Ogbor. It seems someone reported that our parish priest had large stocks of relief and was not giving it out so they came and told him either to feed the people or they would come and break the store and throw everything out.

Later still the word flew round that they were looking for women and the bishop came down to conduct the twenty or so aspirants (girls who were preparing to be nuns), to the Mission House. I worried about Florence, who had gone to return a dress she had borrowed and hadn't returned (it was now noon on Tuesday). She did return safely later.

As soon as Brigadier Effiong's broadcast was made on 15th January, announcing that the Republic of Biafra had ceased to exist, all the refugees started to go back to their homes.

Some of the Biafran soldiers coming back literally fell by the wayside. Many walked as if in a trance, others barely staggered along. The starvation that these boys underwent makes it a miracle they held on so long. There was no orderly retreat; the soldiers were mixed with the refugees, all just heading for their home towns. Uniforms and guns were abandoned.

The announcement by Britain and America that all relief should go through Nigerian Red Cross if they asked for it was viewed with horror here. I knew any delay would lead to more deaths by starvation.

The day after the surrender Len went on the bike to Amaimo. He met many Hausa soldiers and learned that Sister Gabriel Mary travelled out on Saturday. Sister Dorothea and Sister Mary Thomas were there but very agitated and nervous. On his way back the Nigerian soldiers took some of the stockfish he had been given and also took the bicycle and nearly took his watch. He later got the bike and watch back, mainly because he was able to speak Hausa. In the evening we learned that the W.C.C. store at Oka was broken into and looted. I went to see Fr. John S. and arranged for him to baptise Emeka tomorrow. The atmosphere was a bit calmer and people were moving more freely though women and young girls stayed out of sight.

I met a Yoruba (Nigerian) soldier at Father's house who said he had not removed his boots for two months. He could barely walk as his toes were deeply cut on the underside. I gave him penicillin and anti-tetanus serum from the mission supply and the wounds were dressed.

Chapter 13

Picking up the Pieces

The war was over but how were we to face the future? We were all afraid. No food seemed to be getting in and the war-weary soldiers, now all Nigerian, for the Biafrans had evaporated, leaving items of uniform, pay books, guns and other 'incriminating evidence' strewn along every roadside, were celebrating. The victorious soldiers too were very tired of fighting and longing to go back to their families. Meanwhile they 'liberated' goats, chickens, bicycles and cars and 'borrowed' young girls and wives. They had been told there was to be no violence and many shared cigarettes and passed out Nigerian coins, which were now having a terrific purchasing power. The Biafran pound became of less and less use and soon it was only worth 1d in Nigerian currency but it was still all the people had. People with Biafran debts tried to pay them off before the money lost all value. The banks remained closed. The last few plates, radios and irons appeared in the markets as traders arrived in lorry loads from Lagos and the West to buy at rock-bottom prices. Many people who had managed to preserve their car somehow throughout the war had it stolen then.

To motor between two towns one had to have a pass from the Nigerian Army in the nearest camp. Len and I went to Owerri on 28th January. There we met members of an American relief team, a British woman journalist and two foreign Directors of A.G. Leventis Ltd., a Greek Cypriot group of Nigerian companies. The Leventis directors were hoping to recruit back the staff they had been without for the past few years. One, Mr. David, gave Len his business card. We were asked several times if we would go back to Lagos to work but it was too soon for us and we said no. However, we were lucky to be given some Nigerian currency and we went to the main market in Owerri. There were plenty of things for sale by both Yorubas and Hausas. Long-forgotten luxuries like biscuits and beer, sugar and margarine, lamps and batteries. Very few were buying though. In the fresh food section there was little for sale and again there were few buyers. Many walked about just looking, pricing half-heartedly. We got some much-needed petrol from the relief workers and drove back to the village.

One of our first trips after the war was to see Len's mother who was very anxious to see us all and especially to meet baby Emeka. As our car was not really in first class order and Gab had left the keys of his commandeered Peugeot with us, so that we could warm the battery and use it if necessary, we decided then to travel with the children in the Peugeot so we all got in and set off early one morning. Unfortunately, after a few miles we were stopped by soldiers at a checkpoint who asked to see our driving particulars and particularly proof of ownership of the car. Of course we could not produce these and we were told that we must hand over the car at once. Later, mainly in view of the fact that we had such young children and possibly because of my colour, we were given soldiers to accompany us back to Ogbor and they would then take the car. We had no choice. They climbed in and we headed back to Ogbor but on the way we suspected that the engine was going to knock and we had to stop. Another car was waved down and the occupants forced to take us back to Ogbor in return for some petrol and we eventually arrived home tired and weary and a bit shaken. The soldiers we had met had assured us that even if they had allowed us to continue on our way there were so many other checkpoints that we could not have retained the car. Meanwhile, we were assured that efforts would be made to trace the rightful owner of the car and return it to him. Whether or not this was done we never found out so we then decided that our old Volkswagen was possibly less attractive and we made the journey to Azigbo in it without incident.

We stayed for a few days and one day Len and I took Emeka with us and went to Enugu to see if there was anything left of our flat. The baby went along as a kind of insurance policy as there were very few expatriates around and the soldiers suspected those they saw of being mercenaries. We chugged along in our little Volkswagen, hardly recognising the road we had travelled so often. In fact, when we reached the outskirts of Onitsha we took a wrong turning and skirted the town completely. When we re-joined the Onitsha-Enugu road we noticed a lot of troop movement. The stretch of road between Onitsha and Awka had seen some of the heaviest fighting in the war and the whole area was scorched. The trees were all dead and the houses demolished, roofless or overgrown. Around Abagana lay the carnage of the lorry convoy which had been ambushed by Biafran forces early in the war and for several miles the roadside was littered with burnt-out vehicles of all descriptions. There were several checkpoints but most soldiers seeing the two of us with the baby did not delay us. However, we came to one manned by a soldier who demanded of Len:

"Who is this woman?"

"My wife."

"The baby is not white."

"No, the baby is our baby."

"This madam is not your wife."

"She is."

I offered to show my passport but he didn't listen. Then his face tightened and he came out with his demand for my identity.

"Bring receipt," he said. I hurriedly produced my marriage certificate which he examined carefully, turning it round to try and make out the writing. Now that his face had been saved he let us go on. There was so much theft at this time that it was necessary for one to have the receipt available for anything of value – a radio, bicycle, etc. but still, how many husbands have a receipt for their wife!? This was the only time Len was asked for a proof of ownership of me!

We continued our journey. As we approached Awka it seemed there wasn't a house left fit to live in. Driving through the town I counted only five houses which did not need major repairs.

After Awka the road improved and we made good time. The

power station at Oji River which had supplied Enugu was damaged and deserted. We reached Enugu before midday and drove straight to our flat. People were moving back to the town, cutting back tall elephant grass obscuring the roads and in many cases chalking on the door '___ is back' and a date. Our house was the last of four three- and four-storey houses built in a row and as we reached the first one I saw it was fully occupied by troops. I had very little desire now to enter the home we had once lived in; it was impossible that anything worth having would be left. As we started to climb the stairs, I saw the shattered glass of our chandelier. Someone must have tried to take it through the doorway without dismantling it. Upstairs, the doors had been forced open and taken away and the flat was a complete shambles. All the furniture, carpets, curtains, lino, even wall switches and door bolts had been removed; all that was left were torn letters, photos and books. A large photo of me had had the eyes torn out. The gas cooker was in pieces and strewn through all the rooms. The remains of a canteen of cutlery, a wedding gift, was just a charred box on the balcony. The sliding doors of our wardrobes had gone along with all the clothes we had left. I picked, from the wreckage, some of the children's brightly-coloured building blocks while Len gathered up a few documents and receipts, including to our amazement the receipt for the car. Glass cracked underfoot as we looked around. The dining room had been used as a toilet, probably only a few hours before we arrived. I was relieved when we walked back to the car. There was nothing left for us here; nothing of the home we had struggled so hard to make. We would never return to live here again.

We went to the Save the Children Fund team at Aria Road. Some of their staff were based in a house which we had once occupied for a few days before we finally moved to Enugu from Onitsha. The relief workers gave us some tinned food which we hid under the back seat of the car. We were very anxious to get back to Azigbo that night, especially as we had nowhere to stay in Enugu and it was already late in the afternoon when we climbed Milliken

Hill on our way out of the town.

The car was making very heavy weather of the road and we had not managed to get any engine oil, which was very badly needed. We had been told that there was some at Awka and we were determined to get there by any means. As night fell we switched on the headlamps to find only one was working and that only with a beam equivalent to a small torch. We moved along making use whenever possible of the lights of traffic behind us. It was a very dark night and we crept along, trying to avoid potholes and straining to see a few yards ahead. On the outskirts of Awka we stopped and asked our way but no one could help and it was now raining. We were afraid we might miss our destination if we did not see a sign. We pushed on through the town and just on the other side of it we saw a sign pointing to the Christian Council of Nigeria Store. We drove very slowly up a little track past huge lorries until we came to an uncompleted house all lit up courtesy of a noisy generator. The Relief Team quickly grasped the situation and we were soon sitting down to a meal with them. They also arranged for us to spend the night with them and later we were taken to another house which stood on the main road junction and here we were given a bedroom with a single Vono (metal) bed on which we passed the night. The bedroom was in full view of the road and, having no curtains, we had to dodge about in the morning trying to dress without stopping the traffic. After breakfast and with some oil for the car we moved on and made good time on the rest of the journey home. The baby had been very good throughout and we had even managed to wash his nappies before going to bed the previous night.

A few weeks later we left Ogbor and moved to Ihioma, the town near Orlu which had held the biggest Caritas Store for relief supplies during the war and which was now to be the base of a Save the Children Fund team. We had been half promised jobs by them if we could move there but after we moved they found they couldn't employ us after all. During the move all our precious chickens died, probably of asphyxiation. With the high value of each this was a minor tragedy but we had them all plucked and cooked that same night before they went bad and ate them all over the next few days.

The next morning, we were shocked to find our cat, Kim, carrying a small animal in its mouth.

"Look what Kim has done," said Uche.

I thought it was a rat but closer inspection proved me wrong. It was a kitten. Kim, we had been assured, by the Irish priest who gave us the cat as a young kitten, was definitely a male. Now not only was Kim a 'she' – she was a mother! The journey must have accelerated the birth for there was no sign of pregnancy and the kitten was very small. Still, it survived and although we gave it a name, it was always known as 'Smallpuss'.

About two miles from Ihioma was a children's hospital. Here, at Okporo, an Irish priest was still in residence and I was made Welfare Officer at the hospital, thus ensuring I would get some relief supplies. Shortly afterwards he was rounded up along with the other remaining priests and nuns. Some were kept in a prison for a few days before they were all flown out of the country to be repatriated. They were all put on a banned list and told they would not be allowed to return to Nigeria in the future.

There were over 250 children in the two wards of the hospital and most of them were severe kwashiorkor cases. There was also a convalescent home with well over 100 children, many completely recovered but with no home to go to or with homes too far away to be easily reached. German Caritas had planned to build a full paediatric hospital on this site; it was being built when the war ended and much of its equipment was stranded in Gabon.

The first day I arrived there I was shown round. I was prepared for the condition of the children and the overcrowding but the smell was overpowering. A very fine toilet block had been built with imported W.C.s. but there was no water and the whole area was alive with fat white maggots. The children 'went' anywhere and everywhere. Most had diarrhoea and stepping anywhere near the wards was a hazardous operation. There was virtually no disinfectant and children lying head to toe in one cot lay in each other's excreta. The untrained girls looking after them could not keep pace with the mammoth cleaning task. There were no bed sheets except in the intensive care unit, which also doubled as the Sister's office. The cups and plates were so few that less than half the ward could be fed at a time while the other half screamed their heads off, convinced they were being forgotten. The food was being cooked on open fires in oil drums. A kitchen with a zinc roof and wire mesh covering the space between the half wall and roof had been built. It was only feet from the ward and the children hung around it the whole time. They wandered around, picking up scraps of uncooked cereals when the supply lorry came. Many had large external hernia with a loop of bowel sometimes over six inches long protruding from their sunken buttocks. Water was brought by tanker as the tap supply was irregular and inadequate but it was barely enough for cooking and sluicing the linen, while baths were on a rota system. We were lucky, however, to have four doctors and some qualified nurses.

One of the ward sisters was called Ada. She had trained as a nurse in England and married an Igbo eye consultant. She told me they had two young children; she had left them with her husband in London while she visited her mother in the East before secession when the crisis leading to the civil war was at its height. When the embargo was put in place she was unable to return to London and her husband, son and daughter due to the events taking place in the country.

We also had a trained caterer with City and Guilds qualifications. She was originally based at the convalescent home but soon after I arrived she was brought to the main hospital and did her best to produce a mixed diet for the patients with the very limited means at her disposal.

Their laboratory could only cope with routine tests. The X-ray equipment was not complete but a building was being erected for it.

The staff included woodchoppers to provide fuel for cooking, sign writers who marked every item of clothing, bedding and equipment with the hospital's name and the ward number in paint while carpenters, masons, plumbers and electricians struggled to improve the facilities. A minor battalion of washer-men followed the tanker to the stream each day. Gravediggers did their grim work in a far corner of the former football field. There were no coffins, the dead were just wrapped in a cloth and buried under a simple cross; many died without any member of their family knowing even that they had been our patients. Once again Len organised the digging of pit latrines and with the plastic potties, which had been found in a disorganised store, and a massive clean-up with spades there was a marked improvement in sanitation.

Mothers, who had often walked many miles to be with their children, slept under a thatched roof with no walls at the side of the football fields. They usually wanted to take the dead child home if the worst had happened. The wailing of such a mother chilled the whole compound.

Hundreds turned up every day for the outpatient clinic. At first food was frequently prescribed but later, as supplies diminished, only in-patients were fed. Staff, too were given a food allowance instead of a salary. The doctors and those nurses formerly in the employment of the Eastern Nigerian Government were eventually paid salaries irregularly. Those employed in missions and private hospitals had only their ration of food. The local chiefs who had agreed to their land being used for building the hospital also received rations although this was later stopped. As soon as possible I asked the two ward sisters and the sister-in-charge of the Convalescent Home to prepare lists of their more urgent needs for the children.

Stores arrived in a very haphazard fashion, usually delivered by a lorry whose driver and his mate quickly offloaded a number of cartons, bundles, sacks etc., most times with no indication of what we were actually receiving. The delivery was immediately locked in the storeroom to await sorting. I was given permission to try to make some order of this store which was piled high. Going through some cartons I discovered that we had a lot of baby clothes but little for the older children. Then I opened some bales and they were full of stout blue cotton dresses for girls and jumpers (long shirts) for boys. Soon we had tailors and seamstresses working on the store veranda to alter them as they were almost square in shape when they were delivered. Soon every child had a dress or shirt of some kind and the ward sisters had a pile of spares under lock and key. Lots of bedding was discovered. Bed sheets and blankets were cut into two, marked and issued. Towels and soap, hand basins and nail brushes were also discovered in the store as I delved even deeper. Treasure indeed. Plastic cups, spoons and plates were marked and issued so the children could all eat together. I even found some disinfectant. I checked the inventory of all these things every week. Instruments and dressings were very scarce. The dispensary was full of small quantities of many drugs and the doctors spent time almost every day familiarising themselves with the new medicines which all too soon became unavailable.

I busied myself mainly between the outpatient department, where I helped issue cards, and the stores, where I rooted through heaps of cartons and crates, dragging out items desperately needed on the wards. Once, buried deep down, I found cartons of much needed antibiotics which had long expired and were useless. The store had been a nightmare with lorries turning up with no warning. Much of the stuff delivered was not in the original cartons and we often had to open every box before we found out what was inside. I reached the hospital one morning to find six very large cartons had been delivered late the previous day. There were notices in three languages, indicating THIS SIDE UP; HANDLE WITH CARE; STORE AWAY FROM BOILERS; little arrows, glasses and a drawing of a man pushing a wheelbarrow, all indicated that this was indeed a very fragile cargo. The boxes were surprisingly light for their size so we were not surprised when, on opening them, we saw a lot of cotton wool. What could it be? Glass instruments for the laboratory? Part of the missing X-ray equipment? Thermometers? Light bulbs? We removed some of the cotton wool and felt around. Nothing. We removed some more cotton and probed again and again until the box was empty and we had to accept that what we had been handling so delicately was only loose-packed cotton wool. Six boxes of it.

Some local people came forward asking to adopt orphans. There was some reluctance on the part of the hospital authorities as they did not want to give out children who might just be used as house servants or as a means to procure extra relief supplies. However, a few were vetted and felt to be genuine.

One morning I was just arriving at work on my bicycle as a red lorry was going out. I saw it was the Mayflower School lorry. Fortunately, it was going slowly and I managed to stop it. I was very, very pleased to see Mrs. Sheila Solarin climb down from the cab; it was a very happy reunion. She told me they had just delivered some relief supplies to the hospital and were going on to other places on similar errands. After the first exchange of news of our families, I told her where we were staying and she promised to come and see us again on their next trip. As I was again being paid in relief food and this meant that Len had to barter for much of our needs, he was able to change a few Nigerian pounds for Biafran ones at a favourable rate of exchange, which enabled him to cycle to Ogbor one day and pay Fr. Onwumere for the second-hand car engine at last.

The Save the Children Fund teams who had arrived after the end of the war had great difficulties as they had no handover from the missionaries who had been running the sick bays, clinics, orphanages and stores and had all been deported. None of them were familiar with the kind of existence the local people had been living and it took some time for them to even trace all the clinics. However, they were doing their best under most difficult circumstances. They brought with them a fleet of new white

Landrovers, much quieter than the noisy vehicles people had been managing for the last three years. These they drove quickly through un-tarred roads, scattering people and hens who were used to much more warning of an approaching vehicle.

We had hoped that we would make our new post-war home in the eastern part of Nigeria where we were currently based, but there was no sign of re-development or repairs to vital services. The power station at Oji River was still out of action and without electricity industry could not recover and it seemed there was no chance of Len getting back to work in engineering in the short term. Those of our friends who had been back to Lagos urged us to return. We were not very keen but eventually we saw that we had to at least go and try to re-habilitate ourselves. One of Len's school mates from Kaduna, Babs Yahaya, whom we had last seen in Lagos, turned up at the hospital with a film crew to make part of a documentary film for the government. We talked and he invited us to stay with him if we should decide to visit Lagos.

Transport was still a big problem until we heard that the Save the Children Fund team was sending a Landrover to Lagos and, if we wanted, we could get a lift. We grasped this opportunity and, leaving the children and baby Emeka with Chinyelu, Len's niece, we took off early one morning. The roads were still very bad but we made good time and called in at Mayflower School on the way. We had only about £2 in Nigerian money with us.

We found the Yahaya's home in Lagos and spent the night with them. Babs' wife worked at N.P.A. Headquarters at Marina, so in the morning we got a lift there. We hardly knew where to begin. Many of our expatriate friends must have left the country. The only straw we had to grasp was the words of Mr. David of Leventis whom we had met in Owerri just after the end of the war. Len and I walked for two hours in the blazing sun, through Lagos, over the Carter Bridge to the mainland and finally to the Leventis Head Office at Iddo House where we asked for Mr. David and were shown to his office. We had hardly introduced ourselves before he made it quite clear he remembered us well and asked Len, "When can you start?"

We were stunned. To hit the jackpot at the first attempt as it seemed to us was almost unbelievable. When Len got his breath back, he suggested in a fortnight's time. This was to give us time to go back to the East, pack some things and make plans for the family's move back to Lagos.

We were still very much in a daze as we walked out of Iddo House and back over the Carter Bridge to Lagos Island and to Babs' office in Denton Street. It was a real booster for our morale and although there were still many problems to be solved from accommodation and furniture down to shoes for the children, it was clear that Mr. David had given us a great opportunity in our journey back to normal peace-time life. It was also my 26th birthday.

Back in Ihioma it looked as if everything was happening at once. There being no phone or post we had only a rough idea of when we would actually move but in the meantime we were dependent on my payment in kind of relief supplies. I went to work each day on my bicycle, using footpaths rather than the main road. I had conjunctivitis at one time and was unable to see properly but still I was anxious to get to work. One morning, squinting in the morning sun, I cycled into a palm tree! Fortunately, no one saw me and I did no damage to the bike, the tree or myself.

Sheila Solarin came to the hospital again with the Mayflower School lorry and offered to take us all back to Mayflower when she had finished delivering the relief they were carrying. The local Save the Children Fund team kindly gave us the use of a Landrover for a day and we took our few bits of furniture to Len's mother. We also left her most of our relief supplies but we had to keep some for our own use, for the first few weeks would still be difficult until Len had received his first salary. We left our car with the family whose rooms we had rented, promising to make arrangements for it when we could. We were ready to embark on the next of our adventures.

Chapter 14

Starting Again

On 8th May Sheila Solarin finally arrived with the school lorry and seven passengers, mainly staff. It was too late for us to start the journey that day and we all slept on the floor as we no longer had beds. In the morning we packed up our few remaining possessions: cooking pots, foodstuffs, clothes, precious portable radio, the cat and her new-born kitten in a box with holes punched in and tied shut. All were placed in the lorry. Finally, the children and Chinyelu, who was going to be our house-help, baby Emeka in his carry cot, then Len and I joined them all, with the other seven passengers and Sheila. At 7.20am on Saturday May 9th we set off, heading for Ikenne in the former Western Region some 50 miles from Lagos. We made good time until we drove into a storm after Ore in the Mid-West. A large tree had fallen across the road and men from vehicles that had also been stopped and locals, set to clear the road so that we could all continue. We finally reached Mayflower School at Ikenne at 11pm. Tai, Sheila's husband, was very relieved to see us and especially Sheila. He was worried that she might have been locked up because of the pro-Biafra article he had written the previous week in his regular newspaper column in the *Daily Times*. We spent the night at the Solarins' house.

Next day we moved to an empty teacher's house near the junior school and offloaded our belongings. Two volunteer teachers we met there, Linda, who was American, and Susan, a Canadian, were very friendly and interested in hearing a first-hand account of the Biafra experience. On the Wednesday of that week Len went to Ibadan and came back with three LP records he had bought at the university bookshop. I did not see this as a priority purchase; money was still very precious and none of the children even had shoes. However, there was no point in complaining – the deed had been done.

On Monday Len went to Lagos on his own and Susan and I went to the nearby town of Sagamu, where we bought some lengths of cloth which could be made into work shorts for Len and dresses for the girls and me. We sewed until the sewing machine needle broke and, as we had no spare, we carried on by hand. Then Chinyelu got a piece of broken glass in her foot and Susan kindly drove her to the nearest hospital to have the glass removed. Normality was returning. I began helping at the junior school and carried on with the sewing. Once I had finished all the girls, including Chinyelu, had new outfits: a dress and a pair of pants each while a tailor made Len's work shorts; I knew my limits as an amateur seamstress.

Len returned from Lagos on Saturday 23rd May but left again the following morning with a Coca-Cola lorry to go to Ihioma to collect our car, which we had had to leave behind as it needed major work. It was the following Wednesday lunchtime before he returned. We packed what we could on to the lorry, which was carrying the car, and Len climbed aboard. The children and I followed with Sheila in her car, another trusty Volkswagen Beetle.

The keys of the house which we had been allocated by Leventis were not available that day although we were able to look through the windows of a large lounge with a marble floor. Meanwhile, the company accommodated us in the nearby Excelsior Hotel for the night. This was a great novelty for the girls who had never seen a bidet or a lift between floors, or the view from a 3rd floor window. It was also their introduction to air-conditioning. They were all barefoot and one of my first tasks next day was to walk them over to the nearby Bata shoe shop to buy them sandals. Apapa was a big step up from our previous neighbourhood in Lagos. There were three big department stores, Kingsway, UTC and Leventis all very close to the hotel, which even had a swimming pool. A parade of shops including a high class jewellers, textile shops etc. and a large post office, health centre and cinema were nearby. There was also a small local market. One of my first tasks was to write a letter to my parents giving them an update. In this area the sidewalks were paved and there were a lot of expatriates living not far away in the Low Density Area where the houses had large gardens. They did their shopping here in the High Density Area where the houses were built closer together but were still very upmarket compared to where we had lived in Lawanson. Apapa had a large industrial area too, as well as being Nigeria's main port.

Working in the Excelsior Hotel were some Igbo stewards who had remained in Lagos during the war by concealing their origins. The word spread through the staff that we had spent the past three years in Biafra and we had many visitors from the staff asking us about our experiences. There was a young English family, Marilyn and Peter Summers with their little boy Damian staying on the same floor as us and we became friendly with them.

Next day, we were able to move into our furnished company house in Caulcrick Road. We knew we were very fortunate indeed to be given such a house to live in. There was an integral garage and a large lounge/dining room with the said marble floor. Behind this were a big kitchen and utility room. Downstairs there was also a cloakroom and upstairs four large bedrooms, a bathroom and two further toilets. Access through the bathroom led to a large balcony with a children's swing and below this were the boys' quarters. It all took a bit of getting used to. Emeka, who was still waking at night for feeds, shared the main bedroom with us and we tried to split the girls between two of the other bedrooms, leaving the fourth for a playroom, as the previous tenants had created a big blackboard on the wall. For several weeks, each morning we would wake to find the three girls not only in one bedroom but also in one bed!

Directly behind the house and facing the next street was another factory owned by the Leventis group, Apapa Chemical Industries. The Coca-Cola factory where Len was to work was off Malu Road, near the large cattle market (Malu being Hausa for cow). Traditionally these large cows with horns and a hump on their back had been walked the whole distance from the north of Nigeria on a journey taking many months. Understandably there was no fat on them as they grazed by the waysides. Their handlers trudged along with them using a long stick to control them. The men carried the minimum of possessions with them. The Middle Belt area of Nigeria is a tsetse fly zone so cattle were not bred there in any quantity. Later the cows were transported by rail from the North direct to the cattle market. The market itself was a smelly quagmire churned up by thousands of hooves. Butchers from the many local markets would come to Malu Road to buy a cow which would then be walked through the roads to the local market for slaughter. It was not uncommon, when driving along at night, to see two or three cows ahead, being walked along with one man in front with a lighted hurricane lamp and another behind. Motorists gave them a wide berth as, if startled, a cow could do a lot of damage to a car. A different, smaller breed of hornless cow could be found in the area below the tsetse belt. They were considered a prestige purchase and were slaughtered to provide meat for a society wedding, chieftaincy ceremony, or funeral.

The Coca-Cola factory was very new and very modern. Bottles in their thousands passed through a gigantic washer and on several occasions Len had to climb inside the machine to effect repairs. The production line conveyer belts carried the clean bottles to be filled with Coke, Fanta or Sprite and men sat on stools as the bottles raced by picking out any that did not meet the quality criteria, as occasionally one would have a broken off bottle brush in it or be chipped. The noise was considerable to say the least as the bottles jostled each other. The factory operated round the clock. One of the perks of the job for us was that we received more free soft drinks than we could possibly consume. After working at Malu Road for a few months, the manager of ACI (Apapa Chemical Industries) left and Len was moved there. Len's difficulty in working under anyone else, which had cost him jobs in the past and had already threatened his employment in the Coca-Cola factory, was alleviated by this move whereby he managed ACI more directly.

Our house backed on to the premises of the ACI factory and a short cut for easy access had been created by placing a ladder against the wall on our side. From there it was possible to walk along a plank on top of a large (full), uncovered water tank, through a window into the factory and down another ladder. The Greek manager Christo, who lived further along our road, Len and several of the staff used this route regularly rather than walk to the end of the road and round to the main entrance. One of the drawbacks of living so close to his work was that if there was a breakdown at the factory Len was on call and sometimes worked all night through to get production started again.

The factory's main product was cylinders of carbon dioxide for the Coca-Cola factory as well as two other local manufacturers of soft drinks, 7UP and the London and Kano factory known as L&K. Apapa Chemical Industries also produced large blocks of ice which were sold to the local itinerant female fish sellers and people hosting parties who needed a means of cooling quantities of beer and soft drinks. The favoured method of doing this was to obtain an empty 40 gallon oil drum and remove the top, then bottles of beer, soft drinks and broken blocks of ice were placed in the oil drum and often covered with a piece of wet sacking. The fish sellers operated in the evening. Having bought their fish they would place them in a large enamel basin, which they carried on their head, and they would sell them going from house to house. Blocks of ice kept the fish cool and fresh.

In order to have the older children enrolled in school we had to visit the Ministry of Education to obtain the requisite forms. From there we were directed to the office of the East Central State Government, which was the new name for the part of Biafra which included Len's family home in Azigbo. In June, Uche and Nnenna were enrolled in Ladi-lak Primary School, quite close to our house. Still having the hand-driven sewing machine I made their uniforms of white blouses with short sleeves and a 'Peter Pan' collar and deep blue cotton pinafore dresses. Ada, who was not quite 4-years old, was too young and stayed home with Emeka, who loved nothing more than to crawl under the large ceiling fan rotating in the lounge and gaze up at it until he fell asleep.

We met up again with Angus Ferguson and Peter Bell from the Lagos Caledonian Society. We had known them since we lived in Lagos up to 1966 and we attended the society's Chieftain's Ball at the prestige Federal Palace Hotel on 6th June. I had my hair done especially for the occasion at a hairdresser's called Spaniger; it was owned by Maria from Spain who had a Nigerian husband. We arrived at the ball in a Coca-Cola van which Len had the use of as our VW Beetle had still not been fully repaired. I was one of the very few ladies that night not wearing a long evening dress but I had made a cocktail dress from brocade bought locally.

The Caledonian Society's three major events in the year were formal balls with fine food and dancing. Burns Night was held as near to 25th January as could be arranged and British Caledonian Airways flew out traditional haggis for the main course. A guest speaker gave the principal speech to the Immortal Memory of Robert Burns, Scotland's national poet. We were very fortunate to have the Rev. James Currie, a world authority on Burns, flown out especially from Scotland on several occasions. At the end of November we celebrated St Andrew's Night, St Andrew being the patron saint of Scotland. Each occasion was held at the Federal Palace Hotel with over two hundred and fifty people attending who were either members of the society or their guests. Most of the male members wore the kilt in their clan tartan and their ladies wore a tartan clan sash over their evening dress. Dancing went on till after 2am and I noted in my diary that we didn't get home from that first Chieftain's Ball until 3am. We thoroughly enjoyed it. After the meal and speeches there was always music for dancing with Scottish traditional country dances alternating with ballroom.

I was ready to start work again but was finding it difficult. The Spanish hairdresser, Maria, introduced me to her friend Dorothy who was from Aberdeen and was also married to a Nigerian. She worked at the Apapa Club, a popular meeting place for many of the expatriates and better off Nigerians and she said she would make some enquiries for me. The fact that I could not type was a continuing drawback but I really had no interest in typing.

One night we were wakened at 4am by the noise made when the swing door downstairs between the lounge and the bottom of the stairs banged. Thinking it was one of the children looking for a snack Len went downstairs only to confront a thief in the lounge. As Len advanced so the man retreated until he pushed through the glass front door which was concealed behind a curtain, jumped over the gate and ran off. Foolishly we had left the key on the inside of the lock so he had unlocked the door ready for a quick escape and even worse I had left my handbag downstairs. From the bag the thief had taken the red leather purse my mother had given me years before. It contained £4 in Nigerian currency, £5 of old Biafran currency and some postage stamps. I did not mind the loss of the money but the purse had great sentimental value and could not be replaced.

At first we could not find how the thief had got in as there was no sign of a forced entry downstairs but the mystery was solved when we went into the bathroom and saw that the louvred strips from the window had been removed and placed on the balcony outside. Fortunately, nothing else was missing. He probably used the ladder which was always left against the back wall to climb up to the first floor level balcony. On another occasion we were burgled in that house by a thief who had pushed the air-conditioner through the wall of the lounge into the house. As it had been mounted not far from floor level and the outer case was not screwed to a wooden frame cemented into the hole in the wall before the unit was installed, entry was gained without too much difficulty. Bottles of drink were lined up on the dining table but he must have been disturbed as nothing was taken. Another valuable lesson had been learned.

Gradually, people who had fled from Lagos to the East returned and among them was Elizabeth's husband, Francis Ihebom, who went back to his old job with the Ministry of Works. Before the civil war Francis and Elizabeth had bought a house in Apapa. On his return to Lagos he found that while he was away and unable to pay the mortgage, the building society had rented the house out to a Lebanese family, thus ensuring the mortgage continued to be paid. Now he was back but this family were reluctant to move out so Francis was staying with his brother's family elsewhere in Lagos in the meantime. Elizabeth was still in London with the children and was anxious to bring them back. The situation dragged on for over a year and Francis popped in to see us from time to time to keep us informed.

Through another friend of Maria the hairdresser I heard of a job vacancy. Nigerian Book Suppliers Ltd had been set up in Ibadan by Irene Fatayi-Williams, an Englishwoman married to Attanda Fatayi-Williams who had just been appointed a Supreme Court Judge. She was re-locating the business to Lagos while initially keeping on the Ibadan premises. I went for an interview and was delighted to be offered a job in the Lagos office. The company imported books, mainly for libraries, universities and schools and exported Nigerian publications all over the world but mainly to American and British libraries and universities with faculties of African Studies. The company was based in premises just off Broad Street, on Lagos Island, one of the main streets in the city. Our neighbour Mrs. Oladipo, who worked on Lagos Island, kindly gave me a lift in most mornings. The journey to Lagos in the morning was slow, there being only two bridges connecting Lagos Island to the mainland. An alternative journey meant I would walk to the ferry and cross the lagoon and then walk back down Marina, a distance of about a mile, to work.

I really enjoyed working with Irene. Sometimes I went to meet librarians, head teachers and others to discuss their orders. Following the creation of more new states since the civil war ended, there were a lot of new state libraries and each state also needed a law library stocked with legal books from Butterworths, and Sweet & Maxwell in London as the Nigerian legal system was based on the British one. Nigerian Book Suppliers was also the local agent for Harper & Row, a major American publisher, as well as several British publishers. A perk of the job was that when ordering copies of books for customers I was able to add an extra copy of ones that interested me for myself and I was only charged the trade price. So, soon after the civil war, the government was still very sensitive about the Biafran viewpoint. Libraries were, however, able to obtain these for reference only, but not to display them. I was thus able to build up a small private collection of books on the subject which included all the press releases of Mark Press of Geneva, the official press agency for the Biafran government, in three large volumes along with a copy of the verbatim account of the crucial Aburi meeting. Sadly, all of these were later lost. Through the company I was also able to order boxed sets of classical music long-playing records very cheaply from the USA which enabled Len to build up an impressive collection.

Initially there were only a few employees in the company but gradually it expanded. I introduced Len's nephew Adolphus and he stayed for several years before starting his own bookshop. Irene was still keeping the Ibadan side of the business going and visited it regularly, while I was managing the Lagos office when she was away.

Len and I had been planning our first proper Christmas for several years when I received an unprecedented personal phone call at work from Scotland. My sister told me that our mother had

had a severe stroke that morning and died. This was a terrible shock as I had no idea that she had been unwell. I phoned Len to let him know and to ask him to come and drive me home.

I was stunned. A multitude of thoughts chased themselves through my head. Mum was only sixty-two years old. Was it somehow my fault she had died? Was worrying about us in Biafra a factor? Should I have taken Uche and Ada and gone back to Scotland when I had the opportunity during the war? If I had gone would Len, his family and Nnenna have survived? He had said he would not leave even if he was given the opportunity and Nnenna might not have been allowed to travel with me. What would have become of her? I knew Len would not have had the generous relief supplies and support we had benefitted from and which had enabled us to help his family and others if I had left Biafra. What was I to do now? Could I hope to get home in time for the funeral? How were my dad and Sheila coping?

I was tempted to just take a taxi and not wait for Len but he had said to wait so that's what I did. I phoned Irene in Ibadan to let her know. Unfortunately, Len was dealing with a machine breakdown in the factory and it was several hours before he arrived. This was December 15th 1970. The funeral would not take long to arrange in Scotland I knew.

We had been back in Lagos for only seven months and had next to no savings. I had believed that, when our finances improved, we would all visit my parents in Scotland. Now we had just enough money in the bank to buy my return air ticket from Lagos via London to Edinburgh so that I could attend the funeral. Len was adamant, however, that I should return by Christmas.

How different this flight was from the one I had taken five years earlier. This was full of passengers, mainly expatriates, happily going home for Christmas. The plane stopped in Kano and we were allowed off briefly. The American man sitting beside me bought some leather articles and was given his change in pounds sterling. He was transferring in London straight to a plane for the

US and, after we had chatted a little and I had told him the circumstances, he gave me the sterling change he had been given. At the time planes could not fly the whole distance from Nigeria to London without re-fuelling so we landed in Rome and re-fuelled before proceeding to London Heathrow, where I took a flight to Edinburgh. I had been able to write a brief note to Fr. O'Sullivan, who was still in Rome, to let him know. He had visited my parents more than once to give them news of me when he was visiting his uncle who was a priest in Glasgow.

On arrival at Edinburgh Airport on 17th December I was stranded. I did not have enough British currency to take the airport bus to the city centre and then the train to Dunfermline. We did not have a telephone at home but a neighbour, Mrs, Inches, who lived nearby, did have one. Using the coins I had been given by my co-passenger I phoned her and she went to fetch my father to speak to me. I explained to him the predicament I was in and that I had been told that a taxi to Dunfermline would cost £15. He told me to take the taxi and he would pay. It was a very sad homecoming.

Although I had been in regular correspondence with my mother I did not know she was unwell. My sister Sheila, then 19-years old and still living at home, said that mum had been writing letters to go in Christmas cards before posting them and had stayed up late to finish. Shortly after getting up the following morning she collapsed and the doctor was called. He diagnosed a stroke and within a couple of hours she had a second stroke and died at home.

The funeral had been arranged for December 18th, which was also my wedding anniversary. My lightweight clothes and shoes were very unsuitable for the cold winter weather. I had no winter clothes and had to borrow. Dad noticed.

"Why don't you wear your mum's boots? You are the same size."

The day after the funeral we went into town so that I could confirm my return flight. Standing in the travel agents, Dad asked, "Are the boots comfortable?"

I said, "They do pinch a little."

He looked down.

"You have them on the wrong feet."

True, they felt much more comfortable after I switched them round!

The shops in Scotland were all busy with Christmas shoppers. It seemed everyone was so happy and I felt as if there was a huge, frozen empty space inside me. I was numb with the shock of Mum's death. No one, I thought, could feel less like celebrating Christmas than I did. Mum hadn't even been able to draw an old age pension as she did not qualify, having not worked since her marriage in 1940. Dad was several years younger than her and only when he retired would she have been eligible for a small pension. Dad's employers, British Rail, only allowed him one day off with pay although at that time he had worked for British Rail since 1940; the rest of the time he needed to make arrangements for the funeral was deducted from his wages. No compassionate leave allowance in 1970.

All too soon my visit was over and on Christmas Eve I set out on the return journey to Lagos. On a cold clear night I had a clear view of the lights along the coast of Italy as we flew towards Rome. I have never forgotten the sight. It was so beautiful. The plane touched down for re-fuelling at around 12.30am at Rome Airport and shortly after a man in uniform boarded and I saw him asking everyone their name as he worked his way up the aisle. When he reached me he asked me to follow him off the plane. Heads turned as I walked across the tarmac towards a brightly-lit glass corridor extending out towards the runway at first floor level. At the end of the corridor I could see a figure. It was Fr. O'Sullivan who had somehow been allowed air-side although he was not travelling.

He greeted me kindly and after a few minutes chat he handed me some boxes of chocolates to take to two Biafra wives he was still in contact with, Pat Kanu, who was in Biafra throughout and Theresa Opara-Nnadi who had gone back to Ireland during the war but was now in Lagos again. He also took out a package of papers, gave them to me and told me that they were copies of all the letters I had sent him during the civil war and that, once I had recovered from the shock of my mother's death, I should use them to write a book, detailing all that had happened to the family in the past six years. I thanked him for coming out to the airport at a time when he would have been expecting to say Midnight Mass on Christmas Eve.

The uniformed man then took me to re-board the plane where I am sure some of the other passengers must have thought I was being arrested when I was escorted off and were very surprised when I re-appeared with extra hand baggage.

Len met me at Ikeja Airport, Lagos, and drove me home. Dorothy had called with little gifts for the children as she was concerned that I might not get back for Christmas. It was a sad celebration for our first Christmas after the three years of hardship.

A few days later we delivered the chocolates to Pat Kanu and Theresa Opara-Nnadi. I acted on Fr. O'Sullivan's advice and, a few months later and, after returning from work in Lagos each day, I would sit at the dining table writing my experiences of life to date. I was very aware that the children would have very little memory of what we had been through and so I was writing this as part of our family history and I also felt that it helped me emotionally. I was still quite nervous, as I found when, at the end of September, an air force plane flew low over Lagos Island in a rehearsal for the October 1st Independence Day celebration and I instinctively took cover under my desk!

One day in 1971, Len and I were shopping in the main UTC, a big department store on Lagos Island, when we met Ada, the

British-trained nurse with whom I had worked at the children's hospital in Okporo at the end of the hostilities. She had travelled from the East for an interview with one of the pharmaceutical companies. Unfortunately, the friend she had planned to stay with while she went to the interview could not accommodate her after all, so we invited her back to stay with us for a few days while she attended the interview and made other enquiries about employment.

Two days later Francis visited us. It was a Saturday morning.

"Something terrible has happened," he said. "I don't work on Saturdays but this morning my boss sent his driver to my brother's house where I am staying. He told me that his 'master' had been contacted and informed that Elizabeth and my children are at the airport. They arrived this morning from London."

"What are you going to do?" we asked.

"I don't know," he replied. "The Lebanese family have still not moved out and my brother's house is already overcrowded. I can't take them there."

"Well the first thing we must do is collect them from the airport," said Len. "We will bring them here, to our house, while we try to work something out."

They then both drove to the airport. Meanwhile, I explained the situation to our guest, Ada. Soon Len and Francis returned with Elizabeth, Stella, Olive, Barbara and Oscar. The children were delighted to see their friends again but our house was getting rather full now with eight children and six adults.

Once the excitement had died down Elizabeth and I went upstairs for a private chat.

"I haven't come back to stay," she said. "I have not come to Lagos to re-join Francis but to leave the children with him."

I was stunned. This was totally unexpected.

"During the time I have been in London and working there I met an Igbo eye consultant, and we have become very close." She continued: "I am going back to England to live with him." She did not realise how shocked I was because I quickly deduced that there couldn't be that many Igbo eye specialists in London and I remembered that was where Ada's husband and two children lived.

By the greatest of co-incidences I had both Elizabeth and Ada under my roof. It hadn't occurred to me that Ada had not returned to London to re-join her family once the civil war was over. We talked for a while longer but her mind was made up. We went back downstairs to re-join the men, Ada and the children. After I had organised the cooking of a meal I took Len upstairs.

"You are not going to believe this but..." I told him what the situation was. He was as surprised as I was. There was no sound of shouting coming upstairs, which I took as a good sign but we didn't know if Francis had been told. However, we did go down with some trepidation to find Elizabeth and Ada seated at the dining table introducing themselves to each other. Amazingly there was no huge row. They seemed to accept that it was fate that had brought them together on this day. Ada was sure she did not want to stay married to her husband and Elizabeth was willing to take on the care of Ada's son and daughter in London. Nothing that Francis could say would make Elizabeth change her mind, and a few days later she flew back to London. I still have a photo of Ada, Elizabeth and myself taken that week while we were all under the same roof in Apapa.

In time, Francis did manage to get his house back. Our children stayed in touch and Uche and Stella are still close friends and by another bizarre twist of fate, Ada's son Robert (Elizabeth's step-son) is father to my daughter Ada's son, Benjamin. Sadly Ada, did not live long enough to meet her grandson Ben; Elizabeth is his step-grandmother. I don't know what the odds would be for such co-incidences; little did I know, when I met them separately in Biafra how our futures would become so intertwined.

Through Ada, who stayed with us again on subsequent visits to Lagos, we met Pius Okigbo, one of Nigeria's leading economists.

He had been commissioned to prepare a feasibility study on Port and Marine Services Ltd. (known as PMS), which occupied a prominent position on Creek Road. The Nigerian proprietor had been tragically killed in a freak accident on New Year's Eve as he watched his workmen finishing the last job of the year working on a boat they had been repairing. A belaying pin snapped and the broken piece of metal flew into the air and struck him on the head. The champagne he had with him, to celebrate the New Year, was instead used to try to revive him but sadly he died and his wife inherited the business.

Knowing that Len had been trained in the Royal Navy and had worked for Niger River Transport at Burutu, Pius asked Len to assess the engineering side and prepare a report, which he did. Once the full report had been submitted Len was asked to join Port and Marine Services to implement his recommendations. He accepted, and resigned from his position at Apapa Chemical Industries but this meant we had to leave the nice big house at Caulcrick Road and move to a one-bedroom company flat on Creek Road. Creek Road is in the heart of the industrial part of Apapa and very few people lived there. We had the middle flat. Below us lived a British engineer and his wife; he was the Chief Engineer of PMS, and above us a relative of the business owner. The flats overlooked the shipyard. The bedroom was, thankfully, very large and we were able to partition it off with wardrobes to create a separate children's sleeping area.

As there was no garden or play area, and the frontage was the main road, the children often played in the flat. One day the girls were practicing somersaults on their beds when Uche misjudged and put her foot through the window. She had a deep cut on the back of her heel and we had to take her to Apapa Health Centre to have it stitched and a week later to have the stitches removed. The very next day, Nnenna was showing the others how the accident had happened and did exactly the same thing! Len was not amused but had to drive us back to the health centre again for her heel to be stitched. Future gymnastic efforts indoors were forbidden.

Emeka no longer slept in a cot and for some weeks he had a habit of waking in the night and wandering around in the dark. Several times I was wakened by him getting into bed with me and on other occasions he fell asleep on the bedside rug and I nearly stepped on him. One morning he was found fast asleep on the bathroom floor. The girls now had considerably further to walk to school and I had a longer walk to the ferry to travel to work. Living 'above the shop' we were looking out on to the yard with the creek beyond where the company carried out construction and repairs and could also deal with barges very easily. A very large crane adorned with the company's name in large letters was a clear landmark.

While we were staying at Creek Road, Nigeria implemented a change from right-hand drive to left-hand drive on the roads. Being surrounded by French-speaking countries which all drove on the left it was felt that it would make sense to change. The news was greeted with great trepidation. New road signs had been erected and covered until one Sunday when the change took place. Very few people ventured out that day as the country's drivers got used to going the other way round roundabouts etc. There were, initially, far fewer accidents as everyone was being so careful. Pedestrians also had to get used to looking right more carefully before crossing the road. By the time of this changeover we had sold the Volkswagen Beetle and had an old Mercedes Benz car bought from someone who was importing them from Germany.

With Apapa being the main port of Nigeria there were often lorries from across the country parked by the roadside, in both commercial and residential areas, waiting to offload cargo or take on a new load. Repairs were carried out by mechanics on the roadside. Discarded tyres, batteries, sometimes abandoned trailer chassis without wheels and pools of black oil littered the verges.

Waiting drivers would rest under their lorry out of the sun while little basic stalls provided meals. Toilet and washing facilities were lacking and it was not uncommon to see people using the deep storm gutters as a toilet. Volkswagen minibuses, a popular mode of transport known as Kia-Kia buses (Quick-Quick), splashed by, creating waves surging over the legs of pedestrians when it rained. They had no timetable but set routes moving at the whim of the driver and his conductor who would travel leaning out of the open door shouting the destination and often remarking on the passers-by as they went. Lagos Municipal Transport vehicles on the other hand were regular large buses following set routes. Their conductors issued tickets but they had great difficulty keeping to any timetable on the congested roads. Taxi fares had to be negotiated in advance and sometimes the car was shared by strangers going in approximately the same direction. Interstate transport was still conducted from lorry parks where Mammy wagons (lorries with wooden roofs, part sides and seats) carried petty traders and sometimes their livestock, a basket of chickens or even a goat between towns. There were also 7-seater Peugeot 404 taxis which still plied the major inter-state routes. It was all still as it had been when we arrived in Nigeria in 1964 but new luxury coaches were making an appearance for longer journeys. Railways ran from North to South but not West to East. Very few could afford to take an internal flight within the country.

My dad came out to visit us for a few weeks. It was his first opportunity to meet all the children as Uche was only a few weeks old when we left Scotland. We all drove to Ikeja Airport to meet him. This was before the new Murtala Muhammed Airport had been built and it was possible to stand at the perimeter fence and watch the arrivals and departures of the planes so we were clearly able to see 'Grandad's plane' arriving and landing and then we went round to the Arrivals Hall to meet him. It was so good to see him. His plane from Edinburgh to Heathrow had been delayed and an announcement was made during the flight asking those with connecting flights to make themselves known to the crew. When the plane landed, his luggage was quickly off-loaded and he was then driven across the tarmac with an immigration officer filling in the necessary immigration paperwork to where the Lagos plane was waiting. I don't know who they thought he was but I certainly could not see anyone getting that kind of service now.

The children were delighted to see him. The tropical heat of Lagos meant that he stayed indoors mostly in the daytime but we often went for a walk through the yard to the waterside when the main work in the yard had stopped and the temperature dropped before nightfall. I was sorry that Len didn't seem interested in showing Dad more of Lagos. At the end of his stay we drove him back to Ikeja to the airport, said goodbye and went back to the perimeter fence to watch the plane depart. As it climbed into the sky Emeka, with all the curiosity of a two-year old, asked, "Why can't Grandad stay on earth like the rest of us?"

Before long it became obvious that Len's employment at PMS was going to come to an end and, once more having lived in accommodation provided by his employer, we were destined to become homeless again. Len had no new job lined up and I knew in my heart of hearts that he was never going to have a career working for somebody else. He needed to be his own boss. He had very strong opinions and felt bound to express them.

Fortunately, we had been able to save a little from our combined incomes. Len decided that that air-conditioning and refrigeration would be the nature of the enterprise. While we looked around for somewhere to base a small business and a place for us to live, the children stayed for a few days with the Onono family. Mrs. Christine Onono was English and her husband, Lawrence, was Igbo. Len and I spent several nights in a flat above a shop with other friends. Within a few days Len was able to arrange for us to rent the ground floor of a detached house, with garage, on Kofo Abayomi Avenue, which was only a couple of hundred yards from our former home in Caulcrick Road. The house was an older style property with a small veranda at the front. The layout was rather unusual .The front door led straight into the lounge and on the opposite wall two doors led to the rest of the flat. The door on the left opened into our bedroom and the other led into a wide corridor which ran straight to the back of the building. We later positioned an office desk and a piano in the corridor without any inconvenience. A second door led from our bedroom into this corridor and on the right was what became the children's room with their two double bunk beds and a small annexe off it was just big enough for a single bed. This little space was only separated from the children's bedroom by a curtain and was where Chinyelu and later Florence slept. The girls were Len's nieces who came from the village to help us and, in return, be helped with their education. They did most of the cooking, went to market, did the laundry etc. Beyond our bedroom on the left was the bathroom, which was surprisingly large and in time we kept our second-hand twin-tub washing machine, seen as a great luxury, in there. On the right after the children's room was a small galley kitchen. Beyond that again was storage space under the outside stairs which led to the upstairs flat. Opposite was another very small room which we also used for storage. The corridor widened at the end and was roomy enough to take our dining table and chairs. Finally, a door at the far end of the corridor led out to the back yard where there were two further rooms, one much larger than the other and a toilet and separate shower. This was designated as the 'boys' quarters'. Our newly-employed carpenter, Joseph, used the larger room as his workshop. The windows, all wooden framed, were barred for burglar protection.

Len quickly turned the garage into a workshop, employing Francis as foreman. Joseph built most of our furniture as the flat at PMS had been furnished by the company. Apart from dining table and chairs he made an upholstered settee, armchairs etc. He also made the wooden casings which were needed to be cemented into the wall when we were installing air-conditioners and the picture frames to go round the air-conditioning unit on the interior; as the units were of varying sizes the boxes and frames had to be custom made. And so Len's Engineering Services was started.

The company repaired, serviced and sold air-conditioners, fridges and freezers. As we had no real capital, I continued to work full time and from my salary we ensured that the staff could be paid. We also took on some young lads as apprentices and Len taught them the practical skills they would need. Most had only received a primary school education and wouldn't have been able to cope with all the technical terms and theory. They provided their own uniform, a shirt and trousers in strong dark blue cotton. We had woven badges made with the company name in red which were sewn to their blue shirt; once they had completed their apprenticeship they received a certificate and then went on to set up their own workshops or join a larger organisation like the Ministry of Works or the Nigeria Electric Power Authority or NEPA as it was known.

Demand for electricity often exceeded the supply and power cuts were frequent. The locals said that the letters NEPA stood for 'Never Expect Power Always'. Because of this uncertainty we arranged for a three-phase supply rather than the usual domestic one-phase, as at times only the latter would be affected by a power cut. This was important as, not long after we started the business, we had also begun to manufacture ice blocks for sale. What started as a side-line developed into a very successful part of the business. It began when we acquired a large hospital-type fridge with an upper compartment having a glass door and underneath a freezer compartment in which we could make twelve ice blocks, each the size of a large loaf of bread. We bought a big diesel generator which was placed at the back of the house and, in the event of a power cut, this would ensure that we had lights and could run electrical appliances in the flat. We cooked using bottled gas.

After a while, in response to the level of demand for the ice blocks, Len bought a flat-pack cold room and erected it in the small front garden. This was about 6ft. square and big enough to take two sets of metal shelves with copper pipes running in rows underneath each shelf then up to the top where two standard domestic air-conditioners sat on the roof. We had lots of tin moulds made for the ice and bought several large water tanks, each holding about 500 gallons.

If the electricity was erratic so was the water supply and we often bought our water by the tanker load. We also needed a tank of water in which to immerse the tins with the ice so that they would float out and we could then sell them or stack them. There were often times when we couldn't keep up with demand and fish women would knock on the door in the evening begging for us even to sell them blocks which were still only half frozen.

Meanwhile the sales and repairs of fridges, freezers and air-conditioners continued to be satisfactory. We had bought a second-hand Volkswagen minibus which had two rows of seats that we could remove if needed; it was useful to the business. We had some customers who lived locally and who had just noticed the sign while others were recommended to us by friends and later, several embassy residences. With the high temperatures in Lagos and 95% humidity, air-conditioning was becoming very popular. This often meant having to travel from Apapa to Victoria Island (VI) or Ikoyi, which could mean an hour or more's journey each way. On one occasion the team had been over in VI servicing air-conditioners at the residence of the Cuban ambassador. They got back in the early afternoon but then there was a phone call from the ambassador's wife to say that since our men had left her electric sewing machine wasn't working. Back into the minibus and off they went. When they reached the residence they found that the sewing machine wasn't plugged in...

The girls were now very close to their primary school, Ladi-Lak, where the headmaster persuaded us to join the committee of the Parent Teacher Association. I was still working full-time on Lagos Island and Emeka started going to a nursery school in the low density area of Apapa.

Since our return to Lagos in 1970 I had become close friends with Penny Ayara-Ekpe, who, with her Nigerian husband Jerry, owned the Flying Ant. This, although on the first floor of a building and above a shop, was run like an English pub and was very popular both with the indigenous population and expatriates. Penny, who is English, came out to Lagos to work in the British High Commission and while there she met her husband Jerry who was one of the local staff. Their son Dominic is six months younger than Emeka and as my friendship with Penny grew so did that of the boys. Penny and Jerry had two more sons, Sebastian and Benedict, and we often met up. As Dominic and Emeka went to the same nursery in the low density area of Apapa, we shared the role of transporting them to and fro as it was much too far to expect them to walk.

The low density area where management-level staff lived, both local and expatriate, was all built on reclaimed land and was low lying as well as low density. The big houses were often set on large plots of land which were liable to be flooded when the rainy season was at its height. Most of the roads in Lagos had concrete storm drains two feet deep running parallel to the road. The rain and domestic waste water flowed into these open channels leading to the creek. However, the ferocity of tropical rainstorms often meant that these drains could not cope and roads were flooded. If a high tide in the Apapa Creek coincided with heavy rain then the situation became even worse and in the low density area roads, gardens and the ground floors of houses were awash; if a car came down such a road a bow-wave would be created. We had friends who had come downstairs one morning to find their precious rug and books afloat. Generally, there was nothing one could do but wait for the waters to subside and ensure that the drains were not blocked as they often were. The storm drains were bridged to allow residents' cars to be parked off the road but these bridges also sometimes trapped branches of trees, old car tyres, cardboard boxes, carrier bags etc. There would also often be odd shoes where people had misjudged where to cross the roads when they were awash. Fortunately, the houses had septic tanks and soakaways to cope with sewage although for the oldest houses in less affluent suburbs, 'night soil men' collected waste from bucket latrines.

I remember once there was a very heavy rainfall after the children had gone to school and nursery. The road outside our house, like all the rest, was soon completely covered in water. It was no longer possible to see where the road actually stopped and still the rain came down. Penny and her driver set off in a car to pick up Dominic and Emeka from nursery but soon they found that the water was too deep to drive through. They abandoned the vehicle and continued on foot more than knee-high in water and they were soon drenched. More than an hour after they should have been home there was no sign of them but the rain was lessening and I went out to look along the road to see if traffic was moving. To my surprise through the rain came Penny with Emeka on her back. She was soaked through! She said that her driver had carried Dominic while she took Emeka. At one point she had stepped into a storm drain and Emeka had nearly choked her in fright. She reckoned then that she couldn't possibly get any wetter so she might as well bring him all the way home. We invited her in to dry off and have a hot drink but she said she'd rather go straight home. Penny and I remain good friends and often look back at the experiences we shared.

A highlight of the Caledonian Society's year was an all-day barbecue held on an offshore island known as Tarkwa Bay. This event was hosted at his chalet there by the Honorary Chieftain, Angus Ferguson. Transport would be arranged to collect those who didn't have their own boats from the jetty at The Federal Palace Hotel. The journey only took a few minutes as we bobbed up and down on the waves. Visitors had to try to remember all that they would need for there was little to buy on Tarkwa. From the jetty there was a walk of a few minutes across a sandy path beneath palm trees or along the beach to the holiday chalets. Some of the big companies and banks had built holiday homes on the island and it was a popular place for the mainly expatriate managers and their families at weekends. Generators supplied light and boats were often met by local villagers ready to carry cool-boxes and other items for a suitable remuneration. Some chalets had a live-in steward who would also act as a security guard.

On one occasion, having greeted our host, we all went to swim in the clear waters of the sheltered bay. Leaving our sandals at the chalet we set off barefoot carrying towels. It was late morning. In the distance we could see ships at anchor waiting to be allocated a berth at the busy port. It was only when we came out of the water that we realised the sand was now scorching hot and that there was no way adults or children could walk barefoot on it – and we had a fair expanse of beach to cross before reaching the shade of palm trees and buildings. Other families were in the same predicament! Fortunately, we had left towels on the beach close to the sea's edge so we stepped on one end of the towel and, carrying a child each, we then brought the other end of the towel to the front of us and stepped on that. This was repeated until we reached the cooler sand before heading back the same way to fetch the other two children paddling in the shallows. Hearing the squeals and laughter people came out of the nearest chalets and loaned us some flip-flop sandals to wear until we got back to Angus' chalet. There was a lovely big shaded veranda where the stalwarts started the barbecue and got busy cooking while the rest sat with cold drinks enjoying this special day.

During the rest of the year the Caledonian Society remained active, holding weekly Scottish Country Dance classes in Ikoyi and Apapa. In Apapa these classes were held at Apapa Boat Club every

Wednesday evening and Len and I went regularly. We danced outdoors on a lovely terrazzo floor fanned by the night breezes coming off the creek. We became members of the Apapa Boat Club but before doing so we had to own a boat. A Scots Canadian called Ron helped us by finding a 14ft. boat and trailer for sale in Ikoyi and Len and I went to see it. Where the name should be there was a painting of a thistle followed by the two letters 'do'. After a few moments we realised that the boat was actually called 'This'll do' and it did! We had it towed back to Apapa where it took up residence in the front garden from where it never moved in all the time we had it. It had no engine. The children played in it but, as owners of the boat, we now were eligible to join the boat club. I was disappointed as I had really thought that we would use it for its intended purpose but although Len had spent years in the Navy and must have learned some small boat skills he had no interest in us putting the boat in the water.

We also joined the Apapa Club which had a swimming pool. Our Aberdeen-born friend Dorothy Odukoya was manageress for a while and later so was Penny. On Sunday afternoons I often took the children to the club where they learned to swim and we could meet friends, many of them of different nationalities and married to Nigerians. Sometimes Len came with us or dropped us off but on other occasions we would walk there and he might join us later and drive us back in the minibus. To walk to the club following the road meant a loop back on oneself but there was a shortcut where, between two properties, there was an open storm drain with concrete walls a few inches thick. By holding onto the chain-link fence on one side it was possible to walk along the top of the wall and reduce the journey time by a good fifteen minutes. The only problem came if you met others coming in the opposite direction! Later in the afternoon the heat would go out of the sun and sometimes, as a treat, we would walk to the boat club to buy some of their delicious chips and then walk home. It was always important to Len for us to be home before dark if we were out walking and that meant being home by 7pm.

He was a harsh disciplinarian and as this was the norm in Nigeria there was little I could do to stop him punishing the children for what he saw as disobedience or wrong-doing and he would punish the others too if he felt they had tried to conceal the truth to protect their sibling. The children not unnaturally tended to spend a lot of their time at home either doing their homework at the dining table or in their bedroom. They did watch some television with us but Len had had a harsh childhood himself and this affected his parenting skills. Unlike in my childhood, fathers did not play with their children. On one occasion a teacher came to visit Len and apologised for being late. He said that he had taken his adolescent son to the police station for the police to beat him because he felt he was no longer strong enough to deal with him himself.

Len's record collection continued to grow. He spent a lot on the finest record playing equipment and speakers which he purchased from Quintessence, a specialist shop in Victoria Island; each record was carefully polished before and after playing. The music began when he rose in the morning and was the last thing to be switched off at night before the lights. Even the television had to compete with the records. My role was to catalogue the collection as it grew, sometimes by twenty records or more in a week. Len bought a lot of classical music, some in boxed sets, as well as the music of James Last, Jim Reeves etc. When he was home the choice of music was always his. Should I play a record of my choice while he was out, on his return he would quickly change it for one of his selections. He always seemed to know when a record had been moved from its shelf. He repeatedly stated that the music collection was for the enjoyment of all the family and while he had his way it was.

One of the lessons taught by the Biafra experience was that it was important to have a suitable home in the village. Many who had built houses and owned property in other parts of Nigeria had learned to their cost that they had nowhere comfortable to live in when they visited their homes, which were often in villages, so a building programme took off in the post-war years and at one time there were many ships with cargoes of cement lying offshore, waiting to come into port to off-load. Despite appeals from Len's family and kinsfolk and the example of others, Len preferred to spend his money in Lagos rather than start to build a house in Azigbo.

"Don't you think we should think about building a house at Azigbo?" I asked from time to time. For Len there were always good reasons why he didn't want to do that.

We had heard many stories of people who had sent money home to the village for a house to be built only to discover that the work had not been done or was way behind schedule as other priorities at home had needed attention. Len was not keen on making regular day-long journeys to Azigbo to visit his family and to check up on progress, which seemed the best way of project management. I knew very well that local opinion would be that I, as a white wife, was preventing a better house being built for Len's mother and sister and for us to live in when we visited. This was not the case. Perhaps, had he married a local girl, her family would have increased the pressure on him.

Len spoke of building a house for us within the same walled compound and had earmarked a site. However, as the years went by nothing was being done. I did comment at times, at the sight of him returning with more bags of LP records, "That's a few blocks less on the house."

He drew sketches for a circular construction as I think he felt his house in the village should be very different from all the others.

Chapter 15

Home and Away

Nigerians in general did not have holidays as we know them in the West. Employed people had annual leave, which they usually used to visit their extended families. For many this would involve a lengthy journey across the country. Christmas was seen as a time when maximum efforts would be made to return to their parents' home, often in a small town or village.

Big decisions would then be made regarding community projects. These might range from improvements to the local schools, which had been built largely by the community, the church, market, or mending the red clay soil roads, known as laterite roads. These developed deep gullies and potholes during the rainy season if there was any kind of hill or slope and which were sometimes totally impassable to cars due to floodwater not being able to drain off. A large meeting was held in Azigbo just after Christmas, as in many other communities, which was attended by all the men. This lasted for the greater part of the day and, being held outdoors, voices were often raised as everyone wanted to have their say. Priorities were agreed for the coming year and the assembly then imposed a tax on those who remained at home in the village and a larger tax on those who lived away in other parts of Nigeria or overseas. Failure to attend the decision-making meeting resulted in a fine.

In the early years after the Biafran conflict the people of Azigbo were very keen to have pipe-borne water. They could not depend on the government to supply this any time soon and fetching clean water took up a great deal of time for the women and children in particular who had to walk to and from a stream or a nearby village with a clay water pot, a large plastic jerry-can or bucket, balanced on their head. Rainwater from the roof was also channelled into large pots or water tanks. The trek to fetch water would often start before dawn so that the journey could be completed before the sun became too hot, and the trip to the stream was also sometimes used to do the laundry. Occasionally someone with a car would drive to a place which already had piped water and fill containers from a public tap. It was also seen as a prestige project which would raise their stature among surrounding villages. Azigbo's water project had started before the civil war. A site had been chosen for the reservoir to be built at the highest point in the village. A lot of money had also been collected by the neighbourhood, work was advancing and pipes were ready to be laid. However, during the hostilities the pipes were taken away for some war need and it was to be several years more before the project was completed and water finally ran through the pipes in Azigbo and then only briefly at first as I remember.

The women of the village held their own meeting on similar lines during the period between Christmas and New Year and they too taxed themselves.

Although Len was very active in the Lagos branch of the 'Azigbo Improvement Union' and was chairman for years and hosted the meetings each month, we did not often return to spend Christmas in Azigbo. The annual return could be very expensive as one was expected to bring gifts for those at home and to entertain visitors whilst there. Len knew that pressure would always be put on him to build his own house, give more financial support to his family living there etc. The Christmas homecoming was also a popular time for weddings and for young adults to think about marriage.

Our Christmases were usually held in Apapa where, on alternate years, we would have a goat and a turkey. The goat, purchased live, had to be killed and prepared and I always made myself scarce then as I could not bear to hear the animal's cries as it was slaughtered. I didn't much like goat meat either, finding it rather strong in taste and tough in texture. The turkey usually came from the Kingsway supermarket and was already plucked, frozen and ready to cook. Many people bought their turkey live and kept it to fatten up for a few days before Christmas but if this became known it was likely to be stolen and re-sold, particularly if it was housed outside at the rear of the property. I was lucky to have a large fridge and a gas cooker with an oven so could bake a Christmas cake and some sausage rolls in advance and roast the turkey on Christmas Day.

Nigerian children had few expectations of receiving toys or treats for Christmas. A new outfit was on the wish list of most families but in our home there were usually gifts of books and at least one toy each as well as new outfits for the children.

People have asked what we normally ate in Nigeria. Most of the cooking during the week was done by whichever niece we had living with us as I was usually out at work during the day and, in any case, Len preferred our evening meal to be prepared in the traditional way, involving pounding with a mortar and pestle. Nigerian soups are more like stews and Igbos, like Len, enjoy a variety of these stews. Egusi soup which is thickened with ground dried melon seeds: ogbono, thickened with okra and ogbono which give the soup a gummy consistency: bitter leaf soup, which involved very thorough washing of the bitter leaf before cooking: waterleaf (like spinach): and oha, flavoured with a leaf which only enjoyed a brief season but which was my favourite. Onions, chilli peppers and tomatoes were added to some of the soups. Each area seemed to have their own favourites and it was generally agreed that the Yorubas enjoyed a lot more pepper in their food than the Igbos. People living near the sea used fresh fish in their stews more than those living far inland. There were many other regional specialities.

Protein in the soup came from dried fish, sometimes stockfish (imported dried Icelandic cod), dried smoked fish, dried crayfish (prawns), and beef or chicken. A big pot of stew/soup was made to last two or three days but it had to be boiled night and morning to prevent it from going off. In the evening, when we were all together, the soup was served with Semovita (semolina), stirred into boiling water until a dough-like consistency was formed; a bowl of soup and a plate with a moulded round of Semovita was set before each member of the family and, after hands were washed, the right hand was used to dip a piece of Semovita into the soup before popping it in the mouth. I preferred to use a fork. The Semovita mix was made from wheat at the Nigerian Flour Mill nearby in Apapa and was more nutritious than garri, which is made from cassava and was cheaper and more commonly eaten. Other families used pounded yam, cocoyam, or plantain as their carbohydrate. Len, like many Nigerians, rationed meat. He would have two pieces about an inch square while the rest of us had one each. Meat was still seen as a luxury in many homes. Okra soup and bitter leaf soup did not like me, causing an upset stomach, and if that was on the menu I would have something else, sometimes a simple recipe made of tomatoes and onions with waterleaf.

At lunch time we might have rice with a tomato-based stew, black eyed beans, or boiled yam often with eggs, tomatoes, onion and sardines. Breadfruit, which was seasonal, was widely popular. It needed to be thoroughly cleaned and then cooked with a small piece of kaun (alum), which helps to soften the seeds and speed up the cooking. I really enjoyed breadfruit which, when cooked, tastes rather like pea soup. Occasionally we might have spaghetti bolognaise or a casserole if I was cooking the lunch. I usually took a packed lunch to work or bought something light. Len felt he had not had a proper evening meal unless he had his soup and Semovita and there were times when we came back very late having eaten out or even having been to a Caledonian Society dinner dance and he would still have Semovita and soup before going to bed well after midnight.

On Sundays our three daughters took it in turn to make akara for breakfast. This involved soaking black eyed beans overnight and removing the husks by lifting a handful and rubbing between the hands before grinding them. A little pepper and water was added to the bean mixture and spoonsful were fried until golden brown. In time I was able to buy a second-hand Kenwood Chef with a liquidiser and grinder attachment from a departing expatriate lady which made preparation of many meals a lot simpler and quicker. In Lagos, as well as many other parts of Nigeria, roadside hawkers cooked akara and sold the golden fried balls as a popular take-away breakfast. Len and I were invited to a function at one of the foreign embassies and mini akara balls were served with the cocktails. On other days we would have cereal, usually cornflakes. There was no real choice of breakfast cereals in Nigeria then. I was aware that we did not eat much first-class protein so I made sure we ate a lot of eggs. I baked cakes for birthdays and Christmas and sometimes sausage rolls, biscuits and scones etc. In the high temperatures of Lagos cooking or baking in our small kitchen was very hot work indeed.

My weight for many years was under nine stones. The climate and circumstances affected me. On a two or three week leave in the UK I would put on about half a stone, which I soon lost again on my return.

When Len's niece Florence came to live with us she expressed an interest in hairdressing and she became an apprentice in a salon a few doors away owned by Cheryl, a West Indian. After Florence had completed her training we moved the carpenter out of the boy's quarters to a lean-to at the side of the house and turned that room into a salon for Florence with hooded hairdryers etc.

Emeka had now reached school age and he went to the private Corona School in Apapa as we could now afford to pay the fees. A fellow classmate and friend was Joe Bassey, the son of former World Featherweight boxing champion Hogan 'Kid' Bassey, who was our neighbour. After his retirement from fighting in 1959, Hogan returned to live in Nigeria where he coached and encouraged young Nigerian boxers and accompanied the Nigerian squad to the Moscow Olympics in 1980. He was a real gentleman and dropped in for a chat from time to time. He offered to have his driver give Emeka a lift to school along with Joe each day but Len wasn't keen and Emeka had to walk. Len was always very mindful of accepting favours which he couldn't or would be reluctant to return and having had a harsh childhood himself he saw no reason to make his children's lives a lot easier. Each term he threatened to withdraw Emeka from Corona School and it took a lot of pleading by me for him to be allowed to continue and complete his primary education.

We took the children to see their first pantomime, performed at the Apapa Club by an amateur theatre group. It was Cinderella and the kids really enjoyed it. Emeka was particularly captivated by the magic of the story. The following week Emeka and I walked to Kingsway to do a little shopping. We only had a few items in a basket when we joined one of the queues at the checkout. We were standing behind a blonde European lady who had a trolley full of items. When it was her turn to pay she turned and indicated that I should go first. Seeing her face for the first time Emeka exclaimed in a voice full of awe and wonder, "Mummy isn't she just like one of the Ugly Sisters?"

"Not really," I replied, but I could see the resemblance as she was very heavily made up. I was so embarrassed I felt the whole store must have heard him and I couldn't get home fast enough.

On another occasion parents were invited to Corona School to meet the teachers and see the children's work. After perching on a very small chair by what was his desk where his school notebooks were laid out, I read from his English book. The children had been asked to write about 'My Mummy'.

"My mummy is a Scottish lady," he wrote. "She has long brown hair."

"True enough," I thought.

"She wears glasses and Scholl's." (Dr. Scholl's sandals).

What a picture that must have conjured up for the teacher. Thank God for the long brown hair!

The girls were doing well at Ladi-Lak and Len and I were both involved with the Parent Teachers' Association. The school was very basic compared to Corona, which had a mainly expatriate pupil intake and teaching staff. At Ladi-Lak classes were larger and the discipline tougher. The headmaster was impressed when visiting us one day to see Ada perusing the pages of the *Daily Times* newspaper. She was then in Primary One. He asked if she was just looking at the pictures and was so surprised when she was able to read the news stories that he immediately took the decision to promote her to Primary Three. She was then in a class more suited to her reading ability but she struggled with maths for a while as she had not yet done the maths taught in Primary Two.

The Primary classes went up to Level Six and it soon became time for the girls to do their Common Entrance Examination to enable them to go to secondary school. It was by no means automatic for children to move on to secondary education; indeed, having had to buy all their children's school text books, exercise books and uniforms for primary school many parents simply could not afford the fees for secondary education. Only ten percent of children, it was estimated at the time, would further their formal education. Some moved on to a local commercial school and paid fees to learn typing and shorthand, tailoring or dressmaking. Others were apprenticed to learn about car repairs, carpentry etc., while many became petty traders or hawkers, their stock displayed on a round tray balanced on their head or a little wooden table by the roadside. Some were employed as houseboys and girls – domestic servants. The houseboys hoped, in time, to become stewards or cook-stewards to wealthy Nigerians or expatriates.

Emeka was still enjoying his private schooling at Corona School, Apapa and his friendship with Penny and Jerry's three sons Dominic, Sebastian and Benedict continued although they attended a different private primary school, St. Saviours. On a Monday the teachers at Corona often asked the children to tell the class what they had been doing over the weekend and usually the response was that they went to the Apapa Club or to the cinema with their family. On the last day of the summer term Emeka and I were walking to the shops after school and were only about 150 yards from the house when a man crossed the road towards us and snatched the gold pendant and chain from my neck. He then ran past us along the road towards the house. One of our apprentices saw what had happened. He alerted the others and they set of in pursuit. Emeka and I followed as quickly as we could whilst other passers-by joined in too. After a chase the man was caught in the next street and rough justice could have prevailed. Fortunately, he was instead marched to the police station not too far away while we again followed on foot. The man had been taken behind the counter as the mob that had by now gathered could quickly have meted out their own punishment. I made a statement, the man was locked up and we started to walk home. The neck of my dress was torn and I had a weal on the side of my neck where he had pulled the chain and broken it. I was feeling quite shaken by the experience but just as I was wondering if all that had happened would give Emeka bad dreams he turned to me.

"Mummy, what a pity there is no school on Monday. I would have had something good to say for 'News'!" he said sadly.

When the case was heard at the Magistrates Court a few weeks later I had to attend. I had expected that Len would come with me for moral support but instead he sent me with the driver in the company minibus. As I walked towards the court with the driver the accused was being led from the prison van and passed close to us. The man called out to me, "Madam, I beg you."

He looked as if he had already had a good beating but he was sentenced to five months in prison. The medallion that had been on the chain was lost and It was quite a long time before I would felt comfortable wearing any kind of necklace.

The competition to enter the more prestigious secondary schools like Kings College for Boys and Queens College for Girls in Lagos was intense. Each state might have only two such secondary schools funded by the federal government and they conducted their own entrance exams. The churches established very good secondary schools and Muslim students also had prestigious colleges. Private individuals set up others like Mayflower School at Ikenne, owned and run by Tai Solarin and his wife Sheila on strictly non-religious grounds.

My work at Nigerian Book Suppliers had involved me visiting many of the Lagos secondary schools to encourage them to order their text books through the company. Uche, and a year later, Ada were accepted for Holy Child College in Obalende. Nnenna wasn't selected for that establishment and was instead given a place at Aunty Ayo's School, also in the area of Lagos called Obalende. Olive Ihebom was also a student at Holy Child at the same time and they would all travel by ferry and/or bus to their secondary schools together. These schools were close to Dodan Barracks which was the main army headquarters and also close to the Radio Nigeria buildings. Stella Ihebom was attending United Christian Secondary School in Apapa so she didn't have the long commute.

During the 1970s a company in Ikeja was organising cheap charter flights to Stansted Airport in England and I was able to travel to visit family and friends in Scotland and England in 1975 and again a few years later. In Dunfermline I stayed with my dad and was able to catch up with other family members like my Aunts Margaret, Lottie and Jessie and meet old friends, Morag and Rosemary, among others. I was away for only two or three weeks at a time. I had not been able to attend my sister Sheila's wedding in 1971 though. She was now living in Gosport in Hampshire on the south coast of England. Her husband Jim was in the Royal

Navy and had completed the same engineering course as Len had at HMS *Caledonia*. He later completed officer training. I had met Jim at Mum's funeral in 1970. They had a son, Paul, in 1971. I was very anxious to see them and spent a week with them in Gosport. I was particularly glad to see Sheila who had been very ill. She was diagnosed with Crohn's disease while pregnant with her second child and, although the symptoms abated as the pregnancy advanced, they came back with a vengeance once baby Mark was born in December 1974. Early in 1975 she was admitted to Haslar Naval Hospital in Gosport. Baby Mark was taken to spend some months with her husband's parents in Beccles in Suffolk while older son Paul, now four-years old, was sent to live with our dad in Dunfermline. Dad's sister, Aunt Margaret and her husband Uncle Bob, who had returned from Zambia and were now living in Dunfermline, supported Dad in caring for the little boy. Sheila's husband Jim had a compassionate posting to a shore base in Gosport but he couldn't look after the two small children as well. I was able to visit in the summer of 1975 when Sheila had finally been discharged home and Paul and Mark were with them once more. Although she was still weak, having spent several months as an in-patient, she was definitely improving and gradually putting on weight again as she had been down to less than six stones at one point.

This was my first time in Britain since the currency had changed from sterling to decimal in 1971. The day after my arrival in Gosport, Sheila and I went food shopping together. She had asked if there were any particular foods I had been missing and I said Weetabix breakfast cereal and marmalade. We went into Waitrose, which was close to her then home in Kensington Road. After we had completed our purchases we walked back to her house.

"I am not going food shopping with you again," she said very emphatically.

"Why? What did I do?" I asked.

"We got to the cereal section and you picked up a box of Weetabix. Then you put it back and picked up a box of Rice Krispies and put that back and then you did the same with several other cereals before going back to the Weetabix. After that," she continued, "you did the same with the marmalade!"

The choice was just too much for me. I was not used to having such a variety of goods to choose from. In Lagos there was only the choice of one or two cereals in the supermarket and some items, which would be classed as everyday products in Britain, were often totally absent from the shelves; if word got around that a supply had arrived they could be sold out very quickly.

Of course, the new decimal coins were very unfamiliar to me too and, out of embarrassment, I often paid with bank notes and soon had pockets full of the unfamiliar coins as change. The alternative would be for me to hold up the queue while I sorted out the right coins to pay with. I looked British and sounded British but I was a real fish out of water. Everyone else had had several years to become familiar with the new currency.

It wasn't only in the shops that I was seeing life with different eyes. Having uninterrupted supplies of electricity, gas and water was also a novelty to me compared to Nigeria. I really appreciated having water at the turn of a tap and light at the flick of a switch whereas people in the UK take it all for granted. In Lagos we never left lights on when no one was in a room, nor wasted water. We ate all the food on our plates too and food wastage was minimal.

It was during that first visit in 1975 that I was able to take a train to London for the day and to meet Fr. O'Sullivan for a few hours. He had finished his time in Rome and was doing a post-graduate course in London. We took a boat trip on the River Thames, I remember, from Westminster Pier. I had never spent more than a few hours in London up until then and it was very interesting listening to the commentary as we passed places I had only heard or read about before.

Mindful that the last ferry crossing from Portsmouth to Gosport was at 12 midnight I made sure that I was on the second to last train from Waterloo Station in London to Portsmouth Harbour station. This was due to arrive before 11pm, giving me ample time to catch a ferry which made the crossing of Portsmouth Harbour to the Gosport side every fifteen minutes, taking less than five minutes for the crossing. Unfortunately, the train was delayed and it was well after midnight by the time it drew into the Harbour station. There were several other passengers bound for Gosport but the guard, who was the only member of staff still around, said the railway company was in no way responsible for our predicament as we had been brought to the train's destination. Few people had a phone line in their home and of course there were no mobile phones then so there was no way for me to contact Sheila and Jim. In any case, as they didn't have a car, there wasn't much they could do to help.

The distance is less than a half a mile across the mouth of Portsmouth Harbour, while the drive round is about 15 miles. The cost of a taxi round to Gosport was prohibitive for me on my own but several of us, all in the same situation (not in the same boat!), agreed to share a taxi and split the fare between us to take us all on to Gosport. Sheila and Jim had gone to bed as they assumed I must be spending the night in London and it was after 2am when I had to waken them to let me in. I always travelled alone on these trips to the UK. Although I would have wanted to take the children with me to meet my family Len wouldn't allow it, but I always had new clothes and some treats for them in my suitcases when I flew back to Nigeria.

Back in Kofo Abayomi Avenue our upstairs neighbour for a while was a very pleasant, modest man from Northern Nigeria called Tony Lanval. His daughter was married to General Murtala Mohammed. She would visit her father at times accompanied by her children, always with an armed soldier as a security guard. Occasionally, General Mohammed also called on his father-in-law, always with an armed escort. When there was a Muslim festival and Tony killed a goat he always sent us some of the meat in accordance with tradition. General Mohammed had been heavily involved during the Biafra conflict and it was his Nigerian troops who were in the convoy, which included oil tankers, that were blown up at Abagana as they tried to get to Onitsha.

When the first post-war military coup took place in 1975 the children were all at school. The revelation that a coup had taken place was first indicated by the radio station playing military music. An announcement was then made and people who had already left home for work made every effort to get back home. The bridges linking Lagos Island to the mainland were closed and all public transport ceased. Flights to and from the country were suspended and markets, schools and businesses all closed until the situation clarified; at times a night curfew was imposed and sporadic gunfire might be heard from barracks.

General Murtala Mohammed became Head of State in July 1975 when Yakubu Gowon, the previous Head of State, who had lead the Nigerian side from 1966 to date, was overthrown in a coup while attending an OAU (Organisation of African Unity) Conference in Uganda. At the time news of the 1975 coup broke Uche and Nnenna had already reached their secondary schools on Lagos Island. They had to leave very early to make the journey, while Ada was still in primary school and she could get home very easily. No one was quite sure what was happening and whether the soldiers were fighting each other so Nnenna wisely made her way to join Uche at Holy Child where the sounds of gunfire was clearly heard coming from the direction of Dodan Barracks, army headquarters, only a short distance away. The Principal, Mrs. Sosan, and the staff, who included several nuns, started to think about how the students would get home. They were all day pupils and came from all over Lagos. An attempt by some soldiers to enter the grounds of the college and convent was refused by the staff and their own security man. Telephone links were still in place but with so many parents wanting information it was hard to get through and the atmosphere was very tense. Mrs Sosan knew that buses and ferries would not be running and that even parents with cars would have difficulty getting to the school as there would be armed soldiers on the streets and the bridges connecting Lagos Island to the mainland would be closed to all traffic.

Among the students were the children of one of the directors of the Ibru Company which operated a large fishing business from premises on Creek Road, Apapa. A launch was sent by the company across the lagoon to a boat club on the Lagos Island side to collect their children and Mrs Sosan asked if they could also take Uche and Nnenna with them. Thankfully they agreed but it was well into the afternoon when the girls arrived home, having walked for half an hour from the Ibru jetty at Creek Road.

General Mohammed was very pro-active in politics nationally and internationally and he was a popular leader with the common people as he tried to deal with widespread corruption, but his reign was brief. He was assassinated in February 1976 while being driven from his home to work at Dodan Barracks. The Mercedes he was in was later displayed in the Nigerian National Museum where the bullet holes can be clearly seen. The second coup, in February 1976, was dreadful news for Tony Lanval, his daughter and grandchildren. He was no longer living in the flat upstairs by that time but our thoughts were very much with them all. General Murtala Mohammed's successor, General Obasanjo, guided the country to a return to civilian rule in 1979.

Among our friends at this time were Joe and Sheila Kemfa. Joe was Nigerian and a very talented musician. Sheila was English and helped out at the nursery school owned by Irene and Tunde Jones whom we had met when we travelled out from Liverpool to Lagos together on MV *Aureol* back in 1964. Joe played with many different groups but his own group was called Aura. They were given a contract to record a long-playing record at the Decca studio in Lagos and needed some backing singers and he asked Len and me if Nnenna, Uche, Ada and Emeka, who had never sung together seriously, would perform. They became known as 'The Lenleys' and sang on several tracks of the LP, which was titled *Jungle Juice* and was released with pictures of Joe and The Lenleys on the sleeve. The recording was finished in 1978 and was played on the local radio station a few times. On my next trip back to the UK I took some copies with me for family and friends. I still have the disc to this day.

In 1976, the beautiful National Theatre was completed at Iganmu in preparation for the hosting of FESTAC 77 the following year. It was a wonderful landmark with a very distinctive design resembling a hat. The 5,000 seat main hall opened with performances by Ipi-Tombi, a South African musical show. Tickets sold very quickly and we were lucky to be able to see the show twice. It later toured the world and had a season in London's West End. We bought the double long-playing record set and even now, 40 years later the tunes are still in my head.

FESTAC 77 was the second Black and African International Festival of Arts and Culture. The first was held in Senegal and Nigeria had been expected to host it in 1970 but this was postponed because of the situation in the country, which had just ended a civil war. This pan-African celebration celebrated all the arts. To provide accommodation for all the expected 460,000 performers and visitors coming to Lagos, FESTAC, a new town, was built on the expressway between Lagos and Badagry. In all, over 5,000 homes were planned. Accommodation varied from apartments to detached houses and, although they were not all ready in time, over the following years they were completed and provided a lot of necessary housing for Lagos's growing population. After the festival there was a ballot to allocate the homes for which we applied but were not successful.

FESTAC 77 was held from January 15th to February 12th 1977. Other venues in Lagos were used as well as the National Theatre, and in Kaduna in Northern Nigeria, as part of the celebrations, a Durbar was held. This climaxed with a parade of 4,000 horsemen, hundreds of camels etc. Fifty-nine nations participated in the festival and everyone agreed that it was a huge success; Nigeria was keen to promote itself as an African leader in culture and commerce.

On the home front Ada joined Uche at Holy Child College in 1977. They had an early start to get to school on time, sometimes leaving before dawn. It wasn't until Uche was 15-years old that she was permitted to accompany me on a visit to Britain and saw again my home town, which she had left as an eight-week-old baby. Although we were only in Dunfermline for a couple of weeks she joined the local branch of the Carnegie Library and almost every day she borrowed and returned books from the branch library a short walk from my father's house. We visited my aunts and uncles and she met the pen-pals she had been writing to, one of whom was Lyndsey, the daughter of my cousin Bruce and his wife Jennifer. She also had other pen-friends, through my friend and her godmother, Rosemary Archbold, who was a teacher. We went to Edinburgh on a day trip by train and took a coach journey to parts of scenic Scotland with my father and then travelled to Gosport and stayed for a few days with my sister Sheila, her husband, Jim, and their two boys Paul and Mark, before returning to Lagos.

In April 1979, my father reached his 65th birthday and retired. He had few interests outside work and I was pleased when he agreed to make a second visit to Nigeria to see us all in September that year. Earlier in the summer he had travelled to spend time with Sheila and her family. The children were now a bit older and we took Dad to the Apapa Club and the Boat Club. Although these clubs had a mainly expatriate membership we had become friendly with some other families with a Nigerian husband and a foreign wife. When the heat had gone out of the day Dad enjoyed a walk up to the nearby shopping centre with me most days.

He returned home to Dunfermline, where six weeks later he had a heart attack during the night. He had been given a spray to use under his tongue if he felt chest pains but had also been advised by the doctor that, should the pain continue, he should call the emergency services. He still had no telephone at home but there was a public phone box about 50 yards from the house. He decided not to bother anyone and to wait till morning before calling for help. He managed to get to the public phone box about 6.30am but it had been vandalised and he couldn't use it. He then decided to walk to the local newsagent shop and the proprietor immediately saw that he was very unwell and called for an ambulance. He was taken to Milesmark Hospital and his sister, my Aunt Margaret, was informed. She consulted the doctors treating him and was told that Dad was very ill indeed and she should let his immediate family know so she phoned Sheila and me. Sheila was able to leave at once by train with her two little boys and travelled from Gosport to Dunfermline, a journey of almost 430 miles by train. She reached the hospital shortly after he had died that same day. I was unable to reach the family home until the next day. It seemed he had subconsciously been guided to see us all one last time.

His funeral was well attended. His former work colleagues arrived straight from work for the service and interment and he was buried with our mother. Sheila's husband, Jim, travelled up on the day of the funeral but had to leave immediately afterwards to get back to Gosport. Aunt Margaret and Uncle Bob did everything possible to support us. We had to clear Dad's house which was rented from the local council. One of my cousins was getting married and setting up home and we asked her to take anything from the house that she could use. Sheila and I chose some mementoes and small items and my Uncle Tommy, who was a skilled carpenter and furniture maker, made a strong packing case for me, which I filled and had shipped out to Nigeria. Among the items I packed in it was a glass-ribbed scrubbing board. This was an item unknown in Nigeria but extremely useful for getting the dirt out when washing clothes and it certainly earned its keep.

I had continued to correspond with Fr. O'Sullivan and, while in Dunfermline, I tried to phone him. He was then living in Dublin but I was told he was in Scotland to attend the funeral of his uncle who was a priest in Glasgow. I was given a contact number for him and it transpired that the funerals were on the same day. He had gone out of his way to visit my parents several times after he left Biafra to give them first-hand news of us all. Now he arranged to visit a friend living close to Dunfermline for a few days and offered to help us in any way he could. My dad had bought a fine new stair carpet not long before he died and that went into the packing case and graced our corridor in Apapa; we were very glad of Fr. Donal's assistance in taking up that carpet. My parents wedding china was something I did not want to see lost forever but it was bone china so I decided to take only the tea plates and packed them in my suitcase. I was very sad that I could not keep in the family a beautifully carved writing bureau which my grandfather Alexander (Sandy) Wallace had made, but along with most of the furniture and house contents it went to auction. Aunt Margaret and Uncle Bob dug up some crowns of rhubarb and a hydrangea plant and re-planted them in their garden where they flourished.

I remember particularly that, although it was only November, the weather was very cold and the roads and pavements were icy. Sheila and the boys and I were staying with our Aunt Margaret and Uncle Bob who lived on one of Dunfermline's several hills. To get to Dad's house from their home meant walking down one hill and then up another. Having become unused to walking on icy pavements or even on hills as Lagos was very flat, I have a distinct memory of clinging on to privet hedges bordering gardens as I went down the hill to stop myself from slipping. On reaching the bottom I stopped and looked back. There was a trail of privet leaves and twigs behind me; I could only hope that no one had seen my actions!

Within a few days we had to remove all the furniture and house contents. Many items had precious memories and it was very painful to part with them. All too soon the house was emptied and the keys were handed in to the council. I reflected that Dad hadn't had much time to enjoy his retirement, just six months. He had worked all his life since leaving school in 1929. In the worst of weather, dense fog and snow he had often been called out to work through the night having already worked a full shift that day. In return he developed chronic bronchitis, frequent chest infections and later angina. He was a quiet, rather shy man who didn't smoke or drink. He had been fortunate to have his sister and brother-in-law nearby to support him and a couple of friends who would go with him to concerts locally. My grieving was made easier with the knowledge that he had managed to travel to Lagos to spend time with us so recently. I recalled Emeka's question to me as we watched Grandad's plane flew away: "Why can't Grandad live on earth like the rest of us?" He had missed Mum a lot and now, re-united and at peace, their influences are alive and strong in those they left behind.

Back in Lagos life returned to normal. I was no longer working for Nigerian Book Suppliers as Len felt that it would be more useful to him if I was based at home. I had been very happy working there and didn't want to leave but I really had no option than to do as Len wanted. Our business was doing well at that time and my salary wasn't needed as it had been when we started it. So for several years I worked from home answering the phone, writing invoices, issuing spare parts, selling ice and refilling the ice makers etc. Len expected me to be available at home during all working hours although I did go to Kingsway store on a Friday afternoon for the weekly shop and to the post office nearby to check our mail box as there was no house delivery.

Len had become increasingly absorbed in mystical studies, locking himself in the bedroom for hours meditating. He did not want to be disturbed for any reason, whether to speak with customers or to the foreman and apprentices, and on Saturdays he attended lodge meetings of the Rosicrucian Order. He received monographs (lessons) by post from their headquarters in California. There was a strong link to Ancient Egypt in the studies and Len arranged to travel to Egypt where he visited Cairo, Luxor and The Valley Of The Kings. Two years later he arranged to take a group from Lagos to visit the same places. On Sundays after breakfast the children and I were assembled in the lounge while Len tried to pass on his acquired wisdom. Although he would make an initial effort to involve us in discussion it soon turned into a lecture. Len was convinced that he was destined for higher things and that in a previous incarnation he had been a powerful and respected leader.

The business began to suffer as well and his enthusiasm for teaching the apprentices and overseeing their work was waning. We were also having problems with the landlord who wanted to repossess the building. Len knew that this man owned over 50 properties in Lagos and felt that our need of the premises was greater than his. I knew that the other buildings in the area were rented at a much higher rate, which Len decided we could not afford. We were fortunate to be in a position on a busy road which had a fair bit of passing trade.

We both became involved in a campaign to clean up Apapa. There were many streets and roundabouts which had become cluttered with discarded lorry tyres, abandoned parts of lorries and trailers and heaps of refuse. The verges were thick with dirty, used engine oil. Women in makeshift shacks cooked and sold food and some roundabouts had become a prayer area for Moslems. Rats were becoming common and some were as big as cats. Large trailers were parked on residential streets as well in the industrial area. Some of the larger companies were contacted and on a Saturday, with the aid of fork lift trucks and flatbed trailers loaned for the day, a real effort was made to clean up Apapa. The result was noticeable immediately. In a further bid to foster community spirit a Carnival Day was organised with music, decorated lorries and cars in a procession and a Carnival Queen. Posters were printed, hand coloured and displayed around the area, while one company donated a quantity of T-shirts emblazoned with their logo and some sun hats.

A brand new Ford pick-up truck was delivered to our house the day before and we decorated it with streamers and paper flowers and Len's throne-like chair was installed and secured. The Carnival Queen was Uche wearing a dress made by a local seamstress, my grandmother's tiara and a specially made scarlet sash. The local school children were all involved and the procession set off to tour Apapa. From time to time the free T-shirts were distributed to onlookers. I was based at the playing field to which the procession would return. Music played as the procession passed along Marine Road and back through the low density area. This took considerably longer than expected and I was told later that such was the eagerness to get one of the T-shirts or hats the procession was virtually slowed to a halt and then had to speed up to avoid trouble. Back at the field speeches were made and people were extolled to take more pride in their surroundings.

All this re-enforced Len's belief that he had earned the right not to be forced to leave where we had our home and business. The landlord took Len to court and judgement was given in the landlord's favour but Len was determined not to move. He appealed. The landlord stopped cashing the rent cheques in a bid to strengthen his case but Len knew in which bank the landlord had his account and paid the money in direct to the account and kept the receipts so we could prove we were not in arrears of rent.

In October 1979 a general election was held in Nigeria and the military government handed over the leadership of the country to Alhaji Shehu Shagari, ending 13 years of military rule. The new governor of Lagos State was Alhaji Lateef Jakande. He established more primary and secondary schools within the state so that all children could receive free education. It was a year of great activity as land was acquired, contracts awarded and the buildings emerged. They were very basic, being constructed of cement blocks to a half wall height with a gap for a doorway and corrugated metal roofs. Classrooms were liable to flooding and pupils balanced on stepping stones of blocks forming paths to reach their classes in the rainy season. When it rained the noise on the roof was considerable as there were no ceilings for insulation and in the heat of the sun in the dry season the classes were very hot. Pupils continued to purchase their own books and uniforms.

By the following year Emeka was approaching the end of his primary education. He applied for entry at King's College Lagos, the elite boys' secondary school. The entrance examination was held on two successive days. Unfortunately, Emeka had malaria on the day of the exam and though he went in to take the papers he was certainly not a well boy and he didn't score highly enough to be offered a place. Instead of applying to some of the more established secondary schools in Lagos, Len decided that he should attend the brand new Apapa High School opening in 1980, which was one of the Jakande schools. I was a bit apprehensive as this was a brand new venture and no one knew what the standard of teaching would be.

We became involved as part of the PTA (Parent Teacher Association) and helped with the design of the uniform. The colours were green and white, echoing the Nigerian flag and we were able to negotiate good deals on a sturdy green material from the manufacturer for the shorts and skirts and white cotton for the shirts and tops. We also had a contract with a local seamstress to make them at a reasonable price. For several years the students were sent to our house to pay for their uniform and then given a receipt to take to the seamstress in the next street to be measured and kitted out. They could, if they preferred, just buy the cloth and have it made up by someone else. I was always busy.

On one of my trips home to visit my family and friends Len accompanied me. The children were left with his niece to care for them while Edwin, his relation who lived nearby, had promised to keep an eye on them too. Len's main reason for the trip was to enable him to attend a Rosicrucian Convention in London so we spent a few days there staying at the Royal Commonwealth Society in Northumberland Avenue, close to Trafalgar Square. During the days I was free to walk around Central London while he went to the convention and we managed to see a Proms concert at the Albert Hall and another concert at Kennington Oval in the evenings. We were only away for two weeks and it was a real whirlwind tour of family and friends although we did manage a few days in Scotland and to visit Sheila and Jim and their family in Gosport.

One of the friends we saw while in Scotland was my school friend Andrea who now lived in Burntisland, a seaside resort not far away from Dunfermline. Andrea had been chatting to me in the Kinema Ballroom on the night Len and I met in 1962. She and her husband had adopted a Chinese baby girl and she learned Cantonese and taught a Sunday school class of Chinese children. She also had Chinese foster children. Sadly, there was a fair bit of racial prejudice directed against her and her family. Len also renewed his friendship with the photographer Peter Leslie in Dunfermline and he bought some unusual lenses for his camera which he tried out on flowers in Pittencrieff Park and later on our visit to Sheila and family.

On our return to Nigeria our problems with the landlord continued and Len's commitment to his mystical studies resulted in a significant drop in our income.

I had a letter published in a Scottish newspaper in 1981 and shortly after received an air letter from a Mrs. Isa Gordon living in Rosyth, very close to Dunfermline. She told me that her son, Alexander Campbell Gordon, a merchant navy captain of the MV

Cadis I, had died at sea on 28th December 1978 as the ship travelled from Accra, Ghana to Lagos. He had spoken to his wife from Accra on Christmas Day, apparently well. There were many unanswered questions about the cause of his death. His body had been brought ashore in Lagos but by the time the formalities had been completed and the funeral organised the ship and its crew had sailed. Mrs. Gordon did not even know where her son was buried and that was very painful for her, her daughter-in-law and family as they tried to come to terms with their tragic loss. I contacted Angus Fergusson, Honorary Chieftain of the Lagos Caledonian Society, and a lawyer but he had heard nothing of these events. I was sure that if the society had known of this sad occurrence we would have helped to organise the funeral in a fitting way. Apparently the ship's local agent had made all the arrangements as prescribed by law. Len and I made more enquiries and, knowing that most foreign nationals who died in Lagos were buried in a designated part of Ikoyi Cemetery, our search resulted in our finding the grave plot number. Several years had elapsed since Captain Gordon had died and many of the graves were overgrown. We cleared the surroundings and took a photo of the small grave marker.

It was arranged that a more fitting headstone be commissioned and erected and the Caledonian Society offered to fly Mrs. Gordon Sr. and Captain Gordon's widow out to Lagos to spend a few days so that they could see where he was laid to rest. When they decided not to take up his offer we went ahead and arranged for a little ceremony at the graveside when the headstone had been erected. The society's piper came playing the *Flowers of the Forest* lament on the bagpipes. Members of the society, our children and Penny gathered; flowers were laid, photographs were taken and sent to Isa and her daughter-in-law. On my next and subsequent visits home I visited Isa and I know that her mind could rest more easily knowing that we had done what we could to honour her son.

Chapter 16

The Nigerwives Years

In 1981, my close friend Penny and I heard about a group of women of different nationalities, all married to Nigerians, who met one Saturday afternoon a month at Our Lady of Apostles Secondary School in Yaba. It sounded interesting so on the next date she gave me a lift and we duly turned up. There were probably about 20 women and, after we had introduced ourselves, we had an enjoyable afternoon. The following month we returned, this time both bearing a mug for tea or coffee as, while refreshments were provided, crockery wasn't.

The aim of 'Nigerwives', for that was the name of this organisation, was to help foreign wives of Nigerians to adapt to their new lifestyle, to share experiences and offer support to each other. It had started in 1979. We had all realised how strong the Nigerian extended family system is and we saw ourselves as sisters who would also form a bond of support. This included passing on information about jobs, services we could offer each other, like dressmaking and cookery tips, and a charitable focus on Brailling and recording on tape school textbooks for blind students who had been disadvantaged by not having such a service available to them.

The need for practical assistance for blind students was brought to our attention by our member Jean Obi, who was working at the WAEC (West African Examination Council), responsible for conducting the examinations leading to the WAEC Certificate of Education at the end of secondary schooling. Blind students at primary were catered for by a charity but those continuing to secondary education encountered significant difficulties, having no access to suitable textbooks for their courses so Nigerwives volunteers began reading the text books on to cassette tapes. A tape copying machine was then purchased and soon each blind student had his or her own copy of the texts needed. Over 200 titles were produced and costs were kept to the absolute minimum. By the early 1980s Nigerwives Braille Book Production Centre was established and has continued ever since to meet the needs of blind students in Nigeria. Jean Obi, who has been living in Nigeria for over 50 years and was awarded the MBE for her charitable work, remained very much involved with the centre.

Among the other early members of Nigerwives were Josephine Mohammed, Beatrice Ajose, and Isobel Fatogun. Many different nationalities were represented and, as the organisation grew, it seemed that there was nowhere on earth that Nigerian men had not been to and married wives of a different nationality. Indeed, we felt sure if Nigerians ever got to the Moon or Mars they might not return alone!

For some of these women marriage to a foreigner had automatically lost them the citizenship of their own country. This could be a major worry if the marriage wasn't happy. At the time there were many foreign wives of Nigerians living in both Lagos and other parts of the country and some of whom had not come across other foreign wives of Nigerians living near them. Nigerwives wanted to be known as widely as possible and on seeing or hearing of a potential Nigerwife we wanted to make them welcome and feel less isolated. Some of the husbands were initially against their wives coming to our meetings as they feared it would be a place where gossip and complaints abounded.

Some families were living in very poor circumstances while others were very comfortably off. Several of the ladies had gone against their families' wishes in marrying and at times they felt very alone and far from familiar surroundings. Also, the kind of situations they were experiencing were very different from what they had grown up with. There were also aspects around the laws in Nigeria which it was felt discriminated against us as foreign wives. At the time a foreign spouse could only live in the country if a Nigerian (usually their spouse) completed paperwork accepting immigration responsibility for them. If the immigration responsibility was withdrawn, for instance due to the death of the husband or marriage break-down then the wife had no right to remain unless another Nigerian would sign up to accept immigration responsibility for her. In some cases this might even be her son. A residence visa had also to be obtained and if the non-Nigerian left the country on a holiday to visit family, or on any other business, a new application had to be made in advance for each return. Details had to be stamped in or carried with her passport. Children were seen under Nigerian law as belonging to the father, so if the marriage foundered there was no guarantee that, should the wife want to leave the country, she would be able to take her children with her.

Foreign wives of Nigerians who wanted to send money back to their own family living abroad had great difficulty in remitting through the banks. Non-Nigerians could not inherit land or purchase land in Nigeria. Many Nigerwives were professionals, doctors, lecturers and teachers etc., but compared to their expatriate colleagues who had the same qualifications and experience they were treated very differently and were expected to accept considerably lower salaries and poorer conditions of employment. It took many years of campaigning to level the playing field a bit. If the foreign wife wanted to take out Nigerian citizenship the process was long and difficult and might involve her giving up her previous nationality, as dual nationality was not recognised between some countries and Nigeria.

After attending the first few meetings I felt that there was a need for a regular newsletter, which would set out the aims of Nigerwives and also share information and advice. This was supported and on the spot several volunteers came forward to join me in forming a committee. The following month, May 1981, we produced the first Nigerwives Newsletter. Our meetings were held on the last Saturday of each month so the first issue was dated June 1981. In these pre-computer days our contributions were taken to Isobel Fatogun who typed them on to a stencil and ran off copies which were distributed at the next meeting. Anyone on our list of members who didn't attend the meeting had their copy posted to them.

Excerpts from the first issue can be found in the Appendix. There were also children's pages and contact details of area representatives for each suburb of Lagos who, in time, organised local meetings.

The standard of contributions to the Newsletter was very high as members shared their knowledge and experience. A new issue was produced each month and I remained the editor until I left Nigeria in June 1985.

Although I write this mainly in the past tense covering the years I was in Nigeria the organisation is very much alive and thriving in 2019, now has its own website and the aims and values remain the same. There is so much up to date information online and distance is not the barrier it was in the 1980s. To marry outside one's own culture, faith and race etc. is no longer the 'blind leap of faith' many of us took.

As the organisation grew the venue was changed to St Saviours Church Hall on Lagos Island and later still to Corona School in Ikoyi. A free lending library was set up and attendance increased so that most months over 100 women gathered. Each month newcomers were invited to stand up and briefly introduce themselves. Soon we had members from all over the world and those whose first language was not English were particularly pleased to meet others with whom they shared a common language. Some of the women brought their children to the meetings and they too formed enduring friendships, in some cases leading to marriage to another 'Nigerchild'. Once a year husbands were invited to a cocktail party and there was always a big Christmas party for our children.

Living, in many cases, very far from their native land and having experiences which would be unfamiliar to family and friends could make foreign wives feel isolated, confused and worried. Nigerwives became like a new family for many. The knowledge that others had had similar thoughts and experiences was a great support. Many young Nigerian men had travelled overseas for further education and were away for several years and for them too, arriving back in Nigeria often shattered illusions of how they would work or live in a country which was ever changing.

Nigerwives now has branches both throughout Nigeria and overseas. In England there is a group based in London but encompassing the whole of southern England. Another group meets in the Manchester area and people who have been members but who no longer live in Nigeria stay in touch and offer friendship. The newsletter continued for several years but is no longer active, sadly, but Nigerwives remains a support and focal point for its members. As an organisation Nigerwives campaigned to resolve some of the points of law which created difficulties for all those non-Nigerians who had married Nigerians.

[For more up to date information consult the website: nigerwives.wixsite.com/nigeria.]

Nigerwives is very important to its members and their families. Not everyone was able to attend the big monthly meeting due, mainly, to transport problems but area representatives hosted small group meetings in their homes and distributed newsletters to those who hadn't been at the monthly general meeting. At the monthly main meeting I used to turn up with Penny and meet up with Isobel who had brought the newsletters. Those present would take their copy and any for members who lived near them but who hadn't managed to attend. At the end of the gathering I would take home the unclaimed copies and the children helped me to ensure they were folded, stapled, stamped and posted.

While writing this many years later I re-read some of the old newsletters we produced and I am impressed again at the quality of the contributions which were published along with the minutes of the previous month's meetings. We certainly had some very gifted members then and I am sure the same is true now. We were printing 300 copies of each issue after a time and I know that many of those were read by more than one person. Soon branches were established in other parts of the country and this was a big help to those who found their husband's occupation meant they had to move across country to an unfamiliar town or area. We had very interesting guest speakers and the mutual support of members made an enormous difference to us all.

In time, some of the husbands/partners of Nigerwives formed a group too and once a year there was a big family gathering. Nigerians rely a lot on the Old Boys/Old Girls Network, maintaining friendships made in college or university and providing mutual support. Nigerwives was (and is) doing the same.

With a wide fund of talents our members included doctors, nurses, teachers and other professionals. Several were very skilled in arts and crafts. At family occasions, such as a wedding, naming ceremony or funeral etc., Nigerwives offered support just as the husband's family would. Several members found employment by hearing about job opportunities through the group grapevine. We also organised excursions to places of interest, one of which was to the Toyo Glass Company where glass bottles were made. We also held seminars on a wide range of topics. Friendships begun through Nigerwives have endured over the years since and among my cherished friends now are women I first met through the organisation in Lagos. The fact was that despite our different nationalities, education or backgrounds there was a common bond. We were all adapting to life in a different country with unfamiliar customs and traditions. Some of these we could accept without question, others required some support and sometimes a compromise or refusal to comply was decided. It helped to be able to talk privately with someone who had some insight into these situations.

We had several generations becoming members and attending meetings, such as one member, now a grandmother, with her daughter and the daughter's child. When I was editor the newsletter committee met once a month, each of us bringing contributions and adverts. Isobel produced the finished edition, using a Roneo stencil machine and they were collated and addressed by hand. Some copies were posted to other countries including one to Fr. O'Sullivan who was now chaplain to the students at the Royal College of Surgeons in Ireland. Many of those students there were not Irish nationals and he made a particular effort to be their chaplain and counsellor regardless of their religion. He kept all the Nigerwives newsletters copies I posted to him and years later he gave them back to me and I have them still.

Some of the embassies in Lagos also organised small groups for their nationals. The American Wives group, the Goethe Institute, Alliance Française and the British Council, among others, provided active support to those of their nationals who were living in Nigeria. These groups were mainly attended by the wives of expatriates working on contracts in Nigeria but they also welcomed Nigerwives members.

The charitable side expanded considerably until it needed its own premises and staff all dedicated to supporting students in Nigeria with sight loss.

Len and I joined the Nigeria-Britain Association (NBA), which was the mirror image of the Britain-Nigeria Association. In Lagos the association organised concerts in the Nigerian Institute of International Affairs with a mixture of local and guest artistes. One particular British High Commissioner, Sir Mervyn Brown, was very musically talented, as was his wife. As well as composing and playing classical music he enjoyed playing with a local jazz band. We attended several concerts for members of the NBA at his official residence and in time Len became a committee member. The presidency of the association alternated between a Nigerian one year and then a British president the next year. Len was on the committee for several years and served as president from 1985-86. The NBA organised days out for members and their families; on one occasion we visited the former Head of State Olusegun Obasanjo, who had become a farmer and specialised in the production of pigs on a grand scale. There was also an interest in local charities which benefitted from the association's support. All these organisations served a valuable, inclusive service to all who became involved.

Chapter 17

Cracks Appear

Len's mother Nne was brought to visit us in Lagos as she needed treatment for a large infected abscess on her neck. I don't know how long it had been festering in the village before we heard about it but probably for quite some time I imagine. After taking her to see a doctor, who prescribed antibiotics, I cleaned and dressed the area daily until all the sepsis had cleared and the skin had healed. She said that the smell was so bad that no one in the village wanted to go near it or her! We could not speak to each other very well as I had not been able to learn much Igbo; Len had already lost patience in trying to teach me long before as I found the tonal language very difficult to speak. Nne's English was "Please", "Thank You", "Good Morning" and "Good Night". We communicated by signs and gestures and I had the greatest affection and respect for her.

It was her first visit to Lagos and it must have seemed very strange after the life she was used to in the village. She had probably never been further than Onitsha, a town about 20 miles from the village. I remember we took her to Bar Beach at Victoria Island where she saw the sea for the first time. When she had recovered her health and had spent a few weeks with us she was accompanied back to her home to Azigbo. Len's sister Irene also came to stay with us when she was unwell. She had a very severe chest infection when she arrived which did not respond to the treatment prescribed by our doctor. Sadly, she died in our home despite all our efforts to nurse her through her illness.

I had long realised I was no match for Len in any kind of discussion and more and more I was keeping my thoughts to myself. He was very dictatorial and was easily angered and upset and this would at times bring on his migraine headaches. He could justify all his actions, even though some of them were very hurtful to me.

In 1979, Nne told Len that she was not happy about the amount of support she was getting in the village. She was becoming frailer and she asked Len to take a second wife, someone who could stay with her in the family compound and help her. Polygamy was still practised in some parts of Nigeria.

He refused. Marrying under traditional law and custom would be very expensive for him. Nne then said that things could not carry on as they were and she would "marry a wife for herself." This was in accordance with an old Igbo tradition, I was told. A young woman would be accepted into the family to be a support for his mother. She would be free to have children but any child born would belong to the family and not to its father. Len did not think that his mother would find any young woman in the village who would accept the conditions but she went to her old family compound where she had lived as a girl. Shortly afterwards, to our surprise, we were informed that Charity, a young woman of the right age, had agreed to the proposal. On Len's next visit to Azigbo, alone, the remaining formalities were completed according to tradition.

I suspect that Charity had not been happy with her own family and expected that she would have more freedom living with an elderly woman. The new 'wife' was expected to assist with work in the small fields where cassava and yams were grown and to help to look after the few sheep, goats, and chickens. She would also if needed go to the local markets and fetch water if the big galvanized tanks collecting rainwater from the roof became nearly empty. At this time Nne had been spending a lot of time on her own as Helen, her youngest daughter, had a little general store in the village and was there most days from morning until late in the evening. It was not long however before the girl became pregnant by someone in the village and Nne also complained that she wasn't getting the help and respect she should have from her. A baby girl had been born and soon we started to receive messages from Nne that the young mother wasn't coping and the baby was being neglected. By the time we made our next trip to the village for a Christmas visit, the little girl who had been named Ngozi (meaning Blessing), was a toddler and her young mother had gone back to her people, saying she no longer wanted to be married to a woman.

Nne couldn't look after the baby as well as all her other tasks.

"We will take her back to Lagos to live with us," decided Len, deciding there was no alternative.

"If we do, then she will be treated like our own children," I replied. "I don't want to get a message from Azigbo in a few years saying she must be sent back to live in the village when she is old enough to be useful to help with chores."

"That won't happen," was the response.

I had had a similar experience before in 1965 when Len's niece, who had been living with us, was suddenly informed that she should go back to the East as her aunt needed her help. This had caused us a lot of problems as Uche was less than two years old at the time and I was working full-time.

We had travelled in our Volkswagen minibus to Azigbo that Christmas and on the way back with all the children, a niece and Ngozi on board, we hit a problem. Soon after we had crossed the River Niger the front windscreen shattered without warning. There was no place where we could buy a replacement as many businesses closed between Christmas and New Year so we had to drive back to Lagos after having knocked out the shattered glass. It was the dry season and the roads were very dusty. Everything had to be held down inside and we were soon all caked in red dust. The journey took several hours longer than it would normally have done as we couldn't pick up any speed owing to poor visibility, roads full of potholes, and the wind and sand in our faces.

Little Ngozi settled very quickly and soon picked up English. Of course, she had been speaking only Igbo in the village. Life was very different in Lagos but she took it all in her stride and she certainly did not appear to miss her mother or village life. There were certainly things about me however that she found puzzling. One evening, during the rainy season when temperatures had dropped, I wore a pair of black tights acquired during my last winter visit to Scotland.

Ngozi came up to me and asked, "Are these your real legs?"

A few months later I had a bad chest infection and lost my voice. I heard her go running to tell the others a few days later, "Mummy has got her own voice back!"

As the one handling our finances because Len said they gave him a headache, I was extremely concerned that the business in the meantime was hardly making any money. Len had put up the selling price of the ice blocks and sales had slumped. The main side of the business was also generating next to nothing; we felt our staff were clearly diverting customers and the apprentices were not learning much at all. We had to dip into our savings to pay the salaries and rent. Len locked himself in the bedroom each morning for hours in meditation, with instructions that he was not to be disturbed for any reason. He spent the rest of the day reading philosophy, writing discourses, or in long conversations with visitors who were AMORC members.

In July 1982, the Rosicrucian Order held a World Convention at their Headquarters in San José, California, and Len had arranged to attend along with some others from Lagos and the rest of Nigeria.

He was away for a fortnight in all and it had been arranged that our Welsh friend, Elwyn Williams, would drive me to the airport to meet Len on his return. Traffic was unusually heavy for a Sunday and, as we approached the Arrivals Hall, the passengers were already outside, sorting out their transport. In the moment I saw Len, before he had spotted me, I had a very strong, strange feeling that things had changed dramatically between us.

He barely spoke to me, sat in the front of the car with Elwyn, and was animatedly telling him how wonderful it had all been and how he had found people of like minds and several had gathered in his room while he led their discussions after the official seminars for the day. He did not ask about the family or how the business was. Really, I might as well have been invisible.

When we got home, we heard a very detailed account of his experiences and how fantastic it all was. At the event, people from different countries had gathered in his room while he explained matters to them. Several had asked to keep in touch with him and he was going to keep in touch with the delegates who had been so impressed with his reasoning. Some of those who had made an impression on him included a French woman from Strasbourg, France, another from Canada while others lived in America. Len's interest in the Rosicrucian Order had grown even deeper. I did not share his beliefs and we agreed that we were growing apart. He had been drawn to a mystical life while I sought at least a basic financial security. I would not become a member of the Rosicrucian Order (AMORC) and that irked him although I supported him and attended their functions which were open to non-members.

By now, there were times in our lives where the day to day strains of life in Lagos were becoming more frustrating. Several times we were stopped by the police when driving which usually meant that according to them, a traffic infringement had occurred. At the least, an apology to the policeman was expected but the hidden message was that the policeman wanted a small bribe or 'dash' as it was called. That they were poorly paid and often in arrears was common knowledge.

At times his driving licence was seized because Len would never apologise, beg, or bribe. He would then have to go to a police station to get it back, which often required several trips as the person who had seized it was 'not on seat' i.e. conveniently unavailable. He did not like it if I attempted to defuse such situations by intervening or apologising on his behalf.

Uche had by now finished her secondary education and was working in the Lagos office of British Caledonian Airways. The Scottish manager who employed her asked for her Christian names as he thought her Nigerian name difficult to pronounce. "Lesley Ann Jacqueline," she said and he decided to call her 'Jacky' in the office. This spread and so now only her close family and old school friends address her as Uche. Her colleagues and others all call her 'Jacky'. She started as a receptionist and then moved on to Reservations. The company kitted their local front-office staff in the same uniforms as their air crew and she was provided with very attractive kilt-type skirts and matching jackets in several tartans with white blouses, hats, a raincoat, and even court shoes and a shoulder bag. Another bonus was that as an unmarried staff member, she qualified for greatly subsidised air travel for herself and her immediate family.

Nnenna had also completed her secondary education and started a course at the Nigerian Hotel and Catering School in the previous September, which she was due to complete in July. She had a real aptitude for cooking Nigerian dishes. Getting to the school meant quite a bit of travelling to and from Fadeyi in Yaba, another suburb of Lagos.

And still our problems with the landlord continued. At the beginning of 1983, I felt so sure that we would have to move that I packed most of our large collection of books into cartons. Len insisted that right was on our side and told me that we could not afford the rent to stay in Apapa as costs had risen steeply since we moved in. This was true. Inflation was very high. He also argued that we could also not afford to separate business and home premises and he would not consider us moving to a less expensive area to live.

By now he was withdrawing more and more from us. The business was really suffering as he was less and less interested in it. Len's response was that all businesses were suffering and I was basing my decision to get a job on emotion rather than reason.

I started a new job with a printing company after having spent nine years working from home. Len was pleased when I was offered this job as he knew the Managing Director who was also a Rosicrucian. He had submitted some photographs he had taken to the company with a view to them being used for greeting cards. I was just relieved that now I was earning enough to keep us all afloat for the present. But I could not deny that I felt I was trapped; I craved security. Always at the back of my mind was the matter of 'immigration responsibility'.

Our landlord tried a new tactic to persuade us to move out and a lot of squatters moved into the flat above us which he had not re-let. There was no electricity or water upstairs and they used the open gutter at the side of the house as a toilet.

I helped Uche and Ada to apply for British passports. Now that Uche was working for an airline it was possible that she would be sent on courses overseas. I also wanted to take them for a holiday in Britain to meet my family.

Len and I had another long talk. "I want you to be more independent," he told me. "I see us as strangers whose paths met, who have been together for some time (20 years) but whose paths may separate again as each pursues their own destiny. I want the freedom to travel, write, and discuss with people at this spiritual level.

"I still love you and have no intention of marrying anyone else," he went on. "My AMORC studies are the main interest in my life. If I had to sacrifice everything else for them, so be it." I accepted that he would do what he believed in.

Daily life continued. I was taken by the company driver each day to the office and back in the evening. I also had the use of the company car and driver at weekends, should I wish it. However, the end of my working day was flexible as at times I was sharing the use of the car and driver with the Sales Manager. We both had schedules involving visiting clients and prospective clients. The commute was several miles through busy traffic from Apapa to Ilupeju where the factory and my office were.

I continued my involvement with Nigerwives, attending the monthly meetings and editing the newsletters. We held a very successful seminar at the University of Lagos. The theme was 'On being Bi-cultural'. The whole day's events were recorded on cassette tapes. It was very clear that, while Nigerwives were more concerned about how their children were integrating, the children themselves felt they had few problems. Children of mixed race and international parentage are more readily accepted in society in Nigeria than in more developed countries.

We had a number of our teenage and older children contributing to the day. The youngsters made a strong point about the need for them to be able to speak their father's vernacular language, eat and learn to cook local food, and be familiar with local customs.

The love and pride of their homeland was very strong among most of the women. However, it was very evident that children of part-Nigerian origin, whether born in Nigeria or abroad and wherever they went to school, saw themselves as Nigerians and wanted to be accepted as such. At the same time they were proud of being the offspring of two nationalities (or more) and did not at all resent their heritage. They felt there were definite advantages of being part of an international family.

In 1983, life for businesses in Nigeria was not easy, especially for those such as my employer who depended on import licences. Production had to be cut and, to add to the turmoil at home, the company I was working for was reducing staff and could no longer afford to employ me.

Len was completely confident in his right to live the life he chose and which he felt destined to live. However, he did agree that Uche, Ada, and I could travel to Scotland and England on 18th June and return on 5th July, the day before Ada's birthday. Making use of the staff family discounts on British Caledonian flights made this possible.

He had decided that, upon our return, he was going to Strasbourg for three months to visit one of the friends he had made at the AMORC Convention the previous year. Uche, Ada and I flew to London and then on to Edinburgh. Our first visit was to Dunfermline where we stayed with my Aunt Margaret and Uncle Bob. The day after our arrival I phoned Nigeria to let Len know we had arrived safely. After the phone had rung several times it was picked up and I was surprised to be speaking to the neighbour's son, Peter Okome.

"Hello Peter. What are you doing in our house?"

"It's not your house now," he said. "The landlord came yesterday with some men and all your furniture was taken out of the house. Your workers helped Mr. Ofoegbu to put it all into a lorry."

"Where did they all go?"

"I don't know."

I was really shocked by this news but I reasoned that there was nothing to be gained by Uche, Ada, and I returning immediately. As the news sank in I was relieved that I had not been present when the eviction took place. I was angry too that such a humiliation had taken place and that it could have been avoided if Len had not been so stubborn. I also realised that if the incident had taken place a few weeks later Len would have been out of Nigeria in France. The repercussions would all have landed on me. I felt it was really the last straw. I had put up with so much. If Nnenna and Emeka hadn't been in Lagos without passports I doubt if I would have wanted to return to Nigeria but I could not abandon them. I felt such shame for the situation I was in. In all the years that I had lived in Nigeria I had never seen or heard of any family being turned out on to the street and I now had no way of contacting Len either.

It was another two days before Len phoned us. He had gone back to the house and the phone was still connected. He told me that he had still been in the bedroom when the landlord arrived. Emeka had gone to school, Nnenna to the Catering College, and Ngozi was having her breakfast prepared by our house-help. She had been very upset at not being able to finish it! Len had taken personal papers, birth certificates, etc., and my jewellery box (though I had little jewellery of any value) round to his relative in the next street for safe keeping. Fortunately, Elwyn Williams helped him to rent a lorry and all the furniture was put in it and taken to a warehouse for storing in Ikeja. The landlord's men had removed all the doors and windows from the house. Our friend Sam Ijioma, who had a house in Satellite Town off the Badagry Expressway, allowed Len and the children to stay with him while efforts were made to find somewhere for us to live on our return.

Leaving Dunfermline, Uche, Ada and I flew from Edinburgh to London where we met up with my sister Sheila, her husband Jim, and sons Paul and Mark, all of whom were spending a day in London. Uche had included a return flight for me from London to Dublin, Ireland. Fr. O'Sullivan, whom I had stayed in contact with since the end of the civil war, was by this time the first RC Chaplain to students at the College of Surgeons in Dublin. I also met up again with Sister Mary Thomas and some of the Irish missionary priests I had met in Biafra.

When Fr. O'Sullivan and I had a chance to talk and I had related all that was happening, he suggested that I should consider what I felt was best for the children as well as myself. If I still felt the situation was intolerable, then in his opinion, I had done all in my power to sustain the marriage. Len had been in my life since I was 18 years old and had had so much influence on me that my self-esteem was low and I could not see our circumstances improving in any way. He believed he was above the law and that he could never be wrong. We seemed to be so far apart in our beliefs that everyday conversation was now difficult. I had yielded so often I wondered if I was even capable of making a big decision for myself and carrying it through. I did not know what I was going to do but I knew things couldn't continue as they were.

That night I woke in the early hours crying and I wept for a long time as I released all the tension and stress which had been building up. I felt that a great weight had been lifted off me and that, at the age of 39, I could still create a new life for myself and the children if they agreed.

I was still very aware though that I would need to make serious plans and that it would all take time. Nnenna and Emeka did not have passports and Emeka was not due to finish his secondary education for another two years. Ada was about to start a two-year OND (Ordinary National Diploma) General Art Course at Yaba College of Technology.

I knew that in Nigeria there would be no retirement pension when I was too old to work. I was still seen as a 'guest' in the country where I had lived for almost 20 years. I was very aware of my need for a personal feeling of security (apparently an attribute of those who share my astrological sign of Taurus). I had been made redundant just a few weeks earlier and I was still owed a month's salary and was without a new job lined up for my return.

I was still a British citizen and if I returned to live in the UK, I would have some kind of a roof over my head even if it was emergency accommodation to begin with, access to free health care, further education and some sort of pension when I retired if I worked until I reached the state retirement age and had paid contributions through earnings. There was such a lot to think about. When I had left the UK in 1964 there was still considerable racial prejudice. What the situation was now I really didn't know; hope was what I did have and some new belief in my own abilities.

Len phoned again in the final days of our holiday at Gosport. He told me that Sam had a colleague who also been allocated a house in Satellite Town. It was a four- bedroom bungalow and he would rent it to us. On the day of our return, Len picked us up from the airport and drove us to Sam's house. He told me he had decided not to move into the new place until we arrived. This surprised me, especially when he told me that the furniture was still in the store in Ikeja about 20 miles away. An even greater shock was his decision to proceed with his proposed three-month visit to Strasbourg later that week and not postpone it until our situation was more stable.

The following morning we started the move. In the haste of the eviction, there had been no proper packing. Many items had been heaped into sheets and curtains and the corners tied to make bundles. When the seats in our minibus were removed, what had been taken to Sam's house filled the bus twice. This was all deposited at the new house and then Len, Emeka, and Ada drove to Ikeja near the airport and brought back some of the large items that had been taken to the warehouse.

In the mêlée, I had started about six tasks around the house and not finished any. I started to hang clothes in the wardrobe and then noticed ants had already taken up residence so they had to be dealt with first. I started to hang up curtains but then was diverted to wash up dishes and to clean kitchen cupboards before I could put them away. Curtains were badly creased so had to be brought down again, ironed and re-hung. There was a growing pile of rubbish to be burned. There were stacks and piles of books waiting for the bookcases to be brought. Ngozi wandered off and was located playing with our new neighbours' children. Food had to be prepared.

The next day, more of our belongings were brought back from Ikeja. I desperately wanted everything brought to the new home before Len left the country. We were all shattered.

We were now living several miles from Apapa, in Satellite Town off the Badagry Road, in an area consisting of bungalows built by the government and sold mainly to civil servants. I could not drive and was unemployed, nor had I any means of making an income. All the ice-making machines had been left in Apapa as Len had decided that they could not be transported because they had been assembled on site. Also, he thought that there would be no market for ice blocks in Satellite Town.

Although he had his tools he could not start a new business in this area if he was leaving the country in a matter of days. We did not have a telephone in the house either. He drove me back to Kofo Abayomi Avenue where we saw that the landlord had by now removed the roof of our former home.

Len planned to leave four days after our return for his visit to see his Rosicrucian friend in Strasbourg. He could travel on the subsidised staff tickets only if there were not enough fare-paying passengers to fill the plane. However, the planes were full so he did not leave for another two days. By the time he left for France, some of our belongings were still at Ikeja and I had no means of getting to them. The girls and Emeka now had difficult journeys and much further to get to work and school. Indeed, it could involve five changes on the bus each way for the girls and two or three for Emeka. We had to allow at least two hours travelling time each way.

There was just enough money in our bank account to pay the rent for six months but that would not cover food, transport, electricity, gas, etc. Uche was now working, of course, but her salary was certainly not enough to maintain us all. Nnenna's course had ended and soon she was offered a position with Afromedia, an advertising company not too far away, but even adding her salary I knew we would not be able to make ends meet. Certainly, we had to pay the rent. The memory of the shame of the eviction was still very raw.

Soon afterwards I managed to get a job working in the office of the private clinic of a German-trained Nigerian doctor in Creek Road, Apapa, not far from where we had lived when Len worked for PMS. Sam, who lived not too far from us, was sometimes able to give me a lift part of the way to work.

At the time there was a policy to try to reduce traffic on Lagos roads. What it meant was that if your car registration number ended in an odd number you could only drive in the main commercial area of Lagos Island on Mondays, Wednesdays, and Fridays. Those whose car registration numbers ended in an even number, could use the roads on Tuesdays and Thursday. Weekends were free for all. This was meant to lead to a lot of car sharing by those who only had one car but those who could afford to have more than one made sure they had odd- and even-numbered cars. Sam had only the one so he car-shared with a colleague. Public transport remained hit or miss with no apparent timetables or queues. Taxi fares had to be negotiated before you got in the car and white people were expected to pay considerably more for taxi fares than the locals.

I made enquiries about obtaining a British passport for Emeka. This was not straightforward as he had no birth certificate, having been born in the last month of the existence of Biafra when the little matter of survival had pushed any idea of birth registration out of our minds. He was not unique in this regard, however, and I was told that what was needed were letters of 'sworn declaration of age' by people who were around at the time of his birth. Sam Ijioma was able to provide one. The Irish Holy Rosary nun, Sister Mary Thomas, who had visited me in Emekuku Hospital the day after Emeka's, birth, was contacted and obliged with a beautiful affidavit in English and Irish and these were accepted by the British High Commission. Nnenna's case was more difficult, but in time she had a Nigerian passport with a 'right of abode in UK' certificate in it. Ngozi's future would become Len's responsibility.

Len was so confident that we would manage in his absence that he only wrote to us twice from Strasbourg and when he returned in October he made no effort to start a business or find employment.

He had accepted that he and I had little in common any more but he was still assuming we had a future together. He returned to something he had spoken about some months earlier. His mission, he declared, was for us to go and live in Azigbo and help his people there with psychic healing and counselling. I made it clear that I would not go to live permanently with him in the village as I had said when he first spoke about it.

He asked what my plans were. I told him my immediate plan was to find another job as he had made it clear he did not like me working at the clinic. I said I wanted to undertake a training course.

In January 1984 there was another coup d'état. Everyone was stressed and rumours abounded. Life at home was no easier.

Through the husband of another Nigerwife, Prof. Babs Fafunwa, I was offered a position working for Chief Dotun Okubanjo who was chairman of a group of companies including one in which he was a partner with Prof. Fafunwa. There was an office in the prestigious Western House in Lagos but his main base was in a property adjacent to his home in Marine Road in Apapa. By coincidence, Len and I had visited that property when it was owned by the British Council and friends Derek and Jenny Cornish lived there. We had even considered buying it when the British Council placed the property on the market and our business was going well but we had insufficient funds to get a mortgage. It was reasonably easy for me to get there by 'kia-kia' bus (public transport), with several changes.

I enjoyed the work which mainly involved administration as there were several typists and a secretary based in the Marine Road office as well as the chief's own office and a boardroom. He travelled abroad extensively, on average being out of the country for a week in most months. In the school holidays his younger children came back from boarding schools and would pop in to the office. My working day ended at 5pm when the office was locked and by taking public transport with several changes I could be home before 6.30pm. Although Len was not working, neither did he stay at home all day and sometimes he drove to Victoria Island to the television station where some of his friends worked. He would sometimes say that he would pick me up on his way home but I frequently had to wait an hour or more on the roadside before he turned up.

My employer, knowing something of my home situation, let me know that there was a vacancy for an engineer at a company where he was a director. Len duly went for an interview for the job at International Distillers Group at Sango Otta, not far from Ikeja. The interview was held in Apapa and he did not go to see which of the sites the position would be at. Instead, he decided that it was not for him; it was some distance from where we lived so it would not be an easy commute; he said I would not like it. Also he believed that the smell of alcohol (the company produced alcoholic beverages) would affect the development of his pineal gland – this was vital for his mystical development.

Not long afterwards, Len made a brief visit to Azigbo by public transport. On his return, he came straight to my office and we took a taxi home. On the way, he told me that his mother had insisted that Ngozi should be sent back to live with her, by the first available transport.

Despite the assurances when Ngozi came to live with us four years earlier I had suspected all along that this would happen. It was still common for children to live with extended family members when it suited them. Len told me that at present, his mother was alone from about 6am until 10pm as his sister Helen spent all day and early evening at her little shop nearer the village centre. Nne had told him that she wanted company and someone to help with the chores.

Ngozi would have her birthday in early April and Len and I agreed she should stay until after that.

Len was also now full of plans to build a small house in his father's compound before December when the expectation was that all Azigbo people living elsewhere in the country would return to the village for Christmas – referred to as 'Mass Return'. He proposed that we should all spend our annual leave this year in Azigbo doing as much of the physical building work ourselves as possible. This did not happen.

I had no doubt that a lot of pressure had been put on him because 20 years after returning from the UK he had still not built a house at home in Azigbo as was expected.

He was convinced that he was embarking on a great service to mankind and I should be grateful and happy to assist him by removing the burdens of everyday existence. "People keep telling me how well I look considering," he enthused.

Silently I thought, "I have enough worry lines and headaches for both of us."

After Ngozi's birthday, it was arranged and Nnenna took her back to Azigbo, returning with the news that Nne was in hospital, very ill, and 300 Naira was needed to pay for her treatment.

Meanwhile, life was not getting any safer. The family who lived three houses from us was attacked by armed robbers one Friday night. They were rounded up, beaten, and locked into a room in the boys' quarters by a gang of about a dozen men armed with knives and guns. After removing all the valuables and cash they could find the thieves left with all the house keys. Around the same time the Secretary of the Apapa Club was shot and killed by people who stole his car near the airport. A few days later, an American Nigerwife living two streets away was robbed one Saturday afternoon when their house was empty for just one hour. Her jewellery and small valuables were taken. Most robberies were not reported to the police as there was little faith in them doing anything about it.

Len made another visit to Azigbo and to my amazement he returned with a distant relative who very clearly had a significant mental health problem. She spoke no English at all. He believed that he could use his metaphysical power to cure her.

Home life became a farce as she helped herself to the girls' clothing, and often locked herself in their bathroom for an hour in the morning when they were trying to get ready for work or school. All appeals to her to let them in were met by laughter from her. She ate everything she could and we had to start locking the kitchen.

Life became increasingly difficult. She was left to her own devices when the children and I had left in the morning and Len was probably meditating in the bedroom or he went out, leaving her on her own. She used a whole bar of soap for one shower and a whole packet of Omo washing powder when washing clothes. Both of these were scarce commodities. Our neighbours started to complain as she would wander into their homes as well.

Being left alone in the house, Len told me she had stripped naked while the rest of us were out and offered herself to him as thanks! In time, he realised that he could not cure her and she was admitted to Yaba Mental Hospital for treatment where we visited her until she was discharged and taken back to Azigbo.

By August I was feeling close to breaking point. I was told to change my thinking and develop my spiritual self, that I was hampering his progress and my feelings of insecurity were self-induced. Every decision I made was wrong and I should accept that I was committed to the marriage whether I liked it or not.

The next year passed with little change. Len still made no effort to support us financially and spent his time meditating, studying or listening to music from his record collection. Sometimes he had visitors who were interested in his ideas and he would spend hours 'teaching or discussing' with them while I avoided involvement as much as possible.

Meanwhile, I had told all the children of my plans to leave and return to the UK and the reasons for them. Fortunately, they understood and agreed with me, although with some reservations.

I began to make enquiries again about having my memoir published. It had been completed more than ten years previously and was my account of our family's experiences up to the beginning of 1970, including our life in Biafra. I had realised that, as the children had been very young at the time, they were unlikely to remember any of the events which had taken place. It would become part of our family history. So, I wrote the story, partly for them, partly as a type of therapy for myself, and because I knew that in time I too would forget many of the details.

When the country was re-united in 1970, the Central Government was unwilling to permit any criticism of what had been their policy. Over the succeeding years and with the passage of time, however, accounts began to be published. Although there was some interest from a British publisher in the early 1970s, I was advised that it would be unwise for me to proceed if I wanted to remain living in Nigeria. Consequently, the manuscript remained in a box under my bed for over ten years.

I mentioned the manuscript to my employer, Chief Okubanjo and he introduced me to Chief Mrs. Flora Nwapa. She was herself an established author who owned a printing and publishing company in Enugu called Tana Press, which published her books. She is credited with being the first female Nigerian author of a novel in English. Her first book, *Efuru*, was published by Heinemann in 1966. She was also the first Nigerian female publisher and when we met she expressed an interest in reading my book.

Chief Mrs. Nwapa passed the manuscript to her editor who happened to be a fellow Nigerwife, Australian Nina Mba. Nina was an academic who did a great deal to publicise the role of women in Nigeria and had written several books herself. She was well respected throughout her adopted country and her untimely death in 2002 left a great void. There was never any talk of payment. I expected to earn some royalties when the book was published as I was told it would be available in the UK and the USA as well as in Nigeria. When I heard that *Blow The Fire* (which covers the period of the first part of this book) was going to be printed in London by an Indian printer, I wanted to read the proofs myself, so in 1984 I flew to London for a long weekend, again using one of Uche's staff family discount tickets. I had read many Nigerian-published books with many errors in them and wanted to avoid this. I collected the proof manuscript which, at my request, had been sent to The Royal Commonwealth Society in Northumberland Avenue, almost opposite the Nigerian High Commission, and spent most of my short visit in a small hotel at my own expense, proof reading and correcting. I still had no contract from Tana Press although I understood that Chief Mrs. Nwapa wanted to launch my book at the same time as one of her own titles. No date had been decided upon. When it was eventually published it was without the corrections I had made and I never did receive any royalties.

In August 1984 I was paid a cheque for 784 Naira (approximately £700) which had been owed to me for over a year, by a previous employer and, without telling Len, I used it to open a bank account in my name. A few months earlier Len closed our joint savings account we had held for many years with the building society, and rarely used, transferring the balance to an account in his name only. He justified this by telling me that it was inconvenient for us both to have be present to withdraw from the joint account. "Of course if you insist I will change it to a joint account but that would show me that you don't trust me," he said. He had already completed the transfer, though how it was done without my signature I do not know. I made no comment about this.

One Sunday, Len convened a family discussion during which we discussed marriages and the reasons why some do not work.

The children suggested lack of understanding, other women/ wives etc. Len spoke of the sanctity of marriage, the perpetuity of oaths, and the terrible penalties of breaking oaths. He felt that if the unions turned out to be mistakes, they should be worked on to make them durable. He spoke of the Nigerian traditional marriage and the careful investigation of family backgrounds before betrothal, saying that the separating of couples encouraged more and more to divorce who otherwise would have been able to continue if society had been stricter. I told the children to look back at their early school friends, remember how close they were yet how they no longer saw some of them because their interests had changed and they had grown apart. I explained that this was sometimes the same in a marriage. People who married young, matured and sometimes grew apart, developing different priorities and sometimes became incompatible and no longer able to live in harmony or mutual love and respect.

After the discussion, Len told me privately that he saw I was not committed to staying. He felt I would regret rejecting his advice and assistance in my spiritual development and felt that I should seek out what will give me true happiness in life.

As 1985 advanced, so did my plans to leave. A trusted friend, Jenny, had the passports for the three girls and Uche managed to get open-dated return tickets from Lagos to London for herself, Ada, and Nnenna. These were also given to Jenny for safe-keeping and I had tickets for Lagos-London-Edinburgh-London-Lagos for Emeka and I as Len had consented to him making his first trip to the UK. Emeka was sitting the last of his West African Examination Council exams ('O' Levels equivalent) on 13th June; the next day the two of us left. The girls knew that I would not be returning to Lagos.

It was only when we were safely in England that I told Len I was not returning and that I was enrolling Emeka in a sixth form college to further his education. He was thus able to explain

Emeka's absence by telling enquirers that because he was not yet 16 years old I was staying in England for the time being while he was at college. Len was, of course, upset that I had gone, particularly as that autumn he was to become the Chairman of the Nigeria-Britain Association in Lagos for a year by virtue of having been a long-standing committee member.

My Nigerwives friends were shocked at my departure as only a very few knew of my plans. I felt badly about having to leave in such an undercover way but felt I had no alternative.

My life in Nigeria was finally over and a new future beckoned. There was no going back, of that I was sure. I was fortunate that my sister and her family took us in for the first few weeks. My first priority was to enrol Emeka in a school to continue his education. Next, I had to find a job and create a home for myself and all my children, should they want it.

Whatever I did from now on, whether I succeeded or not, would be by my own efforts.

There were faults on both sides. I was a very naive teenager when I met Len in 1962 and allowed myself to be swept along by him and his confidence. Later, my inability to convey my anxieties to him and speaking to sympathetic friends instead was a factor but was essential for my survival.

Although we both spoke English it became like different languages. Our understanding of what we said, implied or did not say fractured our communication and made me bottle things up. Words like 'love' came to mean very different things to each of us.

Len's insistence that there was nothing wrong with his marriage and if there was something wrong with mine then I should sort it, illustrates this. My silences he read as acceptance and permission for him to do whatever he wanted. He had no interest in my opinions and openly said that every decision I had made had been wrong and all that we achieved was by his efforts.

I was constantly aware of the hold he held over me and that my residence in Nigeria with our children lay in his hands. He could at any time have me deported from the country simply be withdrawing his Immigration Responsibility for me and in a society like Nigeria that could happen very quickly. I did not even consider separating from him and setting up a home for myself and the children in his country.

Len continued to see himself as superior to other men in his mystical development. His mission is to enlighten others. Even if he accepted he had a personal problem there was no one he respected enough to take advice from.

Postscript

Since 1985 we have all moved on.

I settled in Gosport, Hampshire, close to my sister and her family. It is a lovely spot on the south coast of England with a long naval history due to its proximity to Portsmouth and with views looking over to the Isle of Wight. Len moved back to his village Azigbo and lives in a house he designed and which the family helped him build. The children have stayed in contact with him although none of them live in Nigeria. He has continued his studies of mysticism and philosophy and has some followers. His mother and sisters, Helen, Rhoda and Irene have all passed away.

Emeka completed his 'A' Level education at Bay House School in Gosport following which he went on to study Business Studies and Marketing at Croydon College. He is now known as Len or Lenny by his friends and colleagues though the Nigerian side of the family and I still call him Emeka. He is married to Milly, an Australian who has now settled in her father's homeland of England, and they both work as Financial Service Managers in the banking industry. They live in Milton Keynes, Buckinghamshire with their two young sons Jayden and Brandon.

Nnenna was the first of my daughters to move to England in 1985 and initially she lived with Emeka and me in Gosport. She later moved to London. She married a Yoruba man, Yinka. They have a daughter, Alexandra, who graduated with an MSc in Violence, Conflict and Development from the School of Oriental and African Studies, University of London in 2018. She is a Fundraising and Communications Assistant at BBC Media Action. Nnenna's son, Connel, is also living in London. Nnenna has been working in secondary school administration for over 18 years and she now has British citizenship.

Uche, now known by friends and colleagues as Jacky, transferred to British Caledonian Airways headquarters, near Gatwick Airport, in England in 1987 and later worked for British

Airways and Delta .Airlines. She lives with her husband Olumide (a Yoruba who she had first met in Lagos and lost touch with for many years) in Port St Lucie, Florida, USA. Her son Denzel, who studied at the University of East London, is now a supervisor at Harbor Freight in Conway, Arkansas. Last year we attended Whitney's graduation with a BSc in Biology from the University of Central Arkansas. She hopes to study for a Master's degree in Zoology next year. Younger sister Maya graduated from high school in Houston last year. Presently they are both working in the hospitality industry in Conway.

Four years ago Uche donated a kidney to her husband while they were living in Texas. Unfortunately, six months later, the donated kidney had to be removed and Olumide has home dialysis five days a week assisted by Uche.

Ada, known as Adaora to friends and colleagues, completed her OND in General Art and HND in Graphic Art in Lagos. After a year's NYSC (Nigeria Youth Service Corps), part of which was spent working in the Nigerian Television College in Jos, she moved to England in late 1989. She has been working for the Crown Prosecution Service for 29 years and is a Paralegal Business Manager. She lives in Gosport, not far from me with her 13 year old son Ben, who is now a student at Bay House School. Ben's father is the son of the Biafran nurse Ada I met and worked with in 1970 and is the step-son of Elizabeth Ihebom (now Iwenofu) who lived with me between1968 and 1969 in Ogbor. (A photo of Ben's three grandmothers taken in Lagos in the early 1970s is on the back cover of the book.)

When I first moved to Gosport in 1985 it took me a few months to find a full-time job although I wrote numerous applications. I signed up immediately for evening classes to get recognised qualifications and, within a few weeks, I was also doing voluntary work with Social Services and the Probation Service. Emeka and I spent three months in bed and breakfast accommodation before being allocated a council house just before Christmas 1985.

After working in a local cafe, and doing occasional consultancy work at the Centre for International Briefing in Farnham, I had a few months clerical work at the DHSS (Department of Health and Social Security) office in Fareham. By early 1988 I had the necessary educational qualifications and I applied to Portsmouth Polytechnic (now University of Portsmouth) to study Social Work. Although I was offered a place that summer I had just begun a new job at St. Petrocs (now All Saints), an organisation providing accommodation and support for homeless men in Portsmouth and I asked for my place to be deferred for a year so that I could gain experience and start some savings. As Mill House, where I worked, was in Portsmouth I bought a moped and commuted on the Gosport Ferry across Portsmouth Harbour. Although I passed my car driving test I could not afford the running costs at that time and was happy on two wheels.

I began life as a full-time student at the age of 45 in 1989. Being a full-time student was not easy as I had never had to write in an academic style but I persevered. In May 1990 I changed my surname by Statutory Declaration from Ofoegbu back to my maiden (family name) of Mitchell. While I was a student I also worked some weekend shifts for St Petrocs and as relief duty manager at weekends and during the long vacation in the summer at Hampshire County Council-owned residential properties to build up some savings. In the summer of 1991 I qualified with a CQSW (Certificate of Qualification in Social Work) and was offered a position in the Older Persons Team, Adult Social Services, Hampshire County Council, based in Fareham, a neighbouring town. I had finally achieved my dream job. As a car was now essential I also graduated to four wheels with a red Vauxhall Nova. I quickly became part of the first of a series of very supportive teams. I still meet with some of my former colleagues every few weeks for coffee. In 1992 I was able to put down a deposit, get a mortgage and move from council accommodation to a home of my own.

My work involved following up referrals and assisting, mainly older people, to access services which would make life easier for them and their families. Individually tailored assessments might lead to assisting with claims for financial support, arranging personal care and meal delivery in their own home if appropriate, applications for day care, residential care and respite care. I worked with families from all walks of life and it was a privilege to be able to offer some level of support. Along the way I acquired knowledge of local and national charities and support groups. Initially, all our work was recorded in paper files and there were no mobile phones or computers. I carried cartons full of leaflets and forms in the boot of the car which I might need on home visits. These had to be taken out every weekend so I could do my weekly shop. l retired as a Senior Practitioner in the Fareham Adults Support Team in 2009 on my 65th birthday.

At that time my sister, Sheila, was ill with terminal kidney cancer and I nursed her until she died in September that year in Countess Mountbatten Hospice where another visitor told me of a need for knitted bonnets for premature babies in ventilators in Special Care Units. My friend Elizabeth Dee and I have over the years since knitted and donated over 2,500 bonnets to Queen Alexandra Hospital in Portsmouth. Father O'Sullivan, who had come to our rescue in Biafra when we were homeless applied for laicisation, leaving the priesthood, and when the family he had been living with moved to smaller accommodation he found himself homeless. He needed a quiet place to write his own book titled *Converting the Convertor – African Spirituality inspires an Irish Missionary* and he moved into my spare room as a paying guest, staying until his death in 2013, aged 92 years. A good friend who I spent many hours with over the years, until her death two years ago, was Jean Boyd. She called me the 'daughter I never had' and was truly a second mother to me. A fellow Scot, living only two miles from me, we were very much on the same wavelength.

Since retirement I am actively involved in voluntary work in the Gosport community. I am a trustee of a small not-for-profit organisation called CHAT2US which helps people to make informed decisions and gives advice and support to those who are socially isolated, struggling with form filling, debt management etc. CHAT2US also does knitting projects, including more baby bonnets, fidget muffs for people with dementia, hats and gloves for refugees etc. We organise litter picks regularly in the town. I have also joined several local social groups through the online organisation Meetup. This gives me the opportunities to meet with friends for meals, walks and outings together. I also carry out voluntary work for the Befriending Service of Gosport Voluntary Action.

I have been fortunate to be able to afford to travel over the years and visited my cousin Helen and her family in Australia four times with my sister as well as holidaying in several European countries.

After I retired I decided that there were many things I had wanted to do but always put off so I vowed to do what I can while I can. I keep fit by swimming a mile three mornings a week and have just started doing Walks for Health with local groups. Living only two miles from the sea I enjoy walking by the shore most weeks.

I have also been able to visit Uche and her family in Texas and now in Florida. Last year I squeezed in a week with my cousin Sandra in Camas, Washington State, meeting her sons and their families for the first time. She took me to my first stadium concert in Portland to see The Eagles. Living within a reasonable distance from London has enabled me to attend several shows and concerts in London too over the years.

My children paid for a flight in a helicopter from our small local airport for my 70th birthday and we flew over the Run for

Life race with the competitors in their pink T-shirts looking like a ribbon along Southsea Common. And the next year I bought myself a gliding lesson. Elizabeth talked me into a Mediterranean cruise which I greatly enjoyed and together we have had three winter holidays in Marsa Alam, a Red Sea resort in Egypt where I spent many hours snorkelling.

Many friends from my years in Nigeria have visited my home in Gosport. Following the death of her husband in Nigeria, Nigerwife and old friend Jenny Erhahon, her six children and her mother stayed for several months, although some of them had to sleep in neighbours' houses, coming to my home to spend their days. A friend of Ada, from her time in Yaba Tech, Anne Iyasele, also spent months with us in 1990 and 1992 and remains her closest friend.

Four of the Biafra foreign wives have remained friends in the years since. Elizabeth Iwenofu (previously Ihebom) lives in Kent. Wendy Ijioma has been settled in Birmingham for many years. Pat Kanu and her late husband Okoro, who was a personal friend of Fr. O'Sullivan, and Rose Umelo are now living in London surrounded by most of their children.

Among the Nigerwives I am still in contact with are my dear friend Penny Ayara-Ekpe who I have known since the early 1970s. She lives with her husband Jerry in Woking and Isobel Fatogun is now living in Belfast with husband Dele. Last year, while visiting Uche in Houston, I was able to meet up with Christine Okpomor who had travelled from Arizona to Houston to attend her daughter's graduation. Penny, Isobel and Christine were all part of the Nigerwives Newsletter committee with me from the first issue in 1981. For a while I attended the Nigerwives London group meetings organised by Ingrid Osunde and several times the group came to Gosport for a summer day out.

Elwyn Williams has settled back in Wales where he has only recently retired from sheep farming. He and his wife Naomi run a small bed and breakfast business and I have visited them twice.

I still travel to Scotland, usually more than once a year. Now I tend to fly rather than drive. My Aunt Margaret still lives in Dunfermline in the same house. My cousins Allan, Margaret and Craig keep an eye on her as she is becoming frailer.

Living in Nigeria and Biafra was an amazing experience and an education in itself but I have no regrets about my decision to leave. I obtained a divorce in 1996 and am very happy to remain single. I feel that I had a second chance to make something of my life and have seized the opportunities that have been presented to me.

From Left: Ada (Adaora), Emeka (Len), Leslie, Uche (Jacky) and Nnenna. Taken in 2010 by The Goodwin Studio, Gosport.

Appendix

NIGERWIVES NEWSLETTER
Number 1 June 1981

All correspondence to P.O. XXXXX, Apapa, Lagos,
Nigeria.
Telephone: Lagos XXXXX

EDITORIAL

To be lonely in a crowd is a feeling all foreign wives have at one time or another, especially in the first few bewildering months and sometimes years in their husband's home country. Our husbands felt the same when they travelled abroad for further studies but for them there was the comfort that their stay was temporary and in time they would return to their native land. Nigerwives aims to help foreign wives to settle down in Nigeria, to tackle common problems and integrate into the Nigerian society. A lot of our tensions and frustrations are relieved by sharing experiences with others who have also been in their time bewildered by local customs, cooking and cockroaches. These seem to be three of the most common adjustment problems. (It's amazing how big a problem cockroaches are!)

Nigerwives gives us a forum to discuss problems affecting ourselves as foreign wives: our legal rights and the rights of women in general in Nigeria. We hope to be able to make a meaningful contribution to Nigeria, to help each other and our hosts see the world as one extended family which we can all understand better by getting to know each other as friends. It is not a hotbed of gossip or general moaning and complaints bureau. We want to solve our problems, not allow them to eat us up.

Membership is open to foreign-born wives of Nigerians, including widows and divorcees who have chosen to make their homes here, and to all other women who share our aims.

We meet on the LAST SATURDAY OF EACH MONTH AT 3 p.m. AT OUR LADY OF APOSTLES SECONDARY SCHOOL, OFF HERBERT MACAULAY STREET, YABA. Potential members and visitors are very welcome. Please bring a tea cup or mug for the light refreshment served during the meeting, when there is a good chance to chat with new friends. If you would like to come but feel shy, or you have no transport, contact your area representative (see list elsewhere in the Newsletter). She will be happy to bring you to the meeting and introduce you to some members. You can bring your children too if you have no-one with whom to leave them.

Membership Subscription is fifteen Naira per year. We plan many more active meetings this year. We have had some guest speakers already, and we are starting a quarterly luncheon, regular "Nearly New" Sales and, of course, this Newsletter.

We plan to put out a Newsletter every month. This will make sure that you are kept

290

up-to-date. However, in order for us to do this we need help from all our readers. Share your thoughts, ideas and experiences with us; write and tell us a favourite recipe, book review, beauty hint, or funny things that happened to your family. The floor is open as they say, so don't be shy. If you prefer not to write in English we'll try to publish if our type-writers can accommodate your alphabet! If your children or your husband or members of the family would like to air their opinions we will be very happy to print their views.

At present Nigerwives is only active in Lagos and Kaduna. It is our ambition to see branches in every State of the Country. To start with we are asking for volunteers in the States to be contact members. Someone we can put other Nigerwives in touch with if they are living in or going to be visiting that area and, if possible, to form a nucleus for a branch of Nigerwives. The Secretary has copies of an introductory leaflet about Nigerwives which can be handed out to potential members when you see them. Area representatives in Lagos also have a supply of these leaflets. There is a section of the form on the back page which you can fill in if you would like to know more about being a contact member.

Please note that we ask Subscribers to send us postage stamps to the value of N2.00. It is unrealistic to send a cheque for two Naira from one State to another; postal orders are not easy to pay into the bank – you have to get forms from the Post Office – and currency notes posted do not arrive at all. So please, send your Subscriptions in the form of 5k or 10k stamps. These will be used to post the Newsletters and any excess will be sold to members at the monthly meetings to enable us to use the cash to buy paper, etc.

Please complete the form on the back page to ensure that future issues of the Newsletter reach you.

My grateful thanks to Penny, Isobel, Chris and Vera who have worked so hard to get this Newsletter ready. May your enthusiasm and inspirations continue to yield fruit! The idea for this Newsletter was raised at the General Meeting on April 25th and here is the first issue ready for the meeting of 30th May. Well done!

Sincerely,

Leslie J. Ofoegbu

----ooOoo----

DIARY OF COMING EVENTS

30th May 1981 May General Meeting

13th Jun 1981 First Quarterly Luncheon Meeting to be held at the Posh Nosh Restaurant at the junction of Broad Street and the Marina, Lagos. Details in the Appendix to this Newsletter.

27th June 1981 2.30 p.m. "Nearly New Sale" – This is the first of these sales. If you have any articles you would like to sell, bring them along with labels attached giving the following information:

(a) Your name

(b) The amount required for the article, taking into account that 10% will go towards Nigerwives' Central Funds. If you don't want money for your article please state that.
All articles should be clean and in reasonably good condition. We don't want "junk". Come along in good time for a 2.30pm start and liaise with Mary Coker who has kindly agreed to be the Co- coordinator

3.00 p.m. June General Meeting

PLEASE NOTE THAT THE VENUE FOR MAY AND JUNE GENERAL MEETINGS HAS BEEN CHANGED TO THE CORONA SCHOOL, 6 MEKUNWEN ROAD, IKOYI, AND PLEASE REMEMBER TO BRING YOUR CUP OR MUG, AND IF POSSIBLE, A FLASK OF HOT WATER.

SEAFOOD STEW

3 or 4 lightly smoked fish (the kind called Sapel fish in Bendel State)	½ to 1 kilo shrimps Chopped onion Chopped fresh tomato
Pepper to taste fresh or ground	1 teaspoon tinned tomato puree
Maggi cube	Other seasonings to taste
Salt	1-2 Cooking spoons red palm oil

Remove heads and bones from fish. Soak in water to cover 15 min. to remove some of the salty taste.

293

Clean shrimps and boil with some onion and lemon (optional) for about 10 min. Put red oil in frying pan. When hot, add chopped onions and fry until tender. Add chopped tomato, tinned tomato puree, pepper, Maggi, seasonings and about 1 cup water. Mix well. Add fish, cover and allow to boil until fish are almost soft. Remove cover, add shrimps and cook until they are hot. You want the sauce to be a bit thick, but add water if necessary. Serve with rice. Serves 4 – 6.

AVOCADO VELVET

| Lemon jelly | 1 good sized avocado pear |
| ¾ cup hot water | 1 teaspoon lemon juice |

Dissolve jelly in hot water. Put in blender. Add flesh of one avocado and 1 tsp. lemon juice. Blend. Put in serving dishes and chill until set.

Serves 4. Serve with cream if desired.

Chris Okpomor

ARE YOU POSITIVE OR NEGATIVE?

I once had a Polish friend – or she could have been French or English or any other nationality. What is really important is her attitude toward life in Nigeria. If the children were fighting she would say if only she was in Poland the children wouldn't fight. If the car had a flat tyre she said that it never happened in Poland. If the neighbours played loud music she would say that she never had noisy neighbours in Poland. In fact anything bad or unpleasant that happened here could never happen in Poland if you believed everything she said.

I'm sure you can guess that before 2 years were up she was back in Poland. We will all agree that life is difficult in Nigeria, but there are good things about life here too. Whether or not you see them depends on your attitude to life here. My Polish friend had such a negative attitude that it was impossible for her to make a good life here.

We have to remember that everything was not always perfect in our native country either. There were good days and bad days just like here. If you have a negative attitude you will not make it. But if you open your eyes and really look around – develop a positive attitude – you will learn to love Nigeria for its good points and try to excuse the bad points.

Chris Okpomor

FOR SALE

Baby's pram in excellent condition – N50.00

Mrs. P. Ayara-Ekpe. XXXXXX, Apapa Tel. XXXXXX

FIRST AID - HEALTH CLUB

This will be a regular column in the Newsletter and is mainly to be a guide to those of us who, sooner or later, will be faced with the task of administering some form of treatment either to ourselves or our families.

This month we are concerned with immediate first aid equipment essential for the home and useful drugs to have at hand. Please remember to always keep these items away from children, preferably in a locked cupboard out of reach.

ITEMS   Thermometer (Oral and Rectal)
Assorted plasters and bandages and cotton wool
1 pair of scissors, assorted safety pins
1 eye bath and lotion e.g. OPTREX
1 bottle of antiseptic e.g. Dettol or Savlon

DRUGS   Anti-malarial elixir and tablets   e.g. Chloroquine, Camoquine Nivaquine, Fransidar, etc.
Pain reliever   e.g. Paracetamol (commercial names Febrilix, Panadol, Pentamol)

Anti-diarrhoea	e.g. Guanimycin, Kaomycin (for children) Thalazole (for Adults)
Sedative	e.g. Phenergan
Cough Mixtures	e.g. Benylin expectorant (for Loose productive cough) Benylin with Codeine (for Dry hacking cough)
De-worm agents	e.g. Antepar, Ketrax, Combantrin

Anti-histamine creams for bites, stings, etc.

Always read the instructions on the bottles and keep strictly to the dosages stated. These are first aid measures and in severe cases, medical aid must be sought.

Going into hospital and want to be the model Patient? Then read the following:-

The Perfect Patient:

Has the bladder of a Camel

Keeps a tidy locker

Will eat anything

Has only one visitor, one vase of flowers and above all, one illness at a time, and doesn't tiresomely go and get 'flu or cystitis if she's down on Sister's list as a broken ankle.

Keeps food in her locker – but only for the ravenous nurses.

Does not terrify the new patients with stories of the last three patients who died in that very bed.

Never calls Sister "Nurse" or the nurses "Girl".

Does not snore.

Is in good health!

Vera Azuike

<u>THE BEST SELLER.</u> Falamo Shopping Centre, Ikoyi, Lagos

For beautiful Books and Greeting Cards and Lots of Lovely wrapping paper

Of special interest to Nigerwives is a good selection

Of children's inexpensive readers with African and

Caribbean backgrounds

Made in Nigeria Birthday and other occasion cards

Open daily except Sundays

Pen-Pals

Nigerwives Newsletter

Would you like to have/be a pen-pal to one or more Nigerwives? If so please write a short letter introducing yourself and your hobbies, etc. and stating if you would like one or more pen-pals. Then send/give the letter marked 'Pen-Pals' to:

P.O. Box XXX,

Apapa

Please allow two months before you receive acknowledgement as I am travelling but will be back early July to settle down to the paper work.

Many thanks. I look forward to hearing from you all.

Vera Azuike

-----ooOoo-----

Points which may warrant further coverage:

Visit to the Senate President – Report in next Newsletter

Save Emeka Fund – Emeka Ogbogoh is the son of Nigerian and British parents.

Emeka suffers from brain damage and he and his mother, Mary, are currently in London where Emeka is undergoing treatment. As the kind of treatment needed is lengthy, Nigerwives contributed N510 (£430) and this amount has been remitted to London.

Project - It was suggested that Mrs Jean Obi should brief Nigerwives on possible assistance which might be given to blind students. Her comments follow:

Suggested projects with respect to blind students:

In many developed countries the needs of the blind in respect of reading materials are met not just by national bodies but by volunteers. Here in Nigeria we have no national body meeting such needs. Pacelli School for the Blind and one or two other voluntary groups do what they can but it only meets the smallest fraction of the need. I believe Nigerwives could do something, possibly in one or more of the following ways:

(a)   Reading books onto cassettes

Apart from a clear reading voice and a cassette recorder/player little else is required for this other than time. Literature books – both French and English – Economics, History and like subject matter can easily be made available to the blind in this form. Subjects like Maths and Science cannot be presented in this way very effectively.

(b) Learning to Braille.

This is not difficult. There is a primer and anybody who can manage to spend 30 minutes a day on it can learn quite quickly. The main problem is the one of obtaining machines. The Perkins Brailer ($200+ in the States) is the best but others are manufactured in the U.K. and Germany for example. Braille paper can be bought locally.

(c) Reproducing copies of Braille books from master copies

The Thermoform Machine ($1250 from the States) is used for this. The paper to use with this is obtained from the States too and costs about $33 a ream of 500 sheets, which is about the number required for an average text book. The machine itself is easy to use.

More information from: Mrs Jean Obi

XXXXXXXXXXXXX

Ikoyi.

The original manuscript of *Blow the Fire* was published in Nigeria in 1986 under my married surname (Ofoegbu) with a launch at the Nigerian Institute of International Affairs in Lagos in 1987, which I did not attend. I was already concentrating on my life in the UK.

PRINTED AND BOUND BY:

Copytech (UK) Limited trading as Printondemand-worldwide,
9 Culley Court, Bakewell Road, Orton Southgate.
Peterborough, PE2 6XD, United Kingdom.